THIS GOD OUR GOD

In this series:

The Face of Jesus Christ

THIS GOD OUR GOD

Creator, Judge, Saviour

Archibald G. Brown

THE BANNER OF TRUTH TRUST

THE BANNER OF TRUTH TRUST

3 Murrayfield Road, Edinburgh EH12 6EL, UK
P.O. Box 621, Carlisle, PA 17013, USA

*

This selection first published 2013

© The Banner of Truth Trust 2013

*

ISBN:

Print: 978-1-84871-297-3
EPUB: 978-1-84871-298-0
Kindle: 978-1-84871-299-7

*

Typeset in 11/15 Adobe Caslon Pro at
The Banner of Truth Trust, Edinburgh

Printed in the USA by
Versa Press, Inc.,
East Peoria, IL

There are two passages in the Scripture which ought never to be separated. One is 'The Lord's portion is his people.' That is God's side. And the other passage is this: 'The Lord is my portion, saith my soul.' God and my soul possess each other. God finds his portion in his people, and his people find their portion in God. This God is mine in all his glorious perfection. His heart is mine, for he loves me. His ear is mine, for I may pour into it all my tales of sorrow and all my songs of joy. His eyes are mine, for they watch me from morning until night. His hand is mine, for it is stretched out to uphold me. Oh, he is a God of infinite glory. Abased in the very dust, and half bewildered by the thought, I yet dare to look up, and say, 'This God is our God.'

Archibald G. Brown, 'This God Our God'.

BROWN, ARCHIBALD GEIKIE, was born in London in 1844. He was impressed in boyhood under the ministry of C. H. Spurgeon in the Surrey Music Hall and Exeter Hall, but was actually led to decision for Christ through a personal appeal made to him by S. A. Blackwood. Desiring to become a minister, he entered Pastors' College, and was sent, before he was nineteen, to start a Baptist cause at Bromley, Kent. He served this Church for four years, and then accepted a call to East London, where he erected the East London Tabernacle, and built up one of the largest churches in the land. Mr Brown held this charge from 1867 to 1896, gaining great influence by his luminous expositions of scripture, his ardent proclamation of Christ, and his winning appeals to the consciences and hearts of his hearers. His name became a household word in East London, and the Tabernacle witnessed many memorable scenes—none, perhaps, more remarkable than the great Saturday evening prayer meetings which formed a fitting prelude to Sundays of grace and power. At length, however, feeling the strain of the work, he removed from East London, and fulfilled faithful ministries at Chatsworth Road, Norwood, from 1897 to 1907, and at the Metropolitan Tabernacle from 1907 to 1910. During the next few years Mr Brown conducted services in many centres, and undertook preaching tours in Australasia and South Africa. The last years were shadowed by affliction, and on 2nd April, 1922, he fell on sleep. He was four times married, his last wife predeceasing him by a few days. He left nine children and many grandchildren. He will be remembered as a preacher of genius, a natural orator, and a man of glowing devotion to Christ and the souls of men. He was an intimate friend and follower of C. H. Spurgeon, whose evangelical and spiritual ideals he deeply shared.—J.W.E.

CONTENTS

PUBLISHER'S INTRODUCTION

ARCHIBALD BROWN'S sermons were in constant publication from 1868 until the outbreak of the First World War in 1914. For the most part they were published individually for wide and cheap distribution; various publishers later brought numbers of them out in bound volumes, details of which will be found in Iain H. Murray, *Archibald Brown: Spurgeon's Successor* (Edinburgh: The Banner of Truth Trust, 2011), pp. 369-71. The disappearance of demand for these sermons over the last century went side by side with an evangelical decline in Britain. Spurgeon said in the 1880s, 'Few men are like-minded with Mr Brown—a brother tried and proved.' In the century which followed the number would be still fewer.

The present volume is a new selection with a new title. We have included Brown's Preface from his book *'Selah' or Think of That* (London: Lovejoy, 1906), on the grounds that what he wrote of the sermons there reprinted is true of all that were published.

Included in the present selection are a number of sermons on the attitude of God towards sin, a theme which will sound very unfamiliar today. It is not that the subject is unbiblical—the fear of God was a characteristic of New Testament believers (*Acts* 9:31; 2 *Cor.* 5:11),—but periods when Christianity is in decline have always seen a neglect of solemn truths. At such times, churches succumb to the temptation to soften or omit what has become unacceptable. Referring to this fact, Brown told his hearers in a sermon on God or Baal?: 'If you always hear from the pulpit just exactly what you desire to hear, in all probability you are listening to one of Baal's prophet; for, as the Lord liveth, if you hear a man who gets his message direct from God you will very often be made to listen to the last thing in the world you wish to hear.' To the objection that it would be 'unloving' to preach all that is in the Bible, Brown replied, 'It is when a man loves another intensely that he will dare even to offend him.' He knew that the saving results of preaching are not dependent on texts congenial to hearers. Before we side with contemporary opinion on this subject, it is well to remember that Brown 'grasped the hands of over four thousand who have been brought out of the world into the church of God by the preaching of the truth of God'. Have the small results of preaching today nothing to do with the absence of urgent warning and the fear of God?

God fits his men for the hour, and these sermons are not reprinted with the thought that they remain a model for us in every respect. For some, who believe that the exposition of passages or books of Scripture, in serial sequence, is the only right way to preach, Brown's approach to preaching may come as a surprise. It is true that such was not his principle. It did not suit his gifts. It did not fit with his desire to take texts which had first gripped him. But before being critical, let us bear in mind that a good sermon is one that does good. Brown's preaching, like Spurgeon's, did good to thousands. Here, as at other points, there is much to be learned from him.

It is with particular pleasure for us that these sermons are now reprinted. May their circulation be made a matter of prayer, with the cry that God will send forth such labourers among the multitudes! When Christ endues preachers with a greater measure of his Spirit it is again found that 'all the people were very attentive to hear him' (*Luke* 19:48).

PREFACE

THESE sermons make no claim whatever to scholarship or literary worth. None of them were written before preaching, but were all delivered from slender outlines. They were taken down in shorthand, and have been printed from the stenographer's copy.

It pleased God, however, to convey blessing, to not a few souls, in the hearing; and our prayer is that the same benediction may rest upon the reading.

None of the sermons were preached with a view to publication, but came to us as messages to deliver in our ordinary ministry of the word.

Your servant in the Lord,

ARCHIBALD G. BROWN

THIS GOD OUR GOD[1]

For this God is our God for ever and ever.
He will be our guide even unto death.
Psalm 48:14.

Thou shalt guide me with thy counsel,
and afterward receive me to glory.
Psalm 73:24.

T HE historical basis of the 48th Psalm cannot be decided. Expositors differ. They all take for granted that there must have been some historic action suggesting this psalm and inspiring this song; but they fail altogether in deciding what that particular history was. So far as the records of the past are concerned, we cannot find any event that exactly fits in with this 48th Psalm. Most historians seek for its explanation in the inroad made by the children of Ammon and Moab and Mount Seir in the days of Jehoshaphat; but, unfortunately for that explanation, those tribes did not surround Jerusalem, and God did not gloriously shine forth and make himself known in her palaces for a refuge. But some persons have gone so far as to say that the psalm must refer to that incident, because of the reference which we have to the ships in the 7th verse: 'Thou breakest the ships of Tarshish with an east wind.' They point out that the 20th chapter of the Second Book of Chronicles, in which we have the account of the invasion, ends with the record that the Lord broke up the

[1] July 12, 1896, East London Tabernacle.

ships. That fact, they argue, is the historical basis of the psalm; but, unfortunately again for those who put forth this explanation, the ships that were there broken up were not those of the enemy, but the ships of Jehoshaphat. We read that Jehoshaphat joined affinity with the king of Israel, and he sent ships to Tarshish, but the Lord broke them up. It was the ships, not of the invader, but of Judah's king, that went to pieces; and therefore we are unable to square the 48th Psalm with that historic incident. I have often wondered that expositors have not been more led to look into the future, rather than into the past, for the explanation of many of the Psalms. My own opinion is that the Psalms stand far more related to history that is to be than to history that has already transpired. All expositors agree that this 48th Psalm is a twin sister to the 46th Psalm, and it looks almost as if it were a continuation of it. But who will pretend to say that the 46th Psalm has yet been fulfilled? Look at the 8th verse: 'Come, behold the works of the Lord, what desolations he hath made in the earth. He maketh wars to cease unto the end of the earth.' When has that been fulfilled? To what particular year, whether B.C. or Anno Domini, can we point as the year in which all wars were made to cease unto the ends of the earth? Has there ever been an age in which some deadly feud or some contemptible squabble has not been embroiling some of the nations? The 46th Psalm looks forward to the time when God shall come and shall make short work of a war-loving earth, when he will break the bow and cut the spear and burn the chariot in the fire, and when war shall be known no more. I believe that this 48th Psalm has its historic basis, not in the ages that are past, but in an age which is yet to dawn.

We are not going to dwell this morning on the dispensational view of the truth, but, personally, I believe that this psalm is yet to be literally fulfilled. Jerusalem is yet to be what we read in the 2nd verse, 'The joy of the whole earth.' She has never been that yet. In her brightest and most glorious times she was a joy to the Jewish race, but she has never yet been the joy of the whole earth as she will be when the Messiah reigns gloriously. And there is to be a time when the nations of the earth shall be confederated against her, and when the kings of earth shall tremble before her; and it is when there is this combination against Jerusalem that the Lord shall come and make himself known in her palaces as a refuge. Then will the ships of Tarshish be broken up with God's east wind, and then we shall have Jerusalem a joy for ever. Now, the writer of this psalm, full of the Holy Ghost, is looking forward to a day which shall yet dawn, when God shall appear in glory and shall deliver Jerusalem from Gentile armies and shall sweep the fleets out of the Mediterranean with his own strong wind; and then so complete shall be the deliverance of the city that there shall be this summons: 'Walk about Zion. Go round about her. Tell the towers thereof.' Count them. Are any of them gone? No, not one. All are complete. 'Mark ye well her bulwarks.' Have any of them been carried? Not one. 'Consider her palaces.' Have any of them been destroyed or riddled with shot? None. Tell it to the generations following that the God who is going thus to preserve this favoured city from destruction is, even now, our God, and he will be our God for ever, and our guide even unto death. We look, then, for the historic basis of this 48th Psalm, not in the past, but in the future.

Having considered the connection of the text, let us now concentrate our thoughts upon these exquisitely beautiful words, 'This God is our God.' This God who has such boundless power, who works such a glorious deliverance, who is known in the palaces of Jerusalem for a refuge—this God is our God, and will be our guide even unto death. And then, speaking in the 73rd Psalm, Asaph puts the finishing touch to this blessed statement. Not only will this God be our guide unto death, but afterward he will receive us to glory.

There are three things which I want you to look at. We have, first, *the glorious fact* that this God is our God. Then we have *the very safe prophecy* that this God will be ours for ever, and will be our guide unto death. Then, as the third point, we have *the crowning mercy,* and this we get from our second text. It is that God will not stop short with guiding us unto death, but that afterward he will receive us into his glory.

I.—Let us look at THE GLORIOUS FACT THAT THIS GOD IS OUR GOD. The text does not say that 'a God' is our God, nor does it say that 'the God of the heavens' is our God. The declaration is very emphatic. It is 'this God;' that is, as Delitzsch renders it in his admirable version of the Psalms, 'such an one'; such a God as has been portrayed in the previous verses of the psalm; the God that has been set forth all the way through the 48th Psalm. '*This* God is our God.' If the Holy Spirit will but help me this morning, I think that I shall be able to show you that the word 'this' is not the least word in the text. It is not an unmeaning little appendage. Everything lies in it. If I am to know how wealthy I am, it is necessary for me to know, not only that God is mine, but what style of God my God is. I will, therefore, ask you to concentrate your thoughts upon the word 'this'. 'This God is our God.'

It is evidently necessary that we should look into the psalm in order to see what is intended by the word 'this'. The very first verse gives you the clue: '*Great* is the Lord; and then our text says, 'this God', that is, *this great God.* The idea is that we have in our God no mere local deity. He is not a second-rate God. He is no manufactured idol which, like the gods of the heathen, has to be carried by his worshippers. He is the great God. The men and the women of Ephesus went mad for many hours, and in their madness they ceased not to cry, 'Great is Diana of the Ephesians'; but their foolish cry at last died out to their own confusion. But God's people are able, not in frenzy, but in much soberness and truth, to declare, 'Great is the God of his people.'

He is *great in himself.* I confess that I never feel so utterly swamped, and so powerless to set forth in language even the thoughts that are in my own mind, as when the theme of my discourse is God himself. You may speak—I was going to say, with comparative ease—about the attributes of God, and about what God has done, but who of us knows who God is or what God is? Are there any frontiers to the greatness of our God? 'Great is the Lord.' How far goes the boundary? How great is he? That he is great in his power and his wisdom all nature declares. I do not need a Bible to tell me that there is a God of infinite majesty. 'The heavens declare the glory of God, and the firmament showeth his handiwork'; and I am persuaded that a little knowledge of astronomy would do untold good to all God's children. I believe that, through our very ignorance of the heavens above us, we have a cramped idea of God. He becomes a sort of parochial deity; for, after all, what is this solar system? We may talk of the sun which walketh forth in his brightness, and we may speak of this system of which our earth forms part, but, after all, what is it? Have you ever marked that sentence in Genesis, 'And he made the stars also?' What an 'also'! We know that each star is itself a sun, and that our sun which blazes every day is only one of millions, and though, up to the present time, no telescope has been able to discover the fact, yet in all probability every star that we see is a sun which is the centre of a system of its own. And, when we have swept the entire heaven with our telescopes, let us remember that we have, in all probability, only just seen the fringe of creation. How far space goes, and how far space is filled up with countless suns more glorious than that which shines overhead, and how many myriads of systems there are revolving in space, God only knows, though I hope to have an idea by and by when I get into the glory. Let our thoughts fly a little way beyond this limited solar system, and be lost for a moment among the myriad suns, those points of light which are known to us as stars, and let us remember that, in consequence of the greatness of God's power, not one of them faileth, and then we shall see that great is the Lord our God. He is great in his power, for he upholdeth all things; and he is great in his wisdom, for he hangeth the heavens upon nothing. Oh, the depth of wisdom by which God has balanced one world against another, so that, by his own law of gravitation, worlds help to uphold each other, and, being hung in space, they revolve round about him. In presence of that starry host our spirits cry, 'Great is the Lord in power and in wisdom, and this God is our God for ever and ever.'

And yet, when I talk about God being great in power and in wisdom, I only say the least that can be said of him, for revelation declares that he is *great in character*. Nature proves that he is great in power; but come to this word where God has been pleased to reveal himself, and what do we find in that? We discover God to be as infinitely sublime in character as he is great in power and wisdom. 'Holy, holy, holy', is the cry of revelation. The infinitely glorious God is as full of love to his people as he is full of power to uphold the stars. And this God is our God.

And not only is he great in character, but he is *great also in all his offices*. As manifested in Christ Jesus, oh how he fills out and expands every office. For listen. Is he a Saviour? I read that he is 'a great one'. Is he a Shepherd? He is 'the great Shepherd of the sheep.' Is he a Priest? He is 'our great High Priest'. Oh, our God is no little deity! All majesty dwells in him. 'Great is the Lord', thunders out the first verse, 'And this God is our God', says verse 14. What a wonderful psalm this is, if we merely take the beginning and the end of it and link them together. 'Great is the Lord', is the shout of the first verse. 'This God is our God', is the declaration of the last verse.

And then God is not only great. The word discovers more than that, for you will see in the 3rd verse that he is *a God who is known and proved to be a refuge.* 'God is known in her palaces for a refuge'; and this God who is known as a refuge is our God. If time sufficed I should like to call up an array of witnesses, and turn this platform into a witness-box so that you might listen to their testimony. Is God known as a refuge? That is the question which has to be decided, and you have to give the verdict this morning. Is God known as a refuge? Let the witnesses come. I can see hoary-headed old Noah coming forth to bear his testimony: 'I trusted God, and, though a world was drowned, he rescued me.' Is God known as a refuge? And the old patriarch Abraham says, 'I proved him to be so. I had my hand upon the knife whilst my boy was on the altar, and in that dread moment God delivered me, and a new name was coined, and I called him Jehovah-Jireh, the Lord will provide.' Do you not think that David would come tripping to the witness-box and say, 'I know God for a refuge. He delivered me from the paw of the lion, and from the hug of the bear; and he delivered me from the might of Goliath'? And I am sure that Daniel would not be left out. He would say, 'I know that I can bear a good witness. I went into a den of lions, and not one of them even breathed his hot breath upon me to discomfort me. I rested as sweetly that night as ever, because God was my refuge.' 'Oh', you say, 'that is very old history.' Come along, then, my friend. Come out of that pew, and stand on the platform here yourself. Come and bear your testimony. Have you known God as a refuge? You have heard others say that he is. Have you ever proved him so? If I were to put it to the vote, I believe that every child of God who is here would be ready to spring to his feet and say, 'I bear testimony that God is known by his people as a refuge.' And this God who is so known is 'our God for ever and ever'.

You will see in the 9th verse that, this God is *a God of*

lovingkindness. 'We have thought of thy lovingkindness, O God.' 'Lovingkindness' is about the most lovely word in the Bible. It is a mixture of two things, both of which are sweet—love and kindness; and when you blend them together you get lovingkindness. I have sometimes received kindness which was not particularly loving, and which on that account lost half its beauty; and I have met some persons who were very loving, but they had not an opportunity to show their love in any practical kindness. But when we get love and kindness mingled, when the kindness has been shown in love, and when the love has manifested itself in kindness, then we have the acme of all that is blessed. Our God, great in nature, power, and wisdom, and great as a refuge, is a God who is known by his lovingkindness.

And, once more, he is *One who is praised as universally as he is known.* That is a big thing which is said in the 10th verse: 'According to thy name, O God, so is thy praise.' And here let me acknowledge again that I have been utterly lost in my theme. Do you catch the thought? 'According to thy name so is thy praise.' I had been looking upon this fallen world, and I felt so disappointed. It seemed to me that it was such a barren bit of ground, and that my Lord reaped such a poor harvest of praise from it, that I almost felt sorry for him. I thought, 'Lord, for one that loves thee on this earth it seems that there are a hundred that are indifferent to thee.' But I looked at this text, 'According to thy name so is thy praise', and my thoughts went up amongst those worlds on high. Is not God praised everywhere? Why, after all, what a drop in the bucket are all the inhabitants of this earth put together. How many myriads of angels are there, think ye? And they all praise him. And who am I that I should think that the poor little world in which I happen to dwell is the only world that is inhabited? I have not a doubt that in every point of light in the heavens there are unfallen beings who bless and praise their Maker. I joy to think that, perhaps, the atoning sacrifice which redeemed one little world keeps myriads of systems from falling, and that through boundless ages their praises will ascend unto God. 'According to thy name so is thy praise.'

And—can we believe it—'this God', who is hymned by pure, bright spirits, of whom we know nothing, and who is worshipped and adored by the inhabitants of a million worlds, 'is our God for ever and ever'? There is not a landowner in England who can say concerning the fields which he calls his own that they are his for ever. No, Mr Landowner. You cannot say concerning your farms or your fields, 'These are mine for ever and ever.' Why, my dear sir, perhaps you will be buried in one of those fields before long. The king cannot say concerning his crown, 'This crown is my crown for ever and ever.' After it has made his head ache enough, it will give a headache to his son, and then it will be passed on again. Business man, you cannot say concerning your business, 'This is mine for ever.' You think that it is yours, and you look at that shop, and you say, 'That is mine.' But for how long will it be yours? There is not a Christian business man here who can say concerning his business what he can say concerning his God. Is not this wonderful? I felt amazed when I thought that I was able to say more concerning my God than I am able to say concerning my own child. I am able to say concerning my God more than I able to say concerning my own home or anything that I possess. 'This God is our God for ever and ever.' He is our God 'for ever', and, as if that were not emphatic enough, the Holy Ghost adds, 'and ever'. It is not fiction; it is not rhapsody; it is a splendid fact. God is the portion of his people for ever. There are two passages in the Scripture which ought never to be separated. One is 'The Lord's portion is his people.' That is God's side. And the other passage is this: 'The Lord is my portion, saith my soul.' God and my soul possess each other. God finds his portion in his people, and his people find their portion in God. This God is mine in all his glorious perfection. His heart is mine, for he loves me. His ear is mine, for I may pour into it all my tales of sorrow and all my songs of joy. His eyes are mine, for they watch me from morning until night. His hand is mine, for it is stretched out to uphold me. Oh, he is a God of infinite glory. Abased in the very dust, and half bewildered by the thought, I yet dare to look up, and say, 'This God is our God.'

The Lord help us to receive this blessed fact. It is not a dream; it is not a metaphor; it is not a poem. It is true of us all as we are gathered here, if only we are believers. This God is our God.

II.—We have also here A VERY SAFE PROPHECY. It is that this God who is ours 'will be our guide even unto death'.

'Our guide.' Then we are a pilgrim company. The wealth of the believer is not discernible. As I look at you from this platform, if I did not know your life and your history I could never guess which was the sinner and which was the saint. One looks quite as respectable as another. I will defy anybody to pick out God's saints by their external surroundings. Indeed, often God's choicest saints are earth's poorest sons. Very often God's most glorious children are earth's sickliest, weakest, humblest, and most despised ones. The men who can lay their hands upon this psalm, and say, 'This God is my God' are but a poor pilgrim host, and they need guidance. Do you grasp the wonderful thought that is contained here? This God, this great all-glorious Lord, this God that is being sung of by a myriad worlds today, takes his place as our guide, and he says, 'I will go before you as I went before Israel. I will mark out your path, and I will lead you along it.' How does he guide us? You will now see why we have added to the first part of our text the words taken from the 73rd Psalm. Those words are very humbling, but they are very instructive. 'Thou shalt guide me with thy counsel.' But who is the one whom God is willing to guide? Now read from the 22nd verse: 'So foolish was I.' Well, I think that a great many of us can say that. That just suits me. I feel that I am amongst God's foolish ones. And what are the next words? 'And ignorant.' Yes, and that word also describes me with remarkable correctness. I am conscious that I am both foolish and ignorant. The man who says this of himself is the man who says that he is going to be guided. But he has not done yet. He says, 'I was as a beast before thee.' You must not call anybody else a beast, but if you like to call yourself one you are at full liberty to do so, and you have given yourself rather a complimentary title, for, in many respects, we are all lower even than the beasts. No man of God who knows anything at all about himself will hesitate to say, 'I was as a beast before thee.' And what does he mean by that? I was as shortsighted as a beast. Just as an ox never looks back through the centuries that have passed, or troubles his bovine brain about the years that are to come, but is occupied with the grass that is at his mouth, so have I often been earth-occupied and shortsighted. I have been like a beast, stubborn and stupid, as if there were no starlit worlds overhead. I have been as a beast before thee; and yet, though I was so foolish and so ignorant, and though I have often been so beast-like, 'nevertheless I am continually with thee. Thou hast holden me by thy right hand. Thou shalt guide me with thy counsel, and afterward receive me to glory.'

III.—Let us pause for a moment here. This leads us up to THE CROWNING MERCY. Our first text only says that God will be our guide unto death, and does not go beyond that goal. A dear brother who is worshipping with us this morning gave me this text. He said to me, 'Has it ever struck you that it is very singular that God should guide anybody unto death?' It does seem strange, does it not? I know very well that the primary meaning there is a reference to time, and that it indicates that God will guide me all my life until I die; but that does not alter the fact that God guides us unto death. We should have thought that it would have been that God so guides us that we should escape death. But no, it is God guiding us unto death. Even the divine leading affords no escape from death. That is a penalty which I have to pay. Wherever there is sin there must be death. Ah, but, if God guides me unto death, I do not think that I need be afraid to die. If God takes me by the hand and leads me, though it be up to that last monster, I will not be afraid. If God guides me even into the sepulchre, I need not shrink back. Death loses its gloom, and the terrors of death depart, the moment that we realize that God guides us unto death. But dear Andrew Bonar, no mean scholar, points out that instead of the word 'unto' it should be 'over' or 'beyond.' 'This God is our God for ever and ever. He will be our guide even over death.' He does not bid me good-bye at the dying moment. He does not guide me into the river, and say, 'Now you must swim that bit for yourself.' He does not guide me into the dying crisis, and say, 'Now that I have brought you up thus far, you must scramble through the remaining hours alone.' He will guide me over or beyond death. And what then? Then Asaph in the 73rd Psalm finishes it: 'And afterward, after he has guided me up to death, and after he has guided me over death, he then will receive me to glory.'

'This God!' Imagine this God receiving me to glory. Can you take in the idea? This God that we have seen to be so majestic all the way through the psalm—this God is going to receive me. But my text says that he is guiding me. How can a guide receive me? Have you never read in the New Testament that he shall present us *unto himself*? That is just what he is doing. God in the Trinity of his persons is guiding me by the Holy Ghost along that blessed way consecrated by the Lord Jesus; and Jesus is going to pass me over unto the Father, a redeemed soul, and this glorious God will receive me. He will receive me into glory at the hands of his own dear Son. *All God's receptions are welcomes.* This is more than can be said of earth's receptions. I sometimes have a card sent me—I suppose by way of compliment—for admission to some reception that is given in connection with religious or social work. I confess that I am afraid of these receptions. I have been to one or two, but I have got so thoroughly frozen that I have steered clear of such refrigerators ever since. If there is anything which is a *de*ception it is what is called a *re*ception, and, if there is anything that does not receive you, it is that which by form and title professes to do so. The Lord Mayor, perhaps, and a few aldermen in big cloaks and golden chains are there to meet you, and your name is shouted out at the door, and somebody bows, and so you are 'received'. A beautiful reception that is! That is not how God is going to receive us. The eternal Jehovah—I say it with reverence—the eternal Jehovah, with a face beaming with delight, will say to me in that day, 'Welcome, welcome, purchase of the blood of my Son. Welcome, trophy of the blessed Spirit's power. Welcome in'; and I, astonished, shall say, 'Where, Lord?' and he will say, 'Into glory. Welcome into the glory.' That is what lies in the 'afterward'. Are you going home depressed? Then ask the Lord to take this morning's text, and to lodge it in the very centre of your being, and you shall sing, 'This glorious God, this great Lord, is mine. He is my own for ever and ever. He will be my God unto and beyond death, and after that he will receive me into glory.'

O Lord, do let every man and woman in this tabernacle this morning know in thine own time what it is to be received into glory, for Jesus's sake. Amen.

THE DEEP THINGS OF GOD[1]

For the Spirit searcheth all things, yea, the deep things of God.
1 Corinthians 2:10.

THIS text is vitally united, you will see, to the verse which precedes it, because this verse begins with 'but,' and that rivets it to the prior verse—it is the outcome of it—and that prior verse has, I suppose, suffered more from misquotation and misapplication than any other verse in inspired writ. You know it well: 'Eye hath not seen, nor ear heard, neither have entered into the heart of man, the things which God hath prepared for them that love him.' That text is always handed over to heaven, and it is read as if it taught that heaven is such a beautiful, such a glorious place, that really we know nothing whatever about it; that no eye hath ever seen, no ear hath ever heard, and no heart can imagine, all the beautiful things that are stored up in an at present unseen heaven.

I need hardly say that heaven was not in the apostle's mind when he penned the words. You will see that so far from teaching that these things are not to be seen or cannot be known, the apostle goes on to say, in the language of our text, which is never quoted, 'But God hath revealed them.' What a pity it is to cry halt and pull up at the end of the ninth verse, and say, 'Eye hath not seen, nor ear heard, neither have entered into the heart of man, the things that God hath prepared for them that love him,' and not to go on to the next verse, 'But God hath revealed them.'

[1] December 17, 1899, Chatsworth Road Chapel, West Norwood, London.

The simple teaching of the passage is this: that mere worldly wisdom can never understand spiritual teaching; that there must be a revelation made by God, and that the work of the Holy Ghost is to make clear to men what they never could learn, either through the eye, through the ear, or by the imagination.

God has made known these glories to us because there is no other way in which we could acquire a knowledge of them but by revelation.

Mental perception, however keen, is not enough; you cannot imagine them. God has to draw the veil over these beauties and reveal the facts in Scripture, and then the Holy Ghost reveals the Scripture again to us. There is thus a double revelation—God revealing his truth in the Word, and then the Holy Spirit revealing the Word unto us. Is it not true that the eye does not see these things? Millions of eyes can see God's work, but they never see the Artificer; millions of ears can hear the voice of God, but they never recognise that which is spoken. God must be revealed to be known.

That brings us right up to this declaration, that the Spirit searcheth all things; those things which the eye cannot see or the ear hear or the heart imagine, God hath revealed unto us by his Spirit, 'for the Spirit searcheth all things, yea, the deep things of God.' What do you understand by 'the deep things of God'? Everything that has to do with God is deep; God has no shallows, but God himself is the greatest depth. In the 11th chapter of Job at the 7-8th verses you have this remarkable utterance: 'Canst thou by searching find out God? Canst thou find out the Almighty unto perfection? It is as high as heaven; what canst thou do? deeper than Sheol; what canst thou know?' I know that we also speak of God's attributes. That is a very easy way of trying to get out of a greater difficulty, but when we have uttered the word 'attribute,' what do we mean by it? We speak of God's omnipotence, his omniscience, his omnipresence; but the dear orphan children can utter all these words, and perhaps know them better than some others here. When you have uttered them, what have you done? You have only, after all, uttered that which you yourself cannot comprehend. Every word in the list of Divine Attributes is an ocean which has neither a bed nor shore; each one is a river that has neither a source nor an estuary. These are the depths of Godhead, but that is not what is intended in the text; it is not the depths of Godhead but the deep things of God that are told to us.

From the 9th verse to the close of the chapter you have the word 'things' over and over again—I think eleven times—and if you have your Bibles with you, will you just for a moment cast your eyes down this portion; it has been called 'the chapter of things.'

Look at the 9th verse: 'The things which God hath prepared.'

10th verse: 'The Spirit searcheth all things, yea, the deep things of God.'

11th verse: 'For what man knoweth the things of a man, save the spirit of man which is in him? Even so the things of God knoweth no man, but the Spirit of God.'

12th verse: 'Now we have received not the spirit of the world, but the spirit which is of God; that we might know the things that are freely given to us of God.'

13th verse: 'Which things also we speak, not in the words which man's wisdom teacheth, but which the Holy Ghost teacheth; comparing spiritual things with spiritual.'

14th verse: 'But the natural man receiveth not the things of God.'

15th verse: 'But he that is spiritual discerneth all things, yet he himself is discerned of no man.'

So that when you come to this portion you are not dealing with an isolated passage; the deep things are referred to all the way through these verses, and things are a short way of saying 'thinkings.' People say things, but when they say things they are really saying thinkings, because every thing was first a thought. This world before it became a thing was a thought in the Creator's mind. Every cathedral that has ever been built was a thought in the mind of the architect before it became a thing in the hands of the builder. Every book of poems was first of all a thought in the poet's mind—it is etherealised thought. The things here spoken of are God's thinkings, God's thoughts, but God's thoughts are realities; they are no mere myths, they are things! God's children are not a number of poor deluded fools that dream of unsubstantial ideas. There are in the gospel wondrous realities, and the work of the Holy Ghost is to search, bring out and teach us these things that are freely given to us, these things that are mentioned in our text as deep things. Let me mention these things that the Holy Ghost wants you to have and wishes you to enjoy. At the head of the list we put God's deep love. 'God *so* loved.' No plummet has ever yet been found capable of sounding the depths of that 'so'—'God *so* loved.'

You cannot learn God's love from nature. I know people often say that they do not go to church or chapel or to the Tabernacle, but they go to worship God out in the fields, in nature. Can you see God's love revealed in nature? I can see God's goodness and God's beauty and God's wisdom, but when I want to see God's love I find that is one of the deep things. Some people may say that the Holy Ghost reveals God's love by the incarnation of Christ. 'God so loved the world, that he gave his only begotten Son.' It is true, that in the birth of the Lord Jesus I do see God's love, but I don't see its depths in the incarnation. Look at 1 John 4:9-10, and there you will see its depth: 'In this was manifested the love of God toward us, because that God sent his only begotten Son into the world, that we might live through him. Herein is love, not that we loved God, but that he loved us, and sent his Son to be the propitiation for our sins.' When the Holy Ghost wants us to know the great depth of

God's love, he points us to Calvary, and standing at the foot of that tree and gazing at that Sufferer, you learn the deep love of God as it can be learned in no other spot.

Then you will have noticed in the reading of that 3rd chapter of Ephesians that there is another deep thing that the Holy Ghost has revealed, and that is this, God's deep wisdom in the church. That is a startling idea of Paul's, the angels studying their God in a redeemed church; those angels that were in existence millions of years before man was made; those beings of purity and light that may have seen countless millenniums, are shown as gazing on redeemed sinners, studying them: why? That they might know the variegated wisdom of their God; the love that prompted such a salvation, the amazing wisdom that devised such a scheme of salvation, just to God and yet kind to man.

I often wish that our services were not so formal, and that pew and platform could talk together. If so, I would like to ask some of you what other things you would name. We have seen that the text means that there are deep things that God wishes us to know; we have deep love, deep wisdom, and I would like to add next, deep mercy. In Psalm 36:5, we read, 'Thy mercy, O Lord, is in the heavens,' and yet it comes down to me. How wonderfully deep it is! Mercy came down from heaven and picked up a poor vile sinner lying at the gate of hell. He who knows anything about himself can only stand amazed that the mercy that has her home up there in the heavens should stoop down so deep to the earth.

But that same 36th Psalm suggests another deep, not only deep mercy, but deep righteousness. That is what people do not like to hear about at the present day. 'Thy mercy, O Lord, is in the heavens; and thy faithfulness reacheth unto the clouds. Thy righteousness is like the great mountains; thy judgments are a great deep.' The great deeps of Divine righteousness are revealed in the gospel. There is nothing in the Old Testament half so terrible as what you can find in the New. Do you want to know the righteousness of God and his hatred of sin? You say, look at the deluge—that proved it; look at those blazing cities in the plain! Ask the Holy Ghost, and he will say, look away from the deluge; look away from Sodom and Gomorrah. Where? At the Cross. There you will see the deep abhorrence of a holy God to sin; there you see the deeps of Divine righteousness and Divine judgment, when he who knew no sin was made sin for us and became a curse that we might have the blessing. People seem to forget in this present semi-infidel age that the gospel is not only the witness of the deep mercy of God, but that it is the most terrible witness of the deep abhorrence that God has to sin to be found anywhere.

What would you put next? I would put next, deep reconciliation, because that is the outcome of the deep mercy and the deep righteousness. Human reconciliation is not a very thorough thing. They say, 'Scratch a Russian, and you find a Tartar', but when God reconciled me unto himself, it was a deep reconciliation. He took away the underlying nature, that which caused the enmity, sin. Christ has taken the sin, and borne it in his own body on the tree, and now the reconciliation between God and the sinner is perfect. This reconciliation is one of the deep things.

If there is deep reconciliation, you will almost anticipate the next point. Is not that accompanied by deep pardon? When God forgives he buries, and there is no future resurrection of sin. In Micah 7:19, you have God's own picture of how he forgives. He says, 'I have cast their sins into the depths of the sea.' God does not throw our sins into the shallows, or on the margin, where an ebbing tide would expose them: they are sunk into the great depths of the ocean of his forgiving love.

As a consequence you and I have deep blessings. There is a deep peace for the believer that flows like a river; a peace that the devil cannot break up, peace that abides when everything else is in turmoil. Some of you will be thinking today what a lot of motion there is on the sea; on the surface the waves are very high, and there is a gale in the Channel, but you only have to go down deep enough to find that the waters that are deep down are never moved; there is perfect stillness down there.

If God's children have deep peace they also have deep joy, a joy unspeakable, and, to crown all they are told by the Spirit that there are for them deep purposes of future glory. Jesus says, 'Father, I will that they also, whom thou hast given me, be with me where I am, that they may behold my glory which thou hast given me'; so that you will see all these deep things of God coming in beautiful succession; and the work of the Spirit is that I might know these things which are 'freely given to me of God.' God does not sell one of them, he freely gives them all, and anyone of us may have all these deep things.

I conclude with this solemn statement of the apostle concerning these things. They are not received by the natural man; he does not understand them. Look at the 14th verse: 'But the natural man receiveth not the things of the Spirit of God.' True, they are revealed in the Word, but the natural man—Calvin puts 'the animal man'—he hears the preacher talking about the deep things, but the words do not convey anything to him; he may perhaps read the chapter right through, and he does not see anything in it, because deep things are spiritually discerned. I am going to quote what is in my judgement one of the most beautiful illustrations ever used, and I acknowledge here again my indebtedness to dear Joseph Parker. I thank God for the marvellous witness he bore in the City Temple (I only wish he were there now!) to the Bible. His commentary on the Scriptures ought to be in every Christian home. He illustrates this very point, that the natural man does not perceive the things of God, because they are spiritually discerned, and such a man is lacking in something which would enable him to understand them; and he says that it was rumoured that underneath a certain piece of ground there was iron to be found, and two men were appointed to go and inspect and investigate the land and see whether there was really iron there. One man, a scientist and mineralogist, was very conscious of his own limitations, and knowing his own weakness, he took with him some scientific instruments. The other man, who was buoyant and self-confident, said, 'I believe what I can see, and what I can't see I won't believe,' and so he walked over the field, and got over it in no time. He said, 'Iron? nonsense! I see no iron; there is no iron here,' and dear Dr Parker says, 'It is almost a pity such men have no wings—they would get over it quicker.' This man went to the syndicate and said, 'There is no iron there: I walked all over the field and I could not see a trace of it.' The other man did not trust to his eye at all. He carried in his hand a little crystal box, and in that little crystal box there was a needle, and he kept watching that needle. He paused, for the needle in that crystal box had pointed down like the very finger of God, and he said, 'There is iron there.' He passed on, until again that needle pointed down, and he said, 'There is iron there,' and when he handed in his report he said, 'From one end of the field to the other there is iron.' 'Oh!' said some of the adherents of the first man, 'how do you know, when you did not see it?' 'Because,' he said, 'that which cannot be seen with the eye can be magnetically discerned.' And so what the eye of the natural man cannot see, and what his ear may not hear, we yet know and know beyond a doubt. The Spirit of God, who is our Guide, he has touched the soul within, and he says, 'Deep things of God here.' Then go and pick them up! Pick them up and make them your own.

GOD THINKS[1]

But I am poor and needy; yet the Lord thinketh upon me.
Psalm 40:17.

ON the evening of September 7th, the passage for reading in *Daily Light* was based on this verse. It is the verse that heads the page, and then, as many of you know, there follows a number of beautifully selected passages, all bearing on the main text. We read this verse that evening, and it suddenly opened up before us a boundless vista; for this morning's discourse will not, I think, go along the lines you anticipate. I am not going to dwell at all upon the grace of the text, but upon its mystery. 'I am poor and needy.' Well, we all know that, and I trust we feel it; but the sentence that rivetted me, and I pray God it may rivet you, is this, 'Yet the Lord *thinketh* upon me.' Then God thinks!! Have you ever allowed this, not only to simmer in your mind, but to go right down into your soul as a fact? God thinks!!! Then God is a thoughtful Being. Surely here is an argument for the personality of our God. To think is an attribute of personality. A mere influence, a subtle force, that which is only part and parcel of created matter, cannot think. It may be moved by laws it has no power whatever to resist; but to think—here we have Jehovah brought before us as a Being, as a person, and as One who thinks. The most wonderful thing you ever do is to think, and when you think, you do that which you cannot explain, and which cannot be explained by anyone else. What

[1] September 13, 1908, Metropolitan Tabernacle, Newington, London.

is thought? All scientists are agreed on this, that thought can never be the product of matter. It is not my brain that thinks—though I may think through my brain—but, as one scientist well says, it is a wrong statement altogether to say that thoughts lie in the brain: thoughts no more lie in the brain than Mendelssohn's oratorio, *Elijah,* lies in the organ or in the piano. By no cerebral convolution, no movement that is muscular, can any thought be generated. Then what is thought? Echo answers,—What? We know this, that God himself is the origin of all thought; and when you have said, 'God thinks', you have said one of the most wonderful things concerning God himself that the lip can utter, except when you have to add, as the Psalmist does, 'He thinketh *upon me.*'

Now before we go right into our subject, I can imagine some here saying, 'Oh, I wish, Mr Brown, you would give us something more practical. We want *"things"*, never mind about thoughts, let us have realities.' And are things more real than thoughts? 'Things' are not the original entity: thoughts are. Thoughts do not come from things, but all things come from thoughts. There never yet was anything that you can see with your eye that was not first seen in some mind; *all 'things' are only materialised thoughts.* You point me, maybe, to a Cologne Cathedral, a masterpiece of architecture— the only building that has ever made tears come to our eyes—and you say, 'What a perfect conception! What a magnificent building!' True, but before ever Cologne Cathedral stood in that square it was in the mind of the architect. It is only a magnificent thought that has become materialised in stone and marble. It was a conception before it was a building. The picture you gaze on was in the artist's mind before any colour was put upon the canvas; the picture is only the materialised thought of the artist. And music— which appeals to some of us even more than the painting—take such an oratorio as I have just mentioned, in our judgment unrivalled, that masterpiece of Mendelssohn, his oratorio, *Elijah,* all those matchless airs, those melodies, those dramatic clashes and pauses, were in his mind before ever there was a minim or a quaver put upon paper. And so, lying at the back of everything is a *think*. There is only the difference of one letter—substitute k for g and you come nearer the truth than perhaps you imagine. The thing is, after all, only the think; all things are the product of thought.

Now, here in our text we have Jehovah spoken of as thinking, and the text, as it gripped me, made me take this form of study:

WHAT DOES THE SCRIPTURE SAY ABOUT GOD'S THOUGHTS? Perhaps some say, 'Is not this rather a dry subject?' I hope it will not prove to be so; but if you come to worship on a Sunday morning, I take it you do not come for a little anecdote, or something that may create a smile: we meet for the study of the word, and a profounder subject than this morning's could hardly be discovered. But I think you will see, the moment we turn to a few passages, that in the light of Scripture we have a most marvellous vision of a thinking God.

What does Scripture say concerning God's thoughts? Let us look at the fifth verse of this Fortieth Psalm, 'Many, O LORD my God, are thy wonderful works which thou hast done and thy thoughts *which are to us-ward.*' God's works and God's thoughts march together. He has done wonderful works,—Why?—because he has had wonderful thoughts; and the wonder of the thought is this, they are thoughts 'to us-ward'. When we think of God upon the throne, the centre of the universe, controlling and governing all, oh the profound mystery and wonder of it—that there are thoughts from that throne to us-ward. I can understand them going out archangel-ward or seraphim-ward; but the psalmist says, 'Thou hast done wonderful works',—Why?—'because thou hast had wonderful thoughts and thoughts about us.' All God's works are God's thoughts carried out, and his thoughts have been and are to us-ward. God's thoughts *imply a purpose,* for in the fourteenth chapter of Isaiah, at the twenty-fourth verse, you read, 'The Lord of hosts hath sworn saying, surely as I have *thought,* so shall it come to pass; and as I have *purposed,* so shall it stand.' There is a divine purpose in all God does, and we are not living in a world where haphazard reigns, we are not living in a world where there is a thoughtless, careless Power above. All God's thoughts are his purposes, and before God does anything—I say it with reverence—he thinks it out. Oh the thought there was ere there was creation: he weighed the mountains in scales, and the hills in the balance, and he so balanced star against star, and world against world, that all the different pullings of gravitation act and re-act so that everything keeps its place. From the suns in the firmament to the daisies in the field, you can see God's thoughts. And are not his thoughts seen in the realm of providence? I do not think there are many here who have been more troubled with sceptical thoughts than the preacher, especially in relation to God's providential dealings. It is so difficult when you see the deck swept of all you love, and it looks as if providence were playing havoc with all your plans, still to realise that everything is being calmly, thoughtfully and lovingly arranged with a view to ultimate good; but the thought that arranged the position of the mountains, the thought that located the worlds in space, that same thought is arranging all things in God's providential realm. Stepping into the brighter and more blessed realm of redemption, I find it is all thought out there: as we read in the Epistle to the Ephesians, it is 'that, by the church might be known'—What?—'the manifold wisdom of God'. Angels and archangels look down and intently study a redeemed church, because there they see the highest and deepest and brightest manifestation of God's thought.

So much for the first reference. Now if you will turn to the NINETY-SECOND PSALM, FIFTH VERSE, you will find another

Scripture ray of light thrown upon a thinking God. 'O Lord, how great are thy works! and thy thoughts are *very deep.'* God's thoughts are very deep. Again, do you see how the Holy Ghost has linked the works with the thoughts. Thy works are very great,— Why?—because thy thoughts are very deep; and there must be harmony between the work and the thought, because every true work is an incarnated thought. But oh, Jehovah's thoughts are very deep! Try and conceive, if you can, of the difference which may be found in the mental powers of men on earth. I was thinking after this style: In yonder house, up in the nursery, is a little child playing. God bless him! I am so glad he has never had any big thoughts yet in that little head, and hope that many years will pass before that little forehead aches through big thoughts that surge. The toy occupies it now. But come into this outer room, that is built from the house, in order that there may be quiet, and here we find the father; he is an astronomer, and I will tell you what he is doing. He has noticed, as he has watched the heavens, that there is a deviation in the course of a planet, and he has argued that the deviation in the course of that planet proves there is another world, which he has never yet discovered, pulling at it, and he is working out a profound mathematical problem; he is going to prove the demonstration of a world he cannot see by the deviation of a world he can see. Is there any comparison between the thoughts of the father and those of the little one up there in the nursery? If that child were to speak it would say, 'Oh, father's thoughts are so deep!' Yes, too deep for your little head, darling. But remember that Jehovah is the origin of all mind, and the difference between the child's thoughts and the astronomer's is nothing compared with the difference that must ever lie between the profoundest thought of a created being and the thought of him who created the mental power. God thinks; and when God thinks I expect him to think something that I cannot always understand. I could not believe that he were God if he did not! *A God who never swamps my intel-lect is a God that shall never have the reverence of my heart.* I expect that when God thinks I shall have to stand amazed and say, 'I have no fathoming line for this.' Thy thoughts are deep.

Now side by side with the passages I have just given you, remem-ber a verse in the fifty-fifth chapter of Isaiah, and how beautifully does it come in: 'For my thoughts are not your thoughts, neither are your ways my ways, saith the Lord. For as the heavens are higher than the earth, so are my ways higher than your ways, and my thoughts than your thoughts.' Oh, it would be almost laugh-able, were it not so unutterably sad, when you see men in the pride of their so-called reason criticising Jehovah, trying to measure up Infinity. Jehovah's thoughts must be deep.

What is the third passage which throws another fresh and beautiful light upon our subject? TWENTY-NINTH CHAPTER OF JEREMIAH AND THE ELEVENTH VERSE: 'I know the thoughts that I think towards you, saith the Lord.' One could very easily get out of one's depth here, because there is not only thinking,—there is knowing that I am thinking; here is God not only having a thought, but he knows he has the thought. 'I know the thoughts that I think toward you, saith the Lord, *thoughts of peace,* and not of evil, to give you an expected end.' The latter clause should be rendered, 'to give you hope'. What is the previous verse? 'Thus saith the Lord, after seventy years be accomplished at Babylon I will visit you, and perform my good word toward you, in causing you to return to this place.' 'I am going to bring you out of your captivity, saith the Lord.'—Why?—'for I know the thoughts that I think toward you,—they are thoughts of peace to give you hope.' I know not, but if there should be some dear child of God here unutterably depressed, almost in despair, Brother, let me throw this passage to you as a lifebelt; put it round you, and rest on it. 'I know the thoughts that I think concerning you.' You were saying, 'but

Lord, I cannot understand them.' 'No', says the Lord, 'very likely not, but I know the thoughts.' You are in your captivity, you are in your Babylon, and you see no deliverance, and you say, 'How can I ever be brought out of this trouble?' The Lord says, 'You shall, for I know the thoughts that I have concerning you—not thoughts of evil but thoughts of peace to give you hope at the end.' It may not be apparent, but God's thoughts do not stop half-way, like ours. My thoughts generally stop before they have gone a few yards into the future; but Jehovah's thoughts travel to the very end; and his thought to us-ward is this, at the end to give us hope. It is alright, Brother, it is alright; at the end you will praise God. 'Dinna weary'; give God time. His thoughts will justify his love.

For a moment, on the fourth passage. It is in the ONE HUNDRED AND THIRTY-NINTH PSALM, the paraphrase of which we sang just now. One Hundred and Thirty-ninth Psalm, seventeenth verse. 'How precious also are thy thoughts unto me, O God! how great is the sum of them.' Before you close your Bibles, read the second verse of this Psalm: 'Thou knowest my downsitting and mine uprising, thou understandest *my thought* afar off.' In this Psalm you have *my* thought, and then you have *his* thought, but the psalmist does not say, 'How precious unto me are my thoughts': it is, 'How precious are thy thoughts unto me.' The reason why we are not happier Christians is this, we so brood over and contemplate our own thoughts, and we shall never get any good out of them. The true attitude is for my thought, like a bee, to find out the flower of God's thought, and then dive down into the flower and get the honey there. Oh, poor self-introspective man, you who are always looking in your own breast, thinking about your own thoughts and analysing them, the object for meditation and contemplation, according to Scripture, is this, Jehovah's thoughts. 'How precious are thy thoughts unto me. My thoughts nestle down in thy thought. I will think about what thou hast thought of me. I will take thy thoughts as expressed in the Scripture, and my thoughts shall cluster round them.'

The last passage is the one we have selected for our text, this last verse of the FORTIETH PSALM. 'I am poor and needy, yet the Lord thinketh upon me.' Thinketh upon me,—How? I believe that Jesus is in this Psalm, not only in the few verses we pointed out in the reading, but very constantly; and this utterance may fall, and I believe does fall, as much from the lip of the Lord Jesus as from David. Jesus could say, 'I am poor.' Yes, he was, 'The foxes have holes, and the birds their nests, but the Son of Man hath not where to lay his head.' 'I am poor and needy, yet my Father thinketh upon me.' If you read the whole of our dear Lord's life, you will see that it was a life of absolute trust in the loving thought of his Father. But let David be the speaker—and without a doubt his own feelings are intermingled—he is speaking of himself not simply by prophecy but by experience, and he finds there are a good many round about who give him trouble. There are some saying, 'Aha! Aha!' Have you ever had people say that to you? There is the scoffer laughing, maybe, at your simple confidence in God, and he boldly says, 'Aha! Aha!' Poor David says, 'Let such as love thy salvation say continually, The Lord be magnified.' But listen how they deride and say, 'Aha, Aha.' And then this thought comes to him, 'I am poor and needy, and there are some who despise me, but the Lord thinketh upon me; I have got a place in his thoughts, and he is *thinking of my deliverance* and my emancipation, so I will send up this prayer: "Make no tarrying, O my God." Do what thou art thinking about; thou hast a thought for me, let it become the "thing"; thou art thinking of my sorrow, deliver me from it.'

Perhaps some will say, 'But, preacher, have you dealt fairly with us? All the passages you have given are out of the Old Testament; are not we New Testament saints? Give us something from the New Testament about God thinking.' The beauty is that you do not find the expression there. I will tell you why. In the New Testament we have *God's thoughts incarnated in the person of the Lord Jesus.* I am so glad that when I pass from the Old Testament, which tells me so much about God's thoughts, and come into the New Testament, I do not find this word 'thought'. I find another word— 'In the beginning was the Word.' What is a word? A word is the incarnation of a thought. I know the thoughts that I have. Yes, but how is anyone else to know them? The thoughts that course through my brain at this moment must be concealed from you until they are expressed in language; then the word becomes the thought manifested. Jesus is the thought of God. I do not need a passage to tell me about God's thoughts. Here are God's thoughts, for listen: 'God, who at sundry times and in divers manners spake in time past unto the fathers by the prophets, hath in these last days spoken unto us by his Son', or, as it should be rendered, 'in his Son'. Look at Jesus, and there you have God's thoughts. I know God's thoughts about sin, I know his thoughts concerning the sinner, his thoughts of mercy, his thoughts of salvation: they are all gathered up in Christ Jesus; he is God's thought, and the thought which is to us-ward. God's eternal thought came to us-ward, and then the manifestation of that thought was Jesus Christ coming to us-ward. 'Lo I come, because the Father's thought has come. I delight to do thy will, O my God.' Is there some poor lonely one here who says, 'I do not think anybody in London thinks of me. I should be so glad if I could only be sure there is some friend thinking about me.' Perhaps you feel as Alexander Selkirk makes that one in the desert island, the true Robinson Crusoe, to feel. Do you remember the passage?—

> My friends, do they now and then send
>   A wish or a thought after me?
> Oh, tell me I yet have a friend,
>   Though a friend I am never to see.

THIS GOD OUR GOD

Does your heart sigh, 'Is there anyone who sends a wish or a thought after me?' You need not say it any more; alter Alexander Selkirk's little verse, and write it thus:—

> My friends, do they now and then send
> A wish or a thought after me?
> Oh tell me I yet have *the* Friend,
> And the Friend I am ever to see.

'The Lord thinketh on me.'

WORSHIP[1]

God is a Spirit, and they that worship him
must worship him in spirit and in truth.
John 4:24.

WE shall only dwell on the one word 'worship'. I can almost imagine that I hear someone saying, 'Only *one* word? Will you be able, preacher, to fill up the allotted time from so small a text?' True, it is only one word, but then it is *such* a word that we need have no fear of exhausting its teaching, did we preach until midnight. The only dread we have is lest the greatness of the word should altogether overwhelm us, for an ocean depth lies in this single word. 'Worship'. Seven letters spell it, but seven millenniums will never exhaust its meaning. 'Worship'. Oh, it is a *sanctuary* word. As the tabernacle of old among the tents of Israel, so is this word 'worship' in earth's vocabulary. It will be a delightful occupation if, this morning, we can walk round about it; but yet shall we not be satisfied, for, as the tabernacle of old could never be comprehended by an outside view, there being but the badger skin covering to be seen, so merely walking round about the word 'worship' will never discover to us all its exquisite loveliness. To understand worship you must worship. To enter into its meaning you must enter into its reality. May the Spirit of truth promised of our Lord, the Spirit which guides into all the truth, guide us into the truth concerning worship this morning.

[1] September 6, 1891, Metropolitan Tabernacle, Newington, London.

No word is more common or more generally heard in almost innumerably different ways of application. We often hear of 'places of worship', and in some cases a more startling misnomer could hardly be found. We read of 'books of worship', and yet perhaps it is often the book of family worship which stands most in the way of the true worship of the family. 'I am going up to worship this morning' is an ordinary expression, and perhaps hundreds who are present have employed it; and yet going up to worship may be the very last motive that prompts the moving steps in the direction of the sanctuary; or, if it be the object in view, it is perhaps the very last attained. We are told, 'The worship at such and such a place is very ornate.' 'Ornate' worship! One might as well talk of an angel in full evening dress. 'Oh', say others, 'in such a place the worship is severely simple.' 'Severely simple' worship! You might as well speak of an angel in morning costume. Worship can be neither ornate nor simple. Those terms belong to externals only, not to spirit.

'Worship'—what is it? This is the question which we ask, and may the Spirit of God lead us into the true answer. 'God is Spirit, and they that worship *him*'—that is something far more than coming to the Metropolitan Tabernacle on Sunday morning. 'They that worship him'—that is something far more than singing, magnificently as you sang that hymn just now. 'They that worship him must worship him in spirit and in truth.' O Spirit of worship, discover unto us the meaning of worship!

We shall this morning ask and try to answer two questions. The first is, *What is worship?* And when we have received the answer to that we shall ask a second question which is suggested by the answer: *Who then are worshippers?*

I. First, WHAT IS WORSHIP? In order to get at the bottom of the matter it will be best to see what is the actual literal meaning of the words which, in our Bible, are translated 'worship'. In the Old Testament there is one word employed almost exclusively, and the literal translation of the word (and I ask you to mark it) is 'to bow self down'. Indeed, it is many times so translated in our version. The word chiefly used in the New Testament and translated worship means 'to kiss the hand towards'. Now, bring the Old Testament and the New Testament definitions together, and you will see that they amount to this, that worship is the prostration of myself before God, and yet it is not a prostration of terror or dread. It is the prostration of adoring love. But bear in mind that, whilst to bow self down is the meaning of the word which is translated 'worship', to worship is something far more than simply *to bow the body*. This comes out, and most strikingly, in one or two passages to which I will now refer. I might give you a dozen, but we will take only three. In the fourth chapter of Exodus, and the last verse, we read:—'And the people believed, and when they heard that the Lord had visited the children of Israel, and that he had looked upon their affliction, then they bowed their heads and worshipped'; or, literally translated, 'they bowed their heads, and then they bowed themselves'. This evidently teaches that it is possible to bow the head without bowing self. They bowed their heads, and then they bowed themselves in worship. In the twelfth chapter of the same book, and the 27th verse, you have this most interesting distinction repeated:—'And it shall come to pass, when your children shall say to you, What mean ye by this service? that ye shall say, It is the sacrifice of the Lord's Passover, who passed over the houses of the children of Israel in Egypt, when he smote the Egyptians, and delivered our houses. And the people bowed the head, and worshipped.' Here, again, they bowed the head, and then they bowed themselves. But if these two references show us that it is possible to bow the head without bowing self, a third reference shows the converse, or the other side of the shield, that it is possible to bow yourself without bowing the body.

In the Ninety-fifth Psalm we have these well-known words, 'Oh come let us worship',' or, as it is really, 'Oh, come let us bow self down', and then it adds, *'and bow down'.* Yes, I can bow the body without bowing the spirit; and I can bow the spirit and worship without bowing the body.

Evidently, therefore, the first answer to our question, 'What is worship?' is, that it is something infinitely more than mere posture. Personally, I think that it is well to be as reverential as possible in external demeanour; but worship consists not in any attitude. Daniel *kneeled* and prayed, and he so worshipped that the Lord came and put his hand upon him as he kneeled, and he arose strengthened. But Solomon *stood* before the altar of the Lord and prayed; and, as he prayed, the glory of the Lord filled the house, and the cloud of the divine presence went rolling through the building, until man was excluded, and the priests could no longer serve there. But I think that one of the most delightful bits of worship on record is that which David had, concerning which I read, 'And David *sat* before the Lord.' The one kneeled, and the Lord bowed over him. The other stood, and the Lord descended and wrapped him about with his glory. The third sat, but his worship was none the less sweet.

What is worship? Worship is *the bowing of the inner self.* It is my innermost self doing that which may be seen done by the Eastern in his external worship. Look at yonder Oriental. Let him be present to our mind's eye. He stands there, and I see him with closed hands. He bends; he bows; he does not stop until his forehead is in the dust. It is when my soul does *that,* that I worship; and, dear brethren and sisters, there can be no worship at all until self bows. But here is just the difficulty. How hard it is to get this wretched *self* to bow. When my self, graciously influenced by the divine Spirit, prostrates itself lower and lower before God until it puts its very brow into the dust with no word to say for itself, but filled with the glorious consciousness of being before God, perhaps too delighted to be able to utter a word, simply prostrate before God, and yet without an element of dread, then I approximate to the meaning of the word 'worship'. Worship is not even a matter of words. There may be words, or there may not be. Worship is not interfered with, either by their presence or by their absence. Very delightful it is to join in singing hymns, and singing them as you sang just now. Yes, but the singing of hymns is not necessarily worship, although we may worship in the singing of hymns. The reading of the word is very precious, but the reading of the word is not necessarily worship, though I may worship in the reading of the word. When our dear brother led us just now in prayer, who of us did not feel that prayer is talking to God?—and that is delightful worship. Yes, but worship is not necessarily prayer, though true prayer will always be worship. The spirit may worship in prayer, but worship is that inner thing that can neither be seen nor heard by our fellow men. It is my self down before God in unspeakable delight.

Now, may I take you a step further, and this will go more deeply into the subject? What is worship? We answer, true worship is *the sovereignty of God recognised in reality*. I am afraid that the phrase the 'sovereignty of God' is not very popular just now. 'The sovereignty of man' commends itself most to this proud generation. Humanity enthroned and worshipped is Satan's present preparation for an actual Antichrist. A day of terrible judgment is at hand for those who, in the pride of their heart, have thus deified humanity, for 'the lofty looks of man shall be humbled, and the haughtiness of men shall be bowed down, and the Lord alone shall be exalted *in that day*. For the day of the Lord of hosts shall be upon every one that is proud and lofty, and upon every one that is lifted up, and he shall be brought low, and the loftiness of man shall be bowed down, and the Lord alone shall be exalted.' They that bow not now before the sovereignty of God can never be his worshippers. Where there is no recognition of divine sovereignty there can be no true worship, for worship is the bowing, not the exaltation, of self. *God's critic can never worship.* He who has a contention with Jehovah concerning his sovereignty cannot worship him, whatever else he may do. In worship my whole self accepts the sovereignty of God, and, without a quibble or criticism, bows in unreserved obedience. There is a very remarkable expression in the book of Genesis, where Abraham says to his servants, 'Tarry ye here while I and the lad go yonder *and worship.*' He does not mean there 'go and pray'. No, Abraham, taught of the Spirit, has entered into the very core of what worship is. He is going now to render a sublime obedience to the word of his God, a surrender which knows no limit. This is worship. It is comparatively easy to surrender one's self to enthusiasm. Let there be a mighty shout of praise such as would fill this building, and he would be a strangely stolid soul who remained unmoved. Let there be a multitude of people brought together, and one thought filling all minds, and, in all probability, 'animal magnetism' will be quite sufficient to account for a good deal of thrilling emotion. Yes, it is not difficult to be moved by enthusiasm; and it is not a very high experience either to be led to break out in a note of praise. But oh, brothers and sisters, to bend the will, to bow my self—this is no easy achievement. For me to sing ecstatically about the greatness, the glory, and the majesty of God, and yet not be surrendered to him, is not worship. I may sing like a seraph of him who rules and doeth as he wills, but, if my proud heart is not in absolute submission to his will, I know nothing whatever of the meaning of this word 'worship'. No proud, no self-satisfied, no God-contending spirit can worship. So long as self lifts up its head, there is no worship. The worship taught in this word is the prostration of self in adoring love before Jehovah. As one has well put it, if my memory serves me rightly, to worship is to plunge with dazzled eyes into the glory of God, and then, with veiled face, to cry, 'Holy, holy, holy.' This prostration before the sovereignty of God, as we have already said, is not a prostration of fear. No. A worshipper would not have God less a sovereign than he is, if he could. The yoke of the divine sovereignty does not gall him. He sings,

> My God, how wonderful Thou art;
>   Thy majesty how bright;
> How beautiful Thy mercy-seat
>   In depths of burning light!

He would not have the burning light less burning. He fears, but, oh, it is with a delightful fear, a fear that has no element of terror in it; for he adds—

> But I may love Thee too, O Lord,
>   Almighty as Thou art;
> For Thou hast stooped to ask of me
>   The love of my poor heart.

May we know, dear brethren and sisters, more and more every day what it is to be in absolute subjection to the sovereignty of God, our wills completely surrendered to his, so that the subjection becomes the soul's delightful rest.

Perhaps the most marvellous picture of worship which we have in this book is that which is found in Isaiah 6. You know it well. The burning ones, the sons of fire, the seraphim, are worshipping; and how do they worship? I hear them cry, 'Holy, holy, holy.' They are not thinking of themselves. They are not concerned about their surroundings. Those seraphim are occupied with One, and that One is 'upon a throne high and lifted up' and, as the cadence of their song rises and falls, 'Holy, holy, holy', what do they do? They veil their faces, though they be seraphic, and they veil their feet, though they are unsoiled. They boast neither of their character, nor of their walk. It is self veiled, self hidden, self forgotten, self

drowned, and God realized. May the Lord grant that when next
we use this word 'worship' there may be a deeper meaning in it
than, perhaps, there has been heretofore.

> And when I cast my *inner* self
> Prostrate before the Lord,
> Earth left behind, alone with Him,
> 'Tis then I *know* the word.

> When, conscious only of Himself,
> Myself is swept away,
> 'Tis then in spirit and in truth
> I worship in His way.

II.—Our second question is, WHO, THEN, ARE WORSHIPPERS?
Bear with me, dear unconverted friend, for a moment. You may,
perhaps, feel wounded at what we say; but if we wound you, as we
hope we may, we do so in deepest love. In answer to the question,
Who are worshippers? we reply that *the unrenewed cannot be*. No
unconverted man in this tabernacle can worship. I will tell you
why. Because 'the natural man is not subject to the law of God,
neither indeed can be'. As long as I have within me a self that is
not subject unto God, how can I worship? That self which lifts
up its head and struts about and is proud of its own righteousness cannot worship. I know when the angels will recognise your
worship. It is when that proud head of yours has been bent before
God, and the last word of self-excuse has been uttered, and when
the brow of your inner soul is down in the dust, as you cry, 'God
be merciful to me the sinner.' Then the angels will begin to rejoice,
and say, 'Behold, he prays at last. Now the man has commenced to
worship.' 'Two men went up into the temple to pray.' Do you see
the one as he says, 'God, I thank thee that I am not as other men
are'? That man does not bow himself before God. Not he, indeed!
Why, his Pharisaical self struts about like a little god, saying, 'I

do this, and I do that, and I give tithes of all that I possess.' The man said his prayer, and he went back, but he did not worship. Do you see that other man? He bows his innermost self as he cries, 'God be merciful to me the sinner.' Christ's comment is this: 'I tell you; *that* man went down to his house justified rather than the other, for every one that *exalteth himself* shall be abased, and he that *humbleth himself* shall be exalted.'

Do you want to know whom you worship? You worship the one to whom you bow down, whatever may be your professions. If I bow down to money, then I worship money. If I bow myself down to myself, I worship myself. Whatever that thing may be to which I prostrate myself, that thing is my idol, O unrenewed man, thou art a worshipper, but thou art bowing down to the works of thine own hands. Self is thy god. The true Christian, also, *so long as he is unsurrendered* cannot be a *real worshipper*. Have you got any little quarrel on with God? You say, 'A quarrel with God?' Yes, are you sure that you have never had one? I do not know the man who could venture to say that he never had. God's thought about some matter is not quite your thought, and his way is not the way that you want to take, and so there is inward contention. Your will is not surrendered to his, and therefore you do not get any refreshment from your devotions, do you? How can there be 'devotion' where there is no devotedness? As long as I am God's critic,—as long as I am God's judge,—as long as I am contending with him about anything, there can be no real worship. Hence we come away ofttimes so unrefreshed in prayer. We go to church and to chapel very regularly, and perhaps we read the word, but we do not get any blessing. Why is this? The answer is simple. We are not worshippers. The moment that miserable 'self' falls down before God, we shall have the blessing, for then are we true worshippers, but not till then.

This word seems to grow on me, but I see that my time has just gone, and therefore I will conclude.

Any heart that *prostrates itself in adoring love* is a true worshipper. I will not ask you to turn to the references now, but will you look up the word 'worshipper' where it occurs in the New Testament, and see who the real worshippers are. To do so is very instructive. I read, for example, in Matthew 8, 'And, behold, there came a leper and worshipped him.' Now, how did that leper worship? Listen. He said, 'Lord, if thou wilt thou canst make me clean.' I have often heard that poor leper abused as if he was a very unbelieving man, because he said 'if'. I think that the man was quite right. He bowed to the divine sovereignty. 'Lord, I have no doubt as to thy ability. If thou wilt thou canst make me clean.' And the Lord has put him down on the list of his worshippers. In Matthew 15 there comes a Syrophoenician woman, and I read, 'And she fell at his feet, and she worshipped him, and said, Lord, help me.' Now, mark, how did that woman worship? See how she won the title of worshipper. Jesus said, 'It is not meet to take the children's bread and to cast it to dogs.' Most of us would have lifted up the head of our paltry little self, and said, 'Dog? Do you call me "dog"? I am not a dog.' Ah, but when self lifts up its head it ceases to be a worshipper. The woman said, 'Truth, Lord, but yet the dogs eat of the crumbs which fall from their Master's table.' The Lord enrolls her amongst his worshippers. And, had we time, we could show you how often persons in the most unexpected quarters yielded to the Lord a worship which refreshed his heart.

Oh, come, let us worship. You know *where* to come. There is the altar; there is the sacrifice; there is the high priest. Behold where Jesus sits still bearing the marks of the thorn-crown and the nails! I will tell you what worship is, then. It is to go to the mercy-seat concerning which God has said, 'There will I meet with thee and it is to cast one's self right down at the feet of Christ, perfectly pros-trate as far as self is concerned, the last idea of goodness taken out of us, the last word of excuse silenced, the brow in the dust, and yet trust and love in the heart. Oh, come, poor sinner. Your life in the past may have been as black as perdition; you may have rejected the word over and over again; but will you worship this morning? Doff your pride. Do not be damned for the sake of your dignity. Down with self before an exalted Christ. Give him love's salute, and the Lord will say, 'That man worships me.'

> Worship is the captive will,
>   Hidden deep in Him;
> Nothing in our hearts but love:
>   These filled to the brim.
> Hearts that bow before the Lord
>   Lost in loving gaze,
> Viewing what a love He gave,
>   Filled with holy praise;
> Looking at His lovely form
>   With an eye of faith,
> Thinking nought of world and self,
>   Only what *He* saith;
>
> Resting in the arms of Him
>   Who o'er all hath sway,
> Willing He should take our wills,
>   Make them will His way.
> Counting self as nothing worth,
>   Jesus Christ as all;
> Losing our whole self in Him,
>   Caught in love's sweet thrall.
> Worship lies in bended wills
>   Rather than bent knees.
> The secret of a life of praise
>   Is Jesus Christ to please.

Spirit of God, give the spirit of worship to every one of us, for thy name's sake. Amen.

A MIGHTY ARM[1]

Thou hast a mighty arm; strong is thy hand, and high is thy right hand.
Justice and judgment are the habitation of thy throne:
mercy and truth shall go before thy face.
Psalm 89:13, 14.

THIS 89th Psalm is a magnificent poem to the praise of the covenant of God—the covenant made with David, and, through David, made with David's greater Son, for all his heirs unto all generations. Without doubt the psalm was penned by a man who was in deep sorrow of heart. Ethan, whoever he may have been—and many suppose that he lived about the time of the Babylonian captivity—looked round about him and saw that the glory of the house of David had waned, and the throne of David, so far from being established, was seemingly tottering. Filled with sore trouble and dismay, Ethan seeks to comfort his soul by remembering what God had promised to his chosen servant. Ah, there is nothing like God's covenant for a troubled heart. You, who have never known the meaning of soul anguish and dark depression—you, whose craft has always glided along in smooth waters, may afford to have a religion which has very little of covenant grace in it. But those who are called to do business in great waters, when all frames and feelings worth having are gone, and the storm king is abroad in his fury, know what a sense of unspeakable relief it brings to fall back upon a covenant that is 'ordered in all things

---

[1] No date, East London Tabernacle.

and sure'. It is delightful to get out of the realm of *ifs* and *perhapses,* and *peradventures,* and just rest upon the *wills* and the *shalls* of a God who cannot lie. Thus Ethan before he makes his complaint, calls to remembrance all that Jehovah had pledged by his word to David. You will find the word 'faithfulness' in verses 1, 2, 5, and 8. It sparkles all the way through the psalm. Ethan continually reminds his soul, 'God is faithful; God is faithful.' This is the sheet anchor of his heart; and, to encourage himself yet more, he calls to remembrance four attributes of God. You have them in the verses which I have selected as our text. 'Thou hast a mighty arm.' Here is God's might. 'Justice', or as it is rendered in the Revised Version, 'righteousness', 'is the basis of thy throne.' Here is right; and 'Mercy and truth shall go before thy face.' Our God is a God of might, and a God of right, and a God of mercy, and a God of truth. On these four attributes, as on four massive blocks of granite, does the soul venture safely to build her eternal hopes.

Let us for a short time look at these four attributes, and then observe, in closing, that these attributes are glorified in God's covenant of salvation, for that is the teaching of the whole psalm.

First, it may encourage our hearts to remember that *our God has a mighty arm.* There is nothing weak about Jehovah. You see that even his left hand is strong. The psalm tells us this: 'Strong is thy hand, and high is thy right hand.' The first hand that is mentioned here must be his left, and even that is clothed with might, while his right hand is lifted up on high. Brethren and sisters, our God is not a weak being who can make promises, but has no power to perform them. Our God is not some merely well-disposed being who has the heart and will to do good to his people, but finds himself unable to carry out all the wishes of his heart. His heart is large to devise, and his hand is equally powerful to execute. Our God has all power. 'Once have I heard this, yea, twice, that power belongeth unto God.' This is one of the articles of our creed. God grant that we may never lose sight of it. Now, the power of our God is not a derived or communicated power. I think it is Charnock, in his wonderful work on the attributes,[1] who brings out the thought that God's power is an essential force—essential to his very being. All the power that man has is derived. Look at yonder piece of machinery. It is in motion. It works mightily. There is power in every cog of that wheel as it revolves, and yet there is not an atom of essential might. The real power lies beneath, in the engine that drives the whole. There is only power in the cogs as that power is conveyed by straps and bands. So with man. But the power which God has is derived from none. From no source does he gather it. It dwells within himself. He is the Almighty. His power is infinite. No language can set this forth, for language is finite, and the finite must break down when it attempts the infinite. Conceive, if you can, of an aggregate of all power, and when your imagination has done its best you will not have begun, for there is no limit to Jehovah's might. Oh, my soul, as these lips speak, fall back upon a power that knows no bounds, and let thy heart rejoice itself in a God who has a mighty arm, whose left hand is strong, and whose right hand is exalted.

If you look into the psalm you will see that the author celebrates the power of God, first, in its destructive work. Look at the tenth verse:—'Thou hast broken Rahab.' I need hardly tell you that Rahab here means Egypt. To the Jew, Egypt was the very embodiment of might; but Ethan, taught of the Spirit, sings this song, 'Thou hast broken Rahab in pieces as one that is slain.' There is the enemy lying dead on the battlefield, and the war chariot comes tearing along, and thunders over the corpses, and its wheels grind the dead, and turn them into the mire of the field; and, says Ethan,

[1] See Stephen Charnock, *Works,* vols 1 & 2 on *The Existence and Attributes of God* (Edinburgh: The Banner of Truth Trust, 2010).

Egypt has no more ability to resist the power of our God than has the dead man on the battlefield to stop the career of the chariot of war that rolls over him. 'Thou scatterest thine enemies with thy strong arm.' This is a very unpopular view of God just now. God has been stripped of almost all his attributes but love and mercy. But turn back, and look at the records of the Book, and thou shalt see that thy God is not one to be trifled with. When he turns out to fight the battle of his people, none can stand against him, for even Rahab is broken in pieces.

The next verses introduce a further manifestation of the might of God's arm, namely, creation. Listen: 'The heavens are thine; the earth also is thine. As for the world and the fulness thereof, thou hast founded them.' Creation sings my text, 'Thou hast a mighty arm.' Give man material to work upon, and I grant you that with wondrous skill he can produce that which delights the eye, but he must have something to begin with. But our God has a mightier arm, for he brings forth wonders from the womb of nothingness. When he took creation work in hand, there was nothing for him to begin with. He said, 'Be', and matter was. Ethan had not a dash of infidelity about him. Looking up at the heavens and out upon the earth, he exclaimed, 'My God has a mighty arm. How strong is the hand that has reared the pillars of the earth, and stretched the heavens like a curtain!' And then in that beautiful sentence that follows, he goes on to say that God's power is seen in the upholding of all that he has made. 'Tabor and Hermon shall rejoice in thy name.' There is not a blade of grass that springs at their feet, or a tree that grows upon their flanks, or a sheep that climbs their summit, which does not testify of the sustaining might of Jehovah's hand. As we read in the Hebrews, 'He upholdeth all things by the word of his power.' Dear brethren and sisters, do you know what it is to get into the great deeps of depression? Some of us know what it is to get 'down' in the fullest and most doleful sense of the word.

Let me recommend to such the cordial of this 13th verse, 'Thou hast a mighty arm.' Oh, child of God, thy Father is not such an one as thou hast taken him to be. Do you say, 'Oh, but I have got to the end of my resources'? I reply, It did not take you long to get there, did it? But have you got to the end of your God's resources? Do you say, 'I am so depressed that I really do not know what to do'? True, but do you not think that God can see what is best to be done for you? Do you say, 'I have done my last stroke to help myself'? Then fall back upon your God. Your arm is weak, but never mind that. Behold, his arm is mighty. Oh, to know how to find a positive pleasure in being weak, a real joy in being in difficulties, a delight in being hedged up all round, just because it gives one a better opportunity for saying, 'Now, Lord, step in; I trust alone in thee. My weakness clings to thy unfailing might.'

Now look for a moment at the next point. In the 14th verse you have *the attribute of righteousness.* 'Righteousness and judgment are the basis of thy throne.' In the East the thrones were often supported by pillars, and we have reason to suppose that Solomon's throne rested upon lions. Do you see how striking is the picture? God has a throne. What does it rest on? God's throne rests on two mighty columns: righteousness and judgment. They are really one. I love that word 'righteousness'. Let me contract it. 'Righteousness' is 'rightness'. Oh, what a mercy that this comes after the 13th verse. Can you conceive a more fearful picture than illimitable power without any sense of right? Is it not one which would defy the genius of a Dante to set it forth? My spirit shrinks from so awful a conception. It outdoes the devil a myriad times. The devil has no righteousness, but, thank God, the devil is not possessed of infinite power. Infinite power without infinite right is something which the mind cannot bear to dwell on. But now let me put the two attributes side by side, and will they not inspire fresh courage in your heart? With infinite might there is associated infinite right;

and the rightness of God is an essential of his nature. He is right-eousness itself. All that he does is right. It is not for me to put down a standard of right, and say whether God comes up to that. God is himself the standard. I have only to know what God has done to find out what is right. God cannot do that which is not right. He must undeify himself before he can do wrong, for, as the fountain, so the stream. He is right; and all his actions are based on righteousness, and are themselves infinitely right.

But I pass on to the next attributes, those of *mercy and truth*. See how these are mentioned: 'Mercy and truth shall go before thy face.' Here is an almighty monarch, and he is on his throne, and that throne is based on righteousness. Now the monarch is going forth, and as he goes, he has two trumpeters marching before him, and these are mercy and truth. Each trumpeter gives a blast, to let us know that the King is coming, and the king never comes out without these two, for 'All the ways of the Lord are mercy and truth.'

How do they go before his face? They do so in the way of warn-ing. When the King rises to do his strange work of judgment, mercy sounds the alarm. The King is coming. Beware! Flee! God never strikes anybody without giving him fair warning. For a hun-dred and twenty years mercy blew her trumpet through the lips of Noah, and warned the world of a coming deluge. But, mark you, mercy is not alone. Mercy gives the warning, and truth fulfils it, for the flood did come. Mercy, you see, will give a fair warning; but be not deluded, and say not that, because God gives a warning, there-fore the threat shall not be fulfilled. Mercy says, 'Be warned', and, if the sinner neglects the warning of mercy, truth comes and fulfils the threat. But, on the other hand, mercy proclaims the promise, and then truth comes and performs it. Oh, it is beautiful to see these two walking together. Proud sinner, art thou here tonight? Remember that, though mercy is warning, mercy does not stand alone. Every threat which God has uttered, truth shall fulfil. Oh, poor anxious soul, you think that the promise of mercy is almost too good to be true. Thou needest have no such alarm, for side by side with mercy promising is truth performing. Do you see the beautiful picture? We have might and right, mercy and truth, a heavenly quartette.

Now, for a minute or two, I will ask for very careful attention, more especially on the part of those of you who are not saved and know that you are not, and those who are not quite sure whether you are saved or not. Oh, to have a clear and intelligent comprehension of God's way of salvation. I have cried much before coming here that God would make this part of our sermon the means of bringing some into perfect rest, and I think that he will; but, at least, will you give me your ears, and let me have your attention on this point. All these four attributes of might, right, mercy, and truth are glorified in God's plan of salvation.

To begin with, you will find all four meeting in Christ—all four meeting in the person of the Lord Jesus. In the Eighty-fifth Psalm you have two or three very remarkable verses, which I think cannot be looked into carefully without at once revealing the person of the Lord Jesus. You read, 'Surely his salvation is nigh them that fear him, that glory may dwell in our land. Mercy and truth are met together; righteousness and peace have kissed each other. Truth shall spring out of the earth, and righteousness shall look down from heaven. Righteousness shall go before *him*.' Oh, it is a person, then, that is spoken of. 'Righteousness shall go before *him*, and shall set us in the way of his steps.' These attributes are all meeting. Here is mercy kissing truth. Here is righteousness embracing peace. Where do we find all these attributes, seemingly at variance one with the other, thus harmonising and blending? The answer is, 'In an incarnate God.' Mercy and truth kiss each other in him. Truth springs out of the ground, and righteousness looks down from heaven. All the attributes of God meet in him, not to wrangle or to war, but to sweetly blend.

Bear with me whilst I remind you that Jesus Christ himself is the mighty arm. 'Thou hast a mighty arm.' I believe that Jesus Christ himself is intended here. Christ is the mighty arm of Jehovah. He is 'the arm of the Lord'. As such he works out salvation, a salvation that is characterized by these three things—righteousness, mercy, and truth. Righteousness, for, in the 42nd chapter of Isaiah and the 21st verse, you have these words: 'The Lord is well pleased for his righteousness' sake. He will magnify the law, and make it honourable.' The salvation of God is not at the expense of law. God has not winked at sin. He saith not to the sinner, 'Well, I will overlook it all. We will not say anything more about it. I feel drawn out in sympathy to you. I will close my eyes to your sin.' No, for his righteousness' sake the Lord has magnified the law and made it honourable. In whom? In the person of his Son. If you want to know what the righteousness of God is like, look at the suffering, bleeding Son of God. Behold in him how much God values righteousness. His throne of mercy has righteousness and judgment for its basis. In the 3rd chapter of Romans and the 25th verse, you read concerning Christ, 'whom God hath set forth to be a propitiation through faith in his blood'. Now note—'to declare his righteousness for the remission of sins that are past, through the forbearance of God; to declare, I say, his righteousness, that he might be just and the justifier of him that believeth in Jesus.' God's salvation is based upon his righteousness. If you had gone into the Holy Place of the tabernacle of old, you would have seen there an oblong box, on the top of which there was a golden slab, and over the golden slab were two cherubim; and if you had asked Aaron, 'What is that golden slab?' he would have told you, 'That is the mercy-seat where God meets with us.' True but supposing that you were to ask another question, 'On what does the mercy-seat rest?' Aaron, had he been allowed to do so, would have lifted up the golden lid, and said, 'Look in'; and you would have found the two tables of stone with the law of God engraved upon them. *Mercy rested on an honoured law.* God met man at the mercy-seat, but the mercy-seat had for its basis righteousness and judgment.

I need not tell you how mercy and truth come into God's salvation. You all know that. Mercy runs and seeks the sinner; mercy brings him home; mercy kisses him; mercy clothes him; mercy takes him into her house and feeds him; mercy puts him among her children; and mercy sets the bells of heaven ringing because he is saved. Yes, but truth has her part. God has kept his word in every part of this salvation. God said that sin could only bring the penalty of death. Has God kept his word? Yes. God never relinquished the penalty. Behold Jesus lying cold and still in the tomb, and then deny it if you can. God has kept his word. Even when the substitute is his own Son, the penalty is not relaxed. I praise God tonight for a salvation that rests on righteousness, honours truth, and sends mercy singing for joy right round the world.

Perhaps some of you have on your bookshelves at home Ralph Erskine's sermons. If so I would advise you to take them down and begin to read them tonight. See whether you have that well-known sermon on the 10th verse of the 85th Psalm: 'Mercy and truth have met together; righteousness and peace have kissed each other.' I know that if you begin to read it you will have to read it right through, for there is a strange charm about it. He works out the idea that all the attributes of God kept meeting in the life of Jesus. He pictures how they all met in the manger. They look at the young babe, and they begin to shake hands. They are all reconciled in him. They met together in Gethsemane, and Ralph Erskine puts it thus (if my memory serves me rightly), that righteousness and mercy and peace so wanted to kiss each other that they pressed Christ between them until great drops of blood did fall to the ground. Righteousness and peace did kiss each other in the breaking heart of Jesus. Their lips met there. And as he hangs upon the tree, righteousness looks up and says, 'I am satisfied', and peace, mercy, and truth all group themselves round about that dying one, and embrace each other as they sing, 'We all meet in him.'

Dear sinner, the salvation which I offer you tonight in my Master's name is not one which rests upon some frames and feelings of your own: 'Blessed are the people that know the joyful sound. In thy name shall they rejoice all the day, and in thy righteousness shall they be exalted.' Does some soul say, 'Oh, sir, tell me how I can be saved'? I will tell you. *Put your faith where God has placed your salvation.* You will find that in the 19th verse of this psalm, God says, 'I have laid help on one that is mighty.' God has put all the help that poor sinners need upon his own mighty One. Go and rest your faith just where God has placed your help. Go, poor, helpless, and weak as thou art, and say, 'O my God, where thou hast put my help I now put my trust; and on Christ's mighty arm do I now put my hand.'

> A guilty, weak, and helpless worm
>   On Thy kind arms I fall:
> Be Thou my strength, my righteousness,
>   My Jesus, and my all.

God bring you to this trust! Trust him, trust him, and thou shalt go out of this building singing, 'Thou hast a mighty arm: it has rescued me. Strong is thy left hand, for it has grasped me. Highly exalted is thy right hand, for it has lifted me up from the pit.' Go, trust the salvation that is based on righteousness, buttressed by truth, and crowned with mercy. The Lord grant that it may be so, for his name's sake! Amen.

NOAH'S TELESCOPE[1]

By faith Noah, being warned of God of things not seen as yet,
moved with fear, prepared an ark to the saving of his house.
Hebrews 11:7.

I SHALL deal mainly with the words, *'things not seen as yet.'*
There is nothing more convincing than sight. When a man
sees a thing, it is superfluous to enter into an argument with
him to prove that it exists. If we do so, he will probably reply, 'My
dear friend, your logic is not wanted; that which I see needs no
proof.' When sight comes in, doubt goes out. In ninety-nine cases
out of a hundred, sight banishes scepticism and makes a matter
realistic. It is hard work to argue a man out of the belief of anything that he has seen. He will meet you with the utterance, 'It is
no use to talk. Seeing is believing. Do you think that I am going
to doubt my own eyes?' Half a minute's glimpse is worth many
hours of proof and argument. I think that none of you will doubt
that the most conclusive evidence possible is that of sight. Do you
think that after I saw the leaning tower of Pisa I could doubt the
existence of such a structure? Impossible. I have seen it, and there
is an end of the matter.

Now, there is another power which makes a thing as certain and
real to us as sight, and that is faith. The word 'faith' has become
a theological term. I am not sure that there is an absolute gain
in that. When I use the word 'faith', you think of it only in the

[1] February 12, 1888, East London Tabernacle.

55

religious sense; but, whilst it is a theological term, it also signifies one of the commonest principles of life. If you believe thoroughly concerning anything, that thing is just as real to you as if you saw it. If it is not, it is because there is something defective in your faith.

You remember that only the other Saturday there was predicted an eclipse of the moon. Now, I noticed that on the morning of that day nearly all the papers had a leading article upon it, but I observed that the word 'if' was conspicuous by its absence. I did not find that any one of the papers said, 'It is stated that there will be an eclipse, and *if* it comes off the public will have an opportunity of seeing an interesting phenomenon.' No, the audacity with which the papers spoke was almost sublime. They told us to the very minute when it would begin and when it would leave off. The whole thing was taken for granted, and I will guarantee that not one of you said on that Saturday, 'I wonder whether there will be an eclipse tonight.' When it occurred no unbelief was removed from your mind, for none had existed; and, though I have no doubt that if some of you had been asked to explain the phenomenon you would have been rather perplexed, yet you had no scepticism concerning its certainty. You thoroughly believed the testimony of the astronomers. My text, slightly altered, would describe your experience: 'By faith, being moved with curiosity concerning a thing not seen as yet, you prepared to witness it.' You took your child to your back door, and said, 'Now, if you look at the moon in five minutes' time you will see that something will appear to begin to eat it away.' You did not say, 'I should not be surprised if such a thing happened.' Not at all; you were sure about the matter, although, perhaps, you could not explain the reason. The thing 'not seen as yet' was visible to your faith.

Now, the whole of this chapter is a splendid argument concerning faith being the eye of the soul. Faith does for a man precisely what sight does: it makes things plain, palpable, real, indisputable.

You have a number of instances recorded in the chapter. There is Enoch. 'No man hath seen God at any time'—that is to say, with the natural eye; but Enoch so believed God that God became a real, living personality to him; and I read that 'Enoch walked with God.' Abraham is called to go out to inhabit a land that he has never seen; and, as geography books were not published in those days, I greatly question whether he had any idea whatever of the locality of that land. But I read, 'By faith Abraham went out, not knowing whither he went.' The land was not seen as yet; but then, he believed what God said, and to him faith was the same as sight. Look at that grand man Moses. I read, 'By faith Moses, when he was come to years, refused to be called the son of Pharaoh's daughter.' Why? 'Choosing rather to suffer affliction with the people of God, than to enjoy the pleasures of sin for a season: for he had respect unto the recompense of the reward.' And then I read in the next verse, 'He endured *as seeing him who is invisible.*' Yes; invisible to these eyes, but plain enough to the eye of faith. I read again, that they 'saw the promises afar off'. Faith does for reason just what the telescope does for the bodily eye. You look up tonight at one of the stars, and all that you can see is just a point of light, seemingly infinitely removed from you. But let the astronomer look through his telescope. That instrument does not add anything to the star, but it reveals what is already there. It brings close to hand that which is far off. It may be interesting to some of you to know that, positively, at the present time there is a published map of the planet Mars in which you can see that there are seas and islands, and mountains covered with snow. A wondrous power is that of the telescope; it makes apparent that which is 'not seen as yet'. Here is our subject. Faith brings the distant near, for 'By faith Noah, being warned of God of things not seen as yet, moved with fear, prepared an ark.'

Let us first note *Noah's telescope;* and then, secondly, *the action that followed his looking through it;* and then I shall close by trying *to put the same telescope to your eye.*

Let us note, then, *Noah's telescope.* He saw a hundred and twenty years ahead. What was it that he saw? 'Things not seen as yet.' I find them in the 6th chapter of Genesis: 'Behold, I even I, do bring a flood of waters upon the earth to destroy all flesh, wherein is the breath of life, from under heaven; and every thing that is in the earth shall die.' God said it; Noah believed it, and his faith became to him the equivalent of sight. Let us carry out the idea. He puts up his telescope to his eye, and he looks one hundred and twenty years ahead; and what a sight meets his view! He can see the black clouds rolling up, and they pass not away before the breeze. He can see the blackness constantly intensifying. He sees now the commencement of that awful downpour. He gazes through that telescope, and he sees a sight that chills the very marrow of his bones. He beholds the waves of the ocean tossing to and fro, and now they burst their bounds. As he watches, he sees the waters, roaring over the earth, and death and desolation reigning everywhere. Looking through the telescope of faith, he was moved with fear because he beheld 'things not seen as yet'.

Now, observe that Noah could see these things *only* by faith. Let him put the telescope down, and he sees no more than any other man. Apart from the simple words of God he had no ground whatever for anticipating a deluge. Morning after morning the sun rose as it only can rise in an eastern clime. Some of you have seen it when you have been on voyages in the east. The sun climbed up from the horizon, blazing in all its brilliancy, and walked its kingly course through the azure, until at night it set again in a blaze of glory. Day after day, it rose and set, and not so much as a fleecy cloud was apparent. I almost imagine that Noah would sometimes say, 'Dear, dear, was not that an ugly dream that I had?' Month after month passed. Sometimes the clouds would gather, and there would be a smart shower, and then they would melt again into light; and I daresay that some of the scoffers would say, 'I say, old Noah, it has not come off yet, has it? You thought that when that rain began you were going to have your prediction fulfilled. Why, it is just as fine now as ever.'

And year after year passed on, and Noah had nothing but the word of God on which to ground his conviction. It might be said that he had a great deal to make it easy for him to doubt. Such a thing had never happened before. The world was not as grey-headed then as it is tonight; but in Noah's day seventeen hundred years had rolled by, and there had never been a deluge or any sign of one; and he might have said, 'Is it not preposterous to think that what never has happened will occur?' The very regularity in the operations of Nature might have suggested a doubt. Spring, summer, autumn, winter followed one another then with just the same beautiful regularity that they succeed one another now. The tides rose and fell, just as they are doing upon our shores today; and it must have been a difficult thing to grasp the idea that a day would come when all this regularity would be broken up.

Methinks that if a doubt ever came into Noah's mind he just took up the telescope and looked again at the 'things not seen as yet'. Yes, there they were. To the eye of faith the heavens were black, and the downpour had commenced, and the floods were rising. Faith was his telescope; and if anyone had said to him, 'Do you not think that, after all, you are mistaken?', he would have replied, 'Do you think that I can doubt my own eyes?' If the sceptic of the day had said, 'Do you not think it is an hallucination after all? Have you not, eaten something that has disagreed with you and made you take a distorted view of things?' I can imagine the old man saying, 'Seeing is believing: and when I look through this telescope which God has put into my hand, I can see the deluge as if it had already begun.'

Now what was the action produced in him by his looking

through the telescope? You read it in my text. 'By faith Noah, being warned of God of things not seen as yet, was *moved with fear*.' This proved the reality of the whole thing. Supposing Noah had not been moved with fear, and had pooh-poohed the idea of building an ark, and yet had said, 'Oh, I believe everything that God says', I think, if I had been alive in those days, I should have said, 'Look, Noah, I believe that you are an old liar.' But Noah proved the reality of his faith by his actions. I am not going to work out this point, but I will leave it with you. The faith that leads to no corresponding action is a sham. I will use an illustration which will show this to you in a moment. I leap upstairs to a man who is lying half asleep in bed, and I say to him, 'That cupboard under the staircase, where you keep your old newspapers and rubbish, is on fire, and the stairs are just catching. Quick! you have not a moment to spare!' He looks up from under the bedclothes, and says, 'My dear Mr Brown, I believe every word you say; I would not doubt any statement of yours for anything. Good-night.' Would he really have believed me? I should say at once, 'Man, you are insulting me. If you did believe that the staircase was on fire, I know what would be the corresponding actions: you would leap at once from your bed and escape for your life.'

When Noah looked through his telescope and saw the deluge coming, he did not hesitate; he did not cavil; he did not suggest to God some other method of deliverance. What did he do? Oh, I wish that I could lead some of you to do the same! He did just what God told him. He fell in with the divine plan and accepted God's method of salvation.

And then Noah became a preacher of righteousness. Why? Because, believing the reality of what he had seen, he would have been something less than a man if he had not warned others. I know that the general idea is that men who preach do so because they are such poor fools that they could not get on at anything else. Let Tom go into the army, and Harry go into the navy, and let Joseph go to the bar, and as for young Archibald, let him go into the ministry, as that is all he is fit for. Now as the Lord liveth, there are hundreds of men who can say before God that they only preach for the same reason that Noah preached. They have looked through the telescope, and they have seen that there is an impending judgment; they have seen that there is a doom hanging over a guilty world. And I put this to you, dear men: granted that you believed what I believe, would you not do what I am doing? If you honestly believed in your soul that there was a day of divine wrath coming, in which men who are out of Christ will be condemned, would you not, out of love to your fellows, do precisely the same as Noah did ages back, and as many of us are attempting to do at the present time? Of course you would.

We are not told what Noah's sermon was, but suppose that it was something after this sort: 'Oh, my dear friends, believe me, this sky is not always going to be blue. The day is coming when this sun will not rise and set as it does today. I have looked through my telescope, and I can see that there is a day coming when the waves, like mad race-horses, shall course over the earth, and when God's judgments shall be let loose. Prepare, prepare for the coming danger!' He was not very successful. He preached for one hundred and twenty years, and he was the means of the salvation of only seven people. He rang the bell of warning for a century, and only a handful of persons received his testimony. But O that God would give us such a handful! He was the means of the salvation of all his own family. If he did not win anybody else, he won those who were nearest and dearest to him.

Have you ever noticed the order? The Lord said to him, 'Come thou and all thy house into the ark.' And I read, 'And Noah went in.' It was quite right that he should be the first. The husband ought to be the leader of the family. The father ought to be the first to accept Christ Jesus. Then the sons of Noah, Shem, Ham and Japheth went in with him. If it were so with hundreds of fathers who hear me, how happy they would be! Then Noah's wife followed him into the ark. And then I can imagine what an expression of gladness overspread Noah's face as his three daughters-in-law entered next; for mark, these women must have left their own relations in order to cast in their lot with their husbands in the ark.

It must have been a tremendous trial to the faith of Noah when the Lord said, 'Come in', for at that moment there was no sign of the deluge. The day was, perhaps, as fine a day as ever God made. But Noah enters the ark, and his family go with him; the Lord shuts the door: and then what happens? They stopped a whole week in that ark before the deluge came. It does not require a very imaginative mind to conceive what a roar of laughter there must have been. I think I can hear the mob saying, 'Look at the old fellow cooped up there. Does he see any deluge coming? What is the old man doing in that great ship built on dry land?' I can imagine their calling out, 'I say, Noah, do you feel your boat rocking much? Are you beginning to feel sea-sick yet?'

The man who takes God at his word will often look very ridiculous in the eyes of worldlings. Faith is always a thing that is misunderstood. I can imagine that as Noah heard their ridicule, he himself sometimes felt almost ready to doubt, until he took up that old telescope that I have mentioned, and had a look through the window, and saw that the flood was awfully near. Then he felt that he could afford to bear their laughter. The seventh day passes by, and now comes to pass that which Noah had seen by faith. The heavens are black; the sea forgets its bounds; the waters rise; the ark begins to move, and at last it floats upon the breast of the deep ocean. God has kept his word, but Noah, by faith having been moved with fear of things not seen as yet, is a saved man.

Now, my brethren, I want *to try to put the telescope to your eyes* for a few moments. 'Things not seen as yet.' There are a good many things not seen as yet, but you would see them directly if you would only use this telescope.

How many of you can see yourselves as old men? There is not a man among all who read this who can see himself as an old man without this telescope. Old age is a thing 'not seen as yet'; but, do you know, there is a passage in the word of God by which if you just look through it, you will be able to see yourself as you will appear some few years hence if you live so long. Look at the 12th chapter of Ecclesiastes, and see a picture of your own old age. 'The day when the keepers of the house shall tremble.' Those are the hands. They are not steady like the thousands of hands that are here this evening. The old man's hands do greatly shake. 'And the strong men shall bow themselves.' That is the bent back when so many Christmases have passed over the old man that he stoops by reason of their weight, and has lost the elasticity that he once possessed. 'And the grinders cease because they are few.' The teeth are wanting. 'And those that look out of the windows be darkened.' The eyes are not so bright and keen as the thousands, that gaze upon me now. 'And the doors shall be shut in the streets, when the sound of the grinding is low.' That is, the teeth being gone, the old man's lips fall inwardly. 'And he shall rise up at the voice of the bird.' You can sleep for ten hours right off now; but how often the old man says, 'Oh, I wish that I could sleep as I used to do!' How light now are the old man's slumbers! 'And all the daughters of musick are brought low.' He does not sing now as he once did. All his notes are 'quavers.' 'Also they shall be afraid of that which is high.' The young man smiles at that which is high. Tomorrow he will be mounting the church steeple, or standing up high on the scaffolding, with no swimming sensations in his head. Fear of that kind is one of the things not seen as yet. 'And fears shall be in the way, and the almond tree shall flourish.' The dark hair of tonight will begin to grow white. The white blossom is already on the heads of some of us. 'And the grasshopper shalt be a burden.' A grasshopper is the very lightest of food. You young men do not know what it is to suffer from a burden of that sort. You can digest anything: I think that I hear a strong, hale, hearty fellow here tonight saying, 'Digest, sir? I could digest a brickbat.' Yes, but the day will come when the grasshopper, the lightest food, shall be a burden. Why is this? 'Because man goeth to his long home.' These are things not seen as yet. It will not do any of you dear young fellows any harm if you put that telescope of the 12th of Ecclesiastes to your eye and take a good long look through its lens.

There is another thing 'not seen as yet': that is *death*. How few men meditate on their own death! 'All men think all men mortal but themselves.' I was talking with a friend only this afternoon about the continual procession of funerals that goes past my house on a Sunday afternoon; and as we were talking I could not help saying to myself, 'I find it so difficult to realize that I may be look-ing on the very hearse which before long will carry me.' Have you ever tried to look at your own death? It will do you no harm; so take up the word of God, and read, 'It is appointed unto men once to die.' Now you know no sickness and no pain. But put your eye to this glass. Do you see that man lying there on that bed? Do you hear how hard his breathing is? Do you see what big drops stand upon his brow? You take him by the hand, and he tries to speak to you, but he cannot. And there in the corner of the room you hear the suppressed sobbing of the wife as she folds her little child to her breast. The dying man's breath gets heavier, and the doc-tor says, 'There is nothing more that I can do.' Do you know that man? Why, it is yourself, man! You are only looking through the telescope at one of the things not seen as yet.

And does not that 3rd chapter of the 2nd Epistle of Peter show you another of the things not seen as yet? The day shall come when the Lord in power will come to judge a guilty world, and the heavens shall be set ablaze, and the sign of the Son of Man shall be in the firmament. You say, 'Well, I do not realize that.' No, nor did the men and women in the days of Noah. They thought that Noah was an old croaker; but then he had looked through his telescope and had seen what was coming. My brethren, in all love I say that I should be less than a man, and utterly unworthy of a gathering like this, if I were not honest about this matter. Before God, I believe that there is a judgment coming upon a guilty world. If I did not believe it I would not preach it. I am as assured as if I had seen the heavens set ablaze that it will come to pass—the day of the perdition of ungodly men; and it is because I believe it that, like Noah, I want to warn you.

Look through the telescope, man. Do you not see the rocks rending and the heavens melting? Can you not see the judgment of God being poured out? Do you say, 'What must I do to be saved?' I will tell you. There is one respect in which you are not to do what Noah did. Noah had to prepare an ark. You have not to do that. Thank God, that is all done. The ark was prepared in the great navy yard of God's sovereign grace. It was prepared by a divine workman. He laid down the keel with many a sigh and many a groan, and he built up the ark of salvation at the cost of his own life. He never ceased until he was able to say, 'It is finished.' He has left the door wide open, and God says to each of you dear fellows tonight, 'Come thou into the ark.' It would not have been any good for Noah to walk all round the ark. No, he must come in. Suppose that Noah had said, as some of you may be saying, 'Well, I will stand close by the door, with one foot on the ark and the other on the ground. I do not want to be pronounced on either side. I will wait until I see the deluge coming, and then I will just step in.' He would have found that he was too late. No, God told Noah that he was to enter the ark a whole week before the deluge came. If any of you are found standing just outside, you will be as much lost as if you were a hundred miles off. The word is, 'Come in.' Ah, then God is inside. It is not, 'Go in.' God himself is in the ark, and he says, 'Come in unto me.' And what is faith? Faith is just taking God at his word, and stepping into the ark, Christ Jesus. As a poor guilty sinner—for that is what thou art—thou must accept God's plan of salvation. Do not hesitate or cavil or disbelieve.

Put the telescope to your eye once more. Turn it towards Calvary. Now look through it. How near is the distant cross! Dost thou see, hanging on that tree, in agonies and blood, the Man, the God-Man? Gaze into those glassy eyes. Behold him marred and heartbroken. Look and look again. The sight ought to fill your eyes with tears, and make you say, 'Lord, didst thou bear all this for me? Didst thou die on Golgotha's cross for me? Art thou my ark of safety? Then, Lord Jesus, as a sinner I come to thee.' Oh, do not go and lose your own souls when you may be saved. Do not go out of this building and say, 'Well, I do not believe a word of it.' Do you want me to doubt my own eyes? I have looked through the telescope, and I have seen that which I have tried to tell you. I have seen a certain doom coming for the sinner. I have seen God's ark of salvation—a Christ who died and a Christ who lives.

I believe that I am in the ark, or I would not dare to speak to you. Dear readers, may God bring you also just where he has put me. Oh, it is a grand thing to be saved. Do not look upon me as if I were a 'professional'. Do not say, 'Oh, well, this is only a pre-pared part of his sermon.' I assure you that it is not. I write to you as a man amongst men—as one who may be preaching his last 'sermon to men'. I want to be able to say to my God in heaven, 'Lord, if those dear fellows are lost at last, put not their blood down to my account.' It is all real. God is real; heaven is real; hell is real; Christ is real; sin is real; the impending doom is real. I have looked through the telescope for myself, and, being moved with fear, I have fled for refuge to the hope set before me, and God has received me. I want you to be saved.

Do not say that you are too old or too far gone to come to Jesus, Whatever the past—though you may have sent your mother down to a premature grave with a broken heart; though you may have dragged a fair name in the mud and mire; though your sisters may be saying of you even now, 'Well, if Tom is converted I will never doubt of anybody'—I tell you, as God liveth, he is able and willing to save every one of you. If you will reject the offer of the gospel, then your doom lies at your own door. May God add his blessing to the testimony. God's doom on sin is coming. Fly to Christ. God save you for Jesus' sake!

AMEN, O LORD[1]

Then answered I and said, So be it, O LORD. [Or, Amen, O LORD.]
Jeremiah 11:5.

FEW, if any, of the characters in Holy Scripture are grander than that of Jeremiah. He was a man among a thousand—indeed, among ten thousand. But, singularly enough, no man has been more misunderstood. The popular idea seems to be that he was on the whole rather a weak character, slightly sentimental, very much addicted to weeping, and sensitive to a degree, if not to a fault; one who took a very gloomy view of affairs; a man who must have suffered more or less from dyspepsia, and one who knew very little of strong, holy, boldness, but was chiefly characterised by that which is plaintive. So far is this from being the case, that Jeremiah stands all but unequalled as a single-handed hero. He was no weeping, retiring prophet, shrinking from delivering his testimony, apologising for his existence, and speaking with bated breath when in the presence of the Lord's foes. God declared that he should be as an iron column and as a brazen wall, and such the Lord made him. We know more of Jeremiah than we do of any of the other prophets, for there is such a strong personal element in his book. Isaiah is all but unknown as a person. Once or twice we get a glimpse of him in his prophecy, as in the 6th chapter, but our conception of Isaiah is really the conception of his writings. But the man Jeremiah is always appearing. The whole book is full of

---

[1] December 2, 1894, East London Tabernacle.

personal incidents, and we are able to look right into his character. He was wonderfully observant, and he seemed to keenly note his own passing thoughts, and he jots down in beautiful simplicity the expressions which fall from his own lips. If ever there was a bold warrior, it was Jeremiah. It is a grand mistake to suppose that in order to be a hero it is necessary to have a hide like a rhinoceros. You will generally find that the most heroic men are the most sensitive. The men who have done the grandest work for God, and borne the most fearless testimony, have not been of hard, unfeeling natures, but men who have worn their nerves outside, and who have known what it is to tremble often with heart agony.

Jeremiah was faithful among the faithless. He lived during the very darkest days of Jewish history. Apostasy was all but universal. The people had forsaken God by the wholesale. But there was one man who stood and faced a mad populace and angry kings for forty years. Never do you find him yielding. In an essentially selfish age he was whole-souled. Amidst utter worldliness he was consecrated; and to the end of the age Jeremiah will stand forth as one of the most splendid men that God ever raised up or used in carrying out his work. And what would poor, erring humanity become if it were not that God is pleased to raise up these elect souls who interpret to others the will of God, and then become in themselves sublime illustrations of whole-souled faith and obedience? Whilst it is true that God works by his word, it is just as true that he does so through human instrumentality. And, if you take the history of Christ's church, you will find it to be the consecutive histories of master-men, choice souls who differed from the common herd; men who were called and equipped by God to bear some peculiar testimony. Oh, may God raise up a race of them today, for I am sure that we badly need them! Such men serve as moral breakwaters, and, when the storm and the tempest and the cyclone of doubt and immorality and scepticism go sweeping over a nation, the waves break on them, and they stand like a Plymouth break-water flinging off the surges amid clouds of blinding spray. They seem almost hidden and half-drowned themselves; but under their lee what a number of little ships find shelter! What a multitude of weaker souls find the force of the tempest broken by them! God grant that now, whilst such a hurricane of doubt, suspicion, 'higher criticism', and all other kinds of devilry, are abroad, there may be still found some who, although they may have to pay an awful price for the honour, may, in some measure, be breakwaters behind which weaker souls shall drop their anchor and ride out the storm.

Jeremiah was all this. He was one of the reminders of God. We see in the 106th Psalm that human nature is quick to for-get that there is a God; and I believe that human nature would forget it altogether if there were not some men to whom God is such a gigantic reality that they make others feel it. As Jeremiah walked up and down in the land, he practically kept saying, 'God is: God is'; and God could not be forgotten whilst there was a Jeremiah ringing out this note. He was just a God-raised witness for despised truth. Whilst he thus interpreted the will of God, he illustrated it in himself.

And *you cannot interpret the will of God unless you are willing to illustrate it.* The mightiest sermon is never the sermon that you preach: it is the sermon that you live; and, whilst Jeremiah kept foretelling and expounding the will of God, he was in himself a magnificent illustration of unbounded consecration, unswerving fidelity, and unrepining obedience.

Do you say, 'Why this introduction?' It is because, as you will see now, it is the explanation of the words of my text. If you read a few verses back, you will see that the Lord is reminding Jeremiah of the covenant that he had made with the people as to their pos-session of the holy land, and he is reminding Jeremiah how they had broken that covenant, and how practically they had brought themselves under the curse; for you read in the 3rd verse that the Lord said to Jeremiah, 'Cursed be the man that obeyeth not the words of this covenant, which I commanded your fathers in the day that I brought them forth out of the land of Egypt, from the iron furnace, saying, Obey my voice, and do them, according to that which I command you: so shall ye be my people, and I will be your God, that I may perform the oath which I have sworn unto your fathers, to give them a land flowing with milk and honey, as it is this day.' It is very terrible language to hear. God says, 'Remember what I said. I said, "Cursed is the man that obeyeth not", and this people have not obeyed the covenant, and I must turn them out from this land, and give it unto others.' And what do you read? 'Then answered I, and said, Amen, O LORD.' If you would come across a grander text than this I think you will have to look a long while to find it. Jeremiah hears the thunder of the curse ringing in his ear. He knows that his beloved people have broken this commandment of God, that they have forfeited all claim upon him for the land, and yet I do not find him quibbling with God. I find him acquiescing. I do not find him protesting against the seeming severity of the word. He simply bows his head and says, 'Amen, O LORD'; that is, 'So be it.'

I.—Here you have THE ONE RESPONSE WHICH A MAN OF GOD MUST EVER MAKE TO THE WORDS OF GOD. When God says anything to him, there is nothing left for him but to bow the head and say, 'Amen, LORD,' and perhaps we shall find out before the sermon is over, whether we have been doing this or not in our past career, and it may be that the secret of many a contention which is going on between God and some of you will be made clear. God has spoken to you, but thus far there has not been Jeremiah's response of 'Amen, O LORD.'

I think that you will see that this response is *the only one that suits a creature's lip.* When God speaks there is nothing left for man but to hear. When God decrees, there is nothing for man to do but acquiesce. When Jehovah gives a command, what is there left for his creature to do but obey? Any other word than 'Amen' springs from rebellion. Any other response to the word of Jehovah simply tells of a spirit that wars with God. It is not for men to judge God's words, far less to amend them. If it pleases Jehovah to say anything, no matter how stern, how terrible, how searching, I contend that there is only one position for man: that is to bow his head and say, 'Amen.' 'Oh', says someone, in the spirit of this proud nineteenth century, 'you are making a bold bid for your God this morning.' I am. *The sovereignty of God needs to be brought to the front.* There has been too much trifling with Jehovah. Man needs to have the peacock's feathers plucked out of his cap and be taught that he is a poor little nothing, and that for God to speak to him at all is infinite condescension, and that for him to say anything else than 'Amen' is boundless impudence. If God condescends to utter a command, am I to go and judge whether the Lord has a right to say it? Shall I take the word of Jehovah my Maker and weigh it in my scales, and bring up his thoughts to the paltry bar of my fallen reason, and virtually enter my protest unless I can see a good reason for God speaking as he does? *When God promulgates a decree he does not send it to man to be revised.* According to the pride of this nineteenth century, the only Bible that is worth reading is one that has been amended by its readers. God has not come down to this yet, and he never will. His claim is this, 'I am Jehovah. I, the LORD, speak that which is right, and let man say, "Amen, O LORD."' We are living in the days of the apotheosis of humanity. One gets sick even of the very word 'humanity'. We hear so much about 'the enthusiasm of humanity', and 'the glory of humanity', and 'the triumphs of humanity', that God has become little better than a very inferior deity who runs after man and touches his cap to him.

This is not the picture which God's Book gives. God's claim is this, 'I am the Lord, and ye are but the creatures of my hand. The brightest of my angels are but sparks struck off from the anvil of my creative omnipotence. When I speak, let men and angels be silent; or, if they must speak, let them say, "Amen, O Lord."' It is the response that suits a creature's lip.

Let me take you but one step further. This response is the only one that can be given if you remember *the character of God*. Here my poor little skiff is launched on a boundless ocean. The character of God! Can you tell me all that lies in those three letters, G-o-d, the most wonderful word that was ever spelt? If you appeal to this platform the answer is, I cannot tell you. I do not know what God is. I cannot conceive what God is. No man has dreamed what God is, save as God has been pleased to reveal himself. Now, what has he revealed himself as? As a God whose wisdom is infinite; and methinks the scientist will grant that, for, after all, what are the triumphs of science but the discovery of those wondrous laws of nature that tell of an infinitely wise law-giver and law-maker? If you can conceive of a being who is infinitely wise, infinitely righteous, absolutely holy, inflexibly just, and all gathered up into boundless love, that is God. If such an one speaks, what is there left for me but to say, 'Amen'? I am stark, staring mad if I can question the utterance of Infinite Wisdom. I am unutterably fallen if I can dare to criticise the utterance of Absolute Love. Idiocy must have taken hold of my brain and, alas! of my heart, if I would amend anything which his untold holiness has declared. The very nature and character of God declare that the only response for man when God speaks is 'Amen, O Lord.'

And yet I must not leave this point until I touch one other aspect of it, and that is that this response *must be universal in its nature*. I am not to give a vociferous 'Amen, O Lord', to one thing, and then keep a total silence when the Lord says another. I am to say 'Amen' all round. You will see that in this particular instance Jeremiah had to say 'Amen' to what was not pleasant. The first word is 'cursed'. Oh, let the dilettante gentlemen of the present century, who have such fine ideas of universal fatherhood and I know not what—those gentlemen who spend their time in blowing bubbles which are not more remarkable for beauty than for the way in which they burst—hear this word 'cursed', and out come their critical amendments. 'Run that word "cursed" through. It is not kind. It must be a mistake. The dear Father could never utter such a terrible word as that.' Jeremiah heard the word 'cursed', and he said, 'Amen, O LORD.' Oh, brethren and sisters, it is not for us to be picking and choosing! It is so easy, is it not, to turn to a nice sweet invitation, such as 'Come unto me, all ye that labour and are heavy laden, and I will give you rest', and say, 'Amen, O LORD'? Or we turn to some precious promise, 'My grace is sufficient for thee', and we say, 'Amen, O LORD.' But when God denounces sin, and your sin, and your besetting sin, and when God tells of righteous judgment for apostasy and unbelief, we are to say, 'Amen, O LORD', to that, and say it as deeply from the heart as when he says, 'Come unto me, all ye that labour and are heavy laden.' Oh, for that grand spirit of perfect obedience to God that bows before every word of God, whether it be a silver note of mercy from heaven, or a thunder-clap of denunciation! We want that spirit which uncovers its head before God, and says, 'Amen', even to the lightning flash which threatens to blast us. 'Amen, O LORD', is the only response which a saint of God can give to the words of God.

II.—My remaining ten minutes shall be occupied in this wise: I will mention SOME LIPS FROM WHICH WE WOULD FAIN HEAR THE RESPONSE. Thus far I have only dealt with the matter in general, and I trust that God has in some measure showed you that it is the only response to be given to any word of his. Now let me try to point out some of the lips from which we long to hear the word 'Amen.'

First, *the lips of the sinner in reference to God's method of salvation.* You will see how the context will help us. God reminds Jeremiah that entrance into the promised land was contingent upon Israel falling in with and accepting God's methods. Now, sinner, would you be saved? Have you any desire to enter into that more blessed land, the heavenly Canaan? Then it behoves you to find out what God's covenant is, and to see how God is going to admit you into that land; and it is for you to say, 'Amen, O LORD', to all the conditions of the new covenant. You will have to fall in with all that God says as to his way of salvation. Let us see how this will work out. I wonder how many of you will say 'Amen' all the way through. May our prayers for souls being ingathered be answered even now. To begin with, there will have to be on your part an acquiescence in the position which God gives you. What position is that? Ruined by the fall of your first father, Adam, perverted through a fallen nature that you received from your own parents with a bias toward evil in you, accompanied by deliberate sin on your part, you have been brought into a condition of being guilty before God; and God, pointing to the sinner, says, 'Sinner, you are lost, you are guilty, you are under judgment, you are under a curse. Do you take the position assigned to you?' The proud sinner says, 'No, Lord, I object to it'; but the humble sinner says, 'Amen, O LORD.' That is the first step. Until you acquiesce in the position which God gives you as a poor, lost, ruined, helpless sinner, there can be no salvation for you. Have not some of you quarrelled with God long enough over that point? When are you going to bow the head and say 'Amen', to it?

What is the next step? *The sweeping away of all supposed human ability.* God says to the sinner, 'You never can save yourself. You have nothing in you that ever can be evolved into salvation. Your holiest things are all defiled, and, if you could work a decent holiness, that would not save you, because my plan is "not of works, lest any man should boast".' And the hand of God comes and sweeps the table. 'Not of works'; and away fly, as a ground of salvation, chapel-going, church-going, baptism, the Lord's supper, Bible-reading, praying, almsgiving. 'Not of works.' The proud soul runs and tries to save the works which have been swept off the table. The humble soul says, 'Amen, O God.' He sees all his supposed good works being swept into the dustbin, and he simply says, 'Amen', and he lets them go.

The third step is this: God says, 'Sinner, in my covenant of salvation I have put *the whole of your salvation in the person of my Son Jesus Christ.* I do not trust you with it at all. I have laid it all up in him. His merits, not yours. His righteousness, not yours. Any acceptance can only be an acceptance in him. Any completeness on your part can only be a completeness in him. It pleases my sovereign will to entrust the whole of your salvation in the person of my Son.' And would to God that with a lowly heart you might respond, 'Amen, O L<small>ORD</small>. So be it.'

And then the Lord will take you one step further, and say, *'The simple acceptance of my Son* is the one condition on which I save you. All the merits which are treasured up in him shall be put down to your account, the moment you trust him.' I wonder whether any man or woman will bow before that word, and say, 'Amen.' If so, you are a saved man. This is a saving 'Amen': Paul's expression in the 10th chapter of the Epistle to the Romans is most remarkable. He says, 'the obedience of faith'; and that defines just what faith is. It is being brought into obedience. God designs to save you in one way, and you want to be saved in another; but God will never give in to you. Then you had better submit to God's method. Drop all your false pride and dignity and bow and say, 'Amen, O L<small>ORD</small>.

No more, my God, I boast, no more,
Of all the duties I have done:

I quit the hopes I held before,
To trust the merits of Thy Son.'

Is that all? A good many of you will not like this next point. The moment a man is saved the Lord adds, 'And now there is one thing more. Go and be baptized.' Surely you think that we should separate baptism from faith. The Lord has not. The answer to 'What must I do to be saved?' is 'Believe on the Lord Jesus Christ, and thou shalt be saved.' That is true; but there is also another passage: 'He that believeth and is baptized shall be saved.' The baptism does not help to save you, but God has linked baptism and salvation together. It is his way of *confession*. But you turn on your heel, and you say, 'I will never say "Amen" to that.' Then you are a rebel. You say, 'I have accepted Christ: I have trusted him.' Then be baptized. 'Oh, but I can get to heaven without it!' Then you are a mean man to want to. Is this your argument—that you will say, 'Amen, O LORD', if you can get anything out of it, but that if it is only a matter of obedience to him you are going to evade it? If the Lord carries this word home to your heart with power, you will turn to such a passage as the 6th of Romans, and say, 'Amen, O LORD', and you will come out and confess his name by his own ordinance. How we long to hear, 'Amen, O LORD', fall from the lips of the sinner in reference to God's method of salvation.

Only a moment. Should we not hear it *from the lips of the saint concerning God's instructions as to daily life?* God says, 'Be ye separate from the world', and the response should be, 'Amen, O LORD.' Only you want to go to a ball, do you not? '"Amen, O LORD", with the exception of that card party.' '"Amen, O LORD", only please let me go to the theatre next Tuesday.' Nay, if you are a real loyal soul, all the diamond dust of God's commands will be infinitely precious to you; and when he says to you, 'Be ye separate', you will say, 'Amen, O LORD'; and when he tells you to think more of him than of your business, you will say, 'Amen, O LORD'; and, instead of worshipping that business as you have been doing lately, you will only toil in trade in order to have the wherewithal to give to glorify him. The idea of amassing wealth for wealth's own sake will be abandoned. You will have heard his word, 'Seek ye first the kingdom of God', and you will say, 'Amen, O Lord.' You will hear him say, 'Be not unequally yoked with unbelievers', and you will break off that engagement with that ungodly young man and you will say, 'Amen, O Lord.' Why is it that there is so much friction and misery and wretchedness abroad? Is it not in great measure because those of us who profess to be the Lord's are so slow to say 'Amen', concerning all that God says as to ordinary every-day life?

But I hasten on to the last point, and I want to put it right down into the very centre of your soul. It is this: these words ought to be heard from the lips of the people of God *in reference to providential dealings*. God does not only speak from the pages of his word; God speaks from providence. Oh, how tough a work it often is to say 'Amen! Is it not so? 'And the Lord said unto Abraham, Take now thy son, thine only son Isaac, whom thou lovest, and go into a mountain which I will show thee, and offer him as a sacrifice.' I think I see the muscles of Abraham's brow knotted with an unutterable agony. And yet he says, 'Amen, O Lord.' The next thing I read is that early in the morning he starts with his son. Now then, sir, the God of Abraham lives still, and he is trying and testing his saints today, as he did then, and he waits for the response of your heart, 'Amen, O Lord.' God has wonderfully prospered you in business. Suppose the Lord just turns the tide altogether aside, and your business ebbs away from you. Do you think you can say, 'Amen, O Lord'? God has wonderfully blessed your home. You have something like a home. There is health, there is rest, there is love, there is joy, there is peace. With what light steps will you go from this tabernacle back to your home? You have every thing there to praise God for. But suppose the angel of death should spread his wings on the blast, and the brightest, fairest, and loveliest of that home should be removed. What if your young wife should be laid low? What if your stalwart young husband should be taken? What will you say then? May God help you just to answer with Jeremiah, 'Amen, O Lord.' Oh, it is this that God is waiting for, and it is to this that he is educating us by losses, by sicknesses, by trials, by deaths—to learn to say 'Amen.' I was so charmed the other day in reading the story of those three Hebrew youths in the book of Daniel. There is the furnace burning. I hear its roar. It has been heated seven times, and Nebuchadnezzar is giving the sign that they are to be cast in. And what do those three Hebrew youths say? 'O king, we are not careful to answer thee in this matter. The God whom we serve is able to deliver us from this fiery furnace.' And then come three grand words: *'but if not,* be it known unto thee, O king, that we will not bow down to this image.' That is what I call grace. Oh, it is so easy to say, 'O Lord, we will worship thee if thou dost help us. We will be true to thee, if thou dost bless us. Only keep us out of the furnace, and we will sing to thee.' But the spirit of Jeremiah is a spirit that says, 'But if not, we will be true to our God still. If he puts his sword to our throat, we will say, "Though he slay me, yet will I trust in him"; and, as the life-blood gurgles from the wound which his own sword has made, my last struggling breath shall say, "Amen, O Lord."'

Fellow workers for God, we ought to be foremost in saying it. I find that Elijah never hesitated. The word of the Lord came to Elijah, and said, 'Arise', and so he got up and went. The word of the Lord said, 'Go to Kishon's brook', and he went. The word of the Lord said, 'Go to the widow who is picking up sticks, and ask for bread', and he went. 'Amen, O Lord', ought to be the characteristic of the Christian worker. Where are you to labour? Well, where would you like to labour? Perhaps you say, 'Oh, I have laboured so long in this sphere that I feel as if my roots had got intertwined with a thousand others, and it would be half death to me to be plucked up.' But if the Lord says, 'Be removed', O worker, there is only one thing left to you to do, and that is to say, 'Amen, O Lord.' If he tells you to step out of the pulpit and teach an infant class, say, 'Amen, O Lord.' If he tell you to give up preaching to that congregation and go and spend your time in the lodging-houses, say, 'Amen, O Lord.' You see that this covers the whole ground. The most perfect example of this is Christ. The clever men, the wise men, and the rich men, all ignore him, and the few that gather round about him are of low caste and ignorant. But is Jesus wounded and hurt? Listen. 'I thank thee, O heavenly Father, that it hath pleased thee to hide these things from the wise and prudent, and that thou hast revealed them unto babes.' Did he murmur? 'Even so, Father, for so it seemed good in thy sight.' There is God's perfect servant saying, 'Amen, O Lord.'

But the last great prophecy remains, and the church of God is to add her 'Amen' to it. He who died for sinners and who for sinners was buried, and he who rose from the tomb and ascended up on high as the true Melchisedec, the combination of high priest and royal king, has left this word, 'Surely I come quickly.' The hope of the church is the return of her Lord. Let the church bow her head, and say, 'Amen, O Lord. Even so come, Lord Jesus.'

The theme is inexhaustible. Whether God is speaking to you by his word, or speaking to you by his providence, or speaking to you through this morning's sermon, bow before the Almighty Sovereign. Let no word of rebellion rise to your lip. Doff your helmet until its plumes trail in the dust, and say with Jeremiah, 'Amen, O Lord.' God help us to add that 'Amen', for his own name's sake.

THE UNGODLY AND THEIR END[1]

The ungodly are not so, but are like the chaff which the wind driveth
away. Therefore the ungodly shall not stand in the judgment,
nor sinners in the congregation of the righteous.
Psalm 1:4, 5.

EVERYTHING shows up best by contrast, and the most startling effects are those produced by suddenly bringing opposites side by side. The artist knows this, and therefore seeks to throw just that particular background into his picture which shall make the leading figures of that picture come out most distinctly, and appear to best advantage. The musician knows it, and therefore, studies to intermingle the most plaintive strains with clarion notes. And the preacher *ought* to know it. Be it his to employ the power or contrasts in setting forth the word of God before his hearers. If he is wise he will endeavour to make the darkness of perdition cause the brightness of heaven to appear all the more lustrous, and he will seek to make the blackness of hell grow gloomier by the force of its contrast with the glory of the saved. It is well, every now and then, to put side by side these things which so differ—the state of the saved with the condition of the unsaved—the glory of being with Christ, with the horror of being with the damned.

Now, you will see that in the psalm from which we have selected this evening's text, we have one of these sudden and striking contrasts introduced. The first few verses are most calm—there is a

[1] October 11, 1874, East London Tabernacle.

peculiar serenity about them; they are gentle as 'a pastoral symphony'. It seems to us as though David were like a shepherd in the field as he sings, concerning the godly, 'He shall be like a tree planted by the rivers of water, that bringeth forth his fruit in his season; his leaf also shall not wither, and whatsoever he doeth shall prosper—the ungodly are not so'! Sudden change; it is like a flash of lightning glaring before your eyes, when there has been no solitary sign of the brewing of a storm. All in a moment, yea, with the rapidity of a storm in the tropical regions, the quietest of calms is broken into, and the roar of the tempest heard. One moment we see a tree growing by a river's side, its roots well watered, its leaves never withering. We think we can hear the music of the brook as it runs by, and we are just ready to say, 'What an exquisite scene of loveliness!' when without a warning, there is brought before our eyes, not a tree, but dry chaff being swept out of the barn door by a very hurricane, whirled up, and carried out of sight,—'And', says the psalmist, 'that is just what the ungodly are like, for the ungodly are not so as I have described the godly, but they are like the chaff which the wind driveth away.'

May God, dear friends, in his great mercy apply this truth to you who are yet without Christ. He is our witness that our only desire is to try and move some of you who have been stolidly indifferent up to the present moment. Our only wish is that many of you who are going to hell asleep, may be woken up; and though, doubtless, some are already saying, 'We wish the pastor had chosen a different kind of text from this', we trust and believe that it shall be proved by God that it is of his selection.

Let us first of all, *try and find out the characters intended in our text;* and then, secondly, *we will listen to the description that is given of them;* and thirdly, *we will remind you of their end.*

I. First of all, LET US FIND OUT THE CHARACTERS INTENDED. The ungodly—who are they? I know full well who are uppermost in your minds. I no sooner mentioned the text, and spoke about the doom of the ungodly, than you began to think of the low and the brutalised characters whose deeds of cruelty make up that shameful list of 'crimes of violence' now appearing in our papers day by day—enough to make a man blush for his country. And side by side with them you doubtless thought of the drunkard, pouring down his throat the liquid fire to better qualify himself for the devil's work. And you thought of brazen-faced harlotry and open licentiousness and of those who are steeped to the lips in sin, and of the men who madly run the black flag up to the mast head, and live, as they say 'for time, and let eternity look after itself'. These are the characters you pictured when we read the word 'ungodly'. Well, you are right, they are ungodly. But I am certain that all I have mentioned fail to compose one tenth part of those who are legitimately to be included in the catalogue of the ungodly. Remember this, that a man may be ungodly without being any of the characters that I have mentioned. An ungodly man is simply a man who tries to get through the world without God. The word is plain enough in its meaning; it is not necessary for a man's life to be a shame and a disgrace for him to be ungodly. It is not necessary for him to be steeped in all sorts of vice in order to be without God. No; all he has to do to earn the title is to leave God *out of his love*. He may have love for wife and children, love for business, love for friends but as far as God is concerned, he has not an atom of affection. It may be said of his heart that it is ungodly—there is no God enshrined in its love. He is ungodly, also, *in his thoughts*. Not ten, no, not two thoughts a day are consecrated unto God. His business, his every-day affairs—these things, he says, are quite enough to occupy him without his troubling his head about religion. Look into his character, and you will find that he is ungodly in every part of his life. Inspect all his *motives,* and you will find that he never does a thing for God's sake. There is no fear of God before his eyes; there is no reverence for God within his heart. He may be gentle, amiable, moral, a good sort of man as far as this world's goodness is concerned. He would be all right, if a man could be all right without God, but he belongs to the ungodly. I will go further, and venture to assert that a man may be *most* moral, and yet *most* ungodly. Whilst hideous immorality has slain its thousands; a godless morality has slain its tens of thousands. And for one that is dragged down to perdition by the mill-stone of vice, there are hundreds who are taken in the meshes of the net of a Christless virtue. A man may be honest in all his transactions, pure in his language, chaste in his thoughts, an honourable man in all his business dealings—just the very one you would like to trade with—his word may be his bond, and all his actions fair, and yet come under the designation of ungodly. It is with him, simply morality, skin deep; there has been nothing of regeneration within, without which it is impossible for a man to enter into the kingdom.

We will go one step further, and say that a man may be most *religiously active,* and yet be ungodly. I can conceive of a man being a most talented preacher, and yet being ungodly. It may be that he has a natural liking and gift for speaking, and he may, perhaps, take a very great deal of interest in the increase of a denomination and the outward mechanism of a church, but for all that he is totally devoid of the life of God within his soul. It is possible for a man to be an enthusiast in committee work—to be a constant worker in the outward details of church life—yea to be a very bigot in maintaining a creed, and yet be ungodly. Oh, pass the question round, I pray you, ye who have made profession of the Lord Jesus Christ for years. Have you got something more than the mere name to live? Are you yet—(oh, can it be?)—ungodly, though a professing Christian—ungodly though once immersed in the name of

Christ—ungodly, though your life is almost a pattern for the very best of Christians? The question is, have you God or not? For my text is not about the licentious, the profane, or the swearer, but about those who, whatever else they have, possess not God.

II. Now, listen to THE DESCRIPTION GIVEN OF THEM. What are these ungodly ones like? Well, you will find that they are the very opposite of all that a godly man is. You have simply to take the picture of the saved man, and then, after every particular, write, 'The ungodly are not so.'

I think it were difficult to find a more solemn or more dreadful description of the ungodly man than given by this short negative sentence. There is not a thing you can say about a godly man, as such, but what you can add, 'The ungodly are not so.' Let us see, then, what is taught in the passage.

Look at the first word of this psalm. It is a grand one for an intro-duction—a word full of all comfort. It is that word 'blessed.' What a precious preface to the description of the child of God! It stands like a herald in the forefront. The Christian is 'blessed', but 'the ungodly are not so'. The godly man is blessed every way. His *person* is—I care not how plain, how unattractive, or even how deformed he may be. It matters not how poor or threadbare the raiment that covers him. Wherever he goes, round about him, but unseen by the worldlings, there is this atmosphere of blessing. Being blessed himself; he carries a blessing with him. It never departs. Whether he is awake or asleep, resting on him, as dew upon the grass in early morning, is the blessing of God that maketh rich. It abides on all his *provisions*, whether it be the stalled ox or the dry crust. The godly cannot partake of a solitary meal but that they have the Lord's blessing resting on their fare. Yea, more, they have God's blessing even on *their trials*, taking all the sting out of them. But 'the ungodly are not so'. No blessing rests either on their persons, their provisions, their homes, or their lives. Why, sirs, if you were to realise this fact, it would he enough to send you down on your knees in the pew at this moment, and cry to God, for his mercy's sake, to make you one of the godly. 'The ungodly are not so.' They live a life devoid of divine benediction. Their bodies may be fed and pampered, but they are not blessed. They may be arrayed in purple and fine linen, as the rich man of old, and yet have no robe of blessing. They may have all that heart can wish, yet be unblessed. Their laugh is laughter under the curse of God. The levity of their speech, that runs like water from their lips—oh, what a mockery it seems! They are joking with the shadow of damnation over their heads, and they let fly their gibes and quips, and make furious merriment, while 'a sword'—a sword is furbished, and it hangs suspended by a hair. The curse of God is out upon them, and upon all they have. Oh, do you say, that is a strong speech? It is not I who said it. These lips would never dare to make such an assertion, unless it were warranted by the divine word. Listen, 'Cursed is everyone that continueth not in all things which are written in the book of the law to do them.' And 'He that believeth not the Son shall not see life; *but the wrath of God abideth on him.*' Oh, dear friend, sad though it may be, it is true; if you are not a converted man or a converted woman you are living with God's curse like a black thunder cloud hanging over you, and it is only through his matchless mercy that the lightning has not flashed forth from it long ere this, and struck you down. God is delaying his judgment in order to lengthen out the time for mercy to be found. Yes, the godly are blest; blest when they fall asleep. All unconscious as they may be of their own existence, the angels watch their slumbers, for God giveth to his beloved sleep. But 'the ungodly are not so'. Young man, will you dare to go to sleep tonight with God's curse for thy coverlet. Can you dare to enter into that strange world which is so nigh akin to death itself, with the thought that when you fall asleep you sleep not like the godly, for they rest beneath the blessing—you beneath the ban.

More than this, you will find, if you look into the psalm, that the godly are like *trees planted*. Here is the picture of a Christian. I care not whether he is high, low, rich, poor, sick, or well: in any case he is like a tree planted by the rivers of water; the roots of which are ever drinking in supplies of luxuriant life. A Christian is an evergreen; his joys in Christ last, though all his other pleasures be taken from him. But 'the ungodly are not so'. If you want to know what kind of trees they are, turn to the Epistle of Jude, and read the 12th verse, and there you will find the contrast. 'Trees plucked up by the roots twice dead, whose fruit withereth.' The ungodly have no root, and no one thanks them for the withering fruit they yield; an accursed fruit that only sets the children's teeth on edge. Put the godly man into never so trying circumstances, and he will triumph, for though the frosts may nip his boughs, his roots find nourishment from hidden springs. But, oh, poor godless soul, what hast thou to fly to when the winter of adversity grasps thy every bough with icy hand? Nothing. For thou art not as the godly.

You see it were easy to talk a long time thus, showing you that no matter what may be said of the godly it may be added, 'the ungodly are not so'. I will only mention two or three points, and I will thank God heartily if you who are unsaved are led to lay hold of them, and think them out at your leisure when you reach your homes. The godly are *saved*, with an everlasting salvation, but 'the ungodly are *not* so'. They are unsaved, lost, dead even whilst they live; under sentence of death. The godly are *forgiven;* there is no charge against them on the Lord's sheet. They have all their iniquities entirely blotted out, but 'the ungodly are *not* so'. Hast thou ever thought, dear friend, that there is not a solitary sin of your entire life yet forgiven? Oh, man, hast thou lived twenty, thirty, forty, fifty years, and is it true that not a solitary sin you have ever committed during all these years has been pardoned, but rests as an accumulated load upon your head tonight? Dreadful indeed is thy condition, passing all description in its horror. And, thanks be unto the Lord, the godly are *conquerors over death*. They know they have to die just as much as the unsaved, but does that thought affright them? No, I think the temptation is more often the other way: they are sometimes in a hurry to depart. So far from fearing death, they look it in the face and say, 'When thou art ready to take us, we are ready to go with thee'; but 'the ungodly are *not* so'. Do you doubt it? Answer me this question, sir, honestly, How would you feel if you had to die tonight? If the message came to you, 'Set thy house in order, for before twelve o'clock this night thou shalt be gone',—how would you take the sentence? Tell the godly man that, and although he might shed some tears on leaving loved ones, he could receive the message without trepidation and say, 'I have a desire to depart, and to be with Christ.' 'The ungodly are not so.' There is their description.

III. Now just for the few remaining moments I want *to remind you of their end;* may the Lord himself strike right home. What is to be the end of these ungodly ones? 'They shall be like the chaff which the wind driveth away, for the ungodly shall not stand in the judgment.'

First of all, then, you see, there will be separation from the righteous. What is the chaff? The chaff is simply the husk that grows on the same stalk as the true grain. They have grown up together, the same sun has shone on both; the same rain has fallen on both. Nay, the husk has been the very cradle of the seed. But at last when the wheat has been reaped and the flail is brought down on it, the grain and the chaff are divided for ever. Oh, there will be some fearful separations on that great day! Father, you know your daughter is a godly girl, and you have lived for her; you have literally been the husk round about her. How you have shielded her; how you have worked for her; and when you have felt weary and tired what comfort you have derived from the thought, 'Well, I am doing it for her.' Yes, poor father, but with all that natural affection you are only the husk while she is the grain, and the wind shall drive you away from her. There will be—unless sovereign grace meets with thee—an eternal separation—the wheat shall be gathered into the garner and the chaff whirled into destruction. You young ones who are present, have you ever thought that you will have to be eternally absent from a godly mother unless her Saviour becomes yours? Young man, young woman present, you live, do you, for your mother? Well, I honour you for that, for no one can love a mother too well. Tell me, then, canst thou bear the thought of mother going to heaven, and you to hell? Can you endure the idea of never seeing her again when once death steps in? Thou mayest seek to cling to her, but thou shalt not be able, for thou art like the chaff which the wind driveth away. Oh, what separations there will be then! The Lord knows that sometimes this thought comes over-poweringly upon our own hearts on a Sunday night. We lie down to rest, but sleep flies, and in thought we see you again, gathered all round us as you are tonight; and from the bottom of our heart we cry, 'Lord, we love them all; may we not meet them all in the glory?' But I know that if many of you die as you are I shall see you standing at the left hand, and I shall hear the sentence of banishment pronounced on you, and shall have to bear witness against you, and say 'Amen' to your condemnation. We shall not be taken to heaven in pews full, or saved as gatherings. It is an individual matter, and though thou mayest have worshipped here never so regularly, yea, become closely linked with us—closely as the chaff is to the grain on the same stalk—the moment shall come when there shall be a final, an eternal separation, 'for the ungodly shall not stand in the judgment'.

Notice too how sweeping and irresistible the ruin. What can a feather-weight of chaff do against the wind? You talk big swelling words now, do you, you, young man? You have had sceptical ideas put into your head. You have been studying, perhaps, Professor Tyndall's lecture at Belfast. You are beginning to talk blasphemously against God and nurturing infidel thoughts within your mind. How soon will these be driven out of you in the day when he saith to thee, 'Depart.' What will thy theories, thy fallacies, thy doubtings, thy excuses, thy bold sayings, be worth then? Thou mayest scoff and jeer in the tabernacle on a Sunday night, it does not need much courage to do that! But when once the Lion of Judah is roused, and thou hast to meet—not a dying Lamb but the angry Lamb, what will thou say to him? Do you feel you are equally matched with omnipotence? Surely not! Then what wilt thou do against the hurricane of Jehovah's wrath? Just as much as chaff can do against the hurricane, and no more,

'The ungodly are not so; but are like the chaff which the wind driveth away.' When? Why, in the judgment, for the ungodly 'shall not stand in the judgment'. Can you imagine that day, and the whole of tonight's congregation, as but a drop in the ocean, gathered there? And now the testing time comes, and there sweeps by a wind more mighty than that which swept past the prophet of Horeb. That was an awful wind, for I read that when it swept by it rent the rocks; but in this great day there shall be a mightier wind than that. It shall come sweeping round the eternal throne, and everything that is not God-built shall be carried away in a moment. I wonder how our modern theologians will be then? Ah, sir, you who have talked about the 'universal fatherhood' of God, deal with the hurricane now. You who have sneered at those who, as you said, 'preached damnation'. What have you to say about damnation now? You considered that God was too kind, and too loving, and too good ever to punish sinners. Where are your delicate ideas now? Oh, how these fine fancies will be swept away, as if they had never been! How all these modern dreams will shrivel up before the hot blast of God's angry 'Depart ye into everlasting fire, prepared for the devil and his angels.' And then with these fancies shall go all excuses. You are a good hand at making them now; I know you could tell me in a minute a 'good' reason for your not being a Christian. Either you have too much business, or you have too little; or you have not time enough to think about these things, or you mean to think about them soon. Yes, how about excuses in that day? How that great wind will catch them all from your lips, and before you have time to give God one of your paltry lies, you with them will be swept with the speed of a hurricane into perdition. There will be only one thing that will stand that mighty tempest, and that will be the soul that rests upon the rock, Christ Jesus. When all false props have gone—when all other dependencies have been swept away, then shall stand immovable the man who flew for refuge to the Saviour. Even then, when the hurricane rends the rocks, and sweeps away the chaff these lines shall be found most gloriously true;—

> Bold shall I stand in that great day,
>   For who ought to my charge shall lay,
>   While by that blood absolved I am,
>   From sin's tremendous curse and shame?

The chaff is to be driven away. Where? Now, I pray you mark this answer. Do let the edge of it be removed by your saying,— 'Oh, that is what Mr Brown says!' It is not. You ask me, do you, the question—'Where is the chaff going?' I will let Jesus Christ himself give you the answer. You will find it at your leisure in the 3rd of Matthew; and the 12th verse; and if, after this, any of you are damned, I am clear of your blood. Where is the chaff going to? The answer is this,—'And he shall burn up the chaff with unquenchable fire.' You may turn round and sneer at it, if you like, and you may reject, and may scoff, and go home and say,—'We had a brimstone sermon tonight.' Say what you will, but remember that God has said,—'The chaff shall be burnt up with unquenchable fire.' Oh, do you think that a heart that has got any feeling in it takes any delight in preaching these things? Do you think that it is any luxury to have to stand before a company like this and tell them that they will be lost? Do you think it is any treat to our heart to have to talk these things? God is our witness, it is the very reverse; but it is not for me to come here and tickle your ears week by week, and select that which I think may please you most. I tell you, if you are unconverted, you are amongst the ungodly, who are not like the saved, and at the last day you shall be carried away like the chaff, and be burnt up with unquenchable fire.

And now, for your soul's sake, flee from the wrath to come. If hell be a reality, shun it. If heaven be a reality, seek it. If God's threatenings be true, fear them. If Christ's invitations be genuine, accept them; and, as a sinner, cast thyself into the arms of him who is willing to save thee tonight, but whose wrath thou canst not bear. 'Today is the day of salvation. Now is the accepted time.' Oh, get ye to Christ quickly, lest the storm break upon thy path, and stop thee. Get thee into the arms, of the Saviour tonight, lest tomorrow thou shouldst be with the chaff which the wind driveth away.

May God in his mercy save you, everyone, for Christ's sake. Amen.

GOD-GIVEN QUIETNESS[1]

When he giveth quietness, who then can make trouble? and when he
hideth his face, who then can behold him, whether it be done
against a nation or against a man only?
Job 34:29.

L AST Thursday was a day of sore trouble to some of us, and
sorrow seemed to reach its climax. When the train steamed
out of Liverpool-street, carrying with it my own bright,
blessed daughter,[2] it seemed for a few moments as if it had left me
on the platform with an empty body. Heart and everything else
seemed to have gone out with that train. I came straight home,
and, on entering my study, I found that, during my absence, some
thoughtful friend had put upon my table, just in front of where I
always sit, a beautifully illuminated card. The words that greeted
my eyes were these, 'He giveth quietness', and underneath was
this text, 'When he giveth quietness, who then can make trouble?'
Whoever it was that deposited that sweet truth upon my table
showed not a little knowledge of heart experience, and of the word
of God. I read the verse, not once or twice only. It came to me as
the very voice of God, and I thought that I could hardly do better
than follow my usual practice of passing on to you everything that
proves of profit to myself. I dare say that, in this morning's gathering, there are hearts that are as sore as mine was on Thursday.

[1] c. 1896, East London Tabernacle.
[2] Miss Gracie Brown started on that day as a missionary to China.

Doubtless, there are not a few here who are as much perplexed, and who know the meaning of 'turmoil' without going to a dictionary. I fain would do for this gathering what that friend did for me. I would put before your eyes these words, 'He giveth quietness, and, when he giveth quietness, who then can make trouble?'

Let us look for a few moments at the passage as it stands related to the whole verse. You will see that it enunciates a great and wide-spreading principle—a principle that is applicable not to a man only, but also to a nation. And the principle is the absolute dependence of individuals, communities, and nations upon God, for quietness, prosperity, and peace. According to this text, God is the great factor in history, and I want you to concentrate your thoughts for a few minutes upon the words, 'whether it be done against a nation'. The principle has no limit. It is as true of the millioned nation as of the solitary man; and yet how completely is this ignored. The gigantic blunders of all past ages, and the huge blunders of today, may all be traced to the fact that nations are trying to do without God in history. They are leaving out the prime factor. They are like boys trying to work out a problem in algebra without the 'x' which stands for the unknown quantity. God is left out, and consequently there is a perpetual entanglement, and bewildered minds say, 'Everything is wrong. What can be done?' Stupefaction comes over some of the clearest brains, and despondency says, 'There is no solution for the difficulties and the troubles of the day.' God is left out. Is not this true of this nation? If you have plenty of time to waste, you will in all probability read through the Parliamentary reports in the daily papers, and wade through all the clever speeches that are made; but, if you are a child of God, you will be forced to the conclusion, 'God is not taken into the reckoning here; the Divine Factor is left out.' Given such an Act, granted such a transaction, and it is supposed that there will be peace and prosperity in the land, and the sun will shine on everyone; but, where is God? This text comes in like a clarion note, and says, 'National prosperity and peace are of God. When he giveth quietness, who then can make trouble unto a nation? But when he hideth his face from a nation, who then can behold him?' Would to God that the day may soon come when our politicians will learn that national prosperity is only a synonym for divine blessing. Look at all the social problems that are distracting minds today. How is it that they remain so insoluble, and that, after all the panaceas that are mooted have been tried, our hearts still feel that failure stamps them all? What is the reason of it? The reason is that God has been left out. God is ignored. History proves it.

As an illustration of this part of our text, look at the history of Israel. Oh, if they had only kept true to God, if only they had been faithful to him, if they had but recognised him in their history, what a different history it would have been! Read the 32nd chapter of the book of Deuteronomy, from the 7th verse. It is a weird story. God tells them how he brought them up out of Egypt, how he nursed them as a child, how he bare them as upon eagle wings, how he fed them from the skies, how he quenched their thirst from the rock, and how he brought oil out of the flinty rock. One man could put a thousand to flight in those days, for God was with his people. Now go on, and see what happens. Jeshurun (the nation) waxed fat, and kicked, and rebelled against God, and the Lord said, 'I will hide my face from them; I will see what their end will be; for they are a very froward generation, children in whom is no faith.' And when God hid his face from Jeshurun, prosperity departed, and the nation was powerless to restore it. Now, what was true of Israel will be true of England, unless she takes warning. There are dark clouds gathering over Britain, and she would do well to have a time of national humiliation and confession. Were this nation to act with true political wisdom and true social economy, she would cast herself down before God, and acknowledge, 'We have sinned;

we have ignored thee; we have departed from thy counsel; we have not honoured thy word or kept thy Sabbaths. Thou art beginning to hide thy face from us. Lord, turn us again that we may be saved, and let the trust of the nation be in thee; for when God giveth quietness, who then can make trouble? And when he hideth his face, who then can behold him, whether it be done against a nation or against a man only?'

Now, taking the text apart from its setting, there is one unspeakably sweet truth taught, and I want to take you all round about it and into it, and then may the Spirit of God take it into you. The thought is this, that *God-given quietness is indestructible*. 'When he giveth quietness, who then can make trouble?' Was there ever a lovelier word than 'quietness'? Linger for a moment on it, and repeat it over. It is more musical than a silver bell. 'Quietness'—the very word is eloquent of its own meaning. There is a ripple as of a peaceful brook about it. 'Quietness'—it is the world's great need; it is what everyone is dying for want of; it is what all hearts sigh for; it is what weary brains crave; it is what the world hunts after; but it is what few find.

And yet, if you look outside the circle of poor, fallen man, and take the wider circle of nature, you will see that there is not only the demand for quietness, but there is the provision for it; and there is not only the provision, but there is the acceptance of the provision. Walk with me for a few minutes along a delightful path of thought. God, knowing the need that all nature has for quietness, has very graciously provided it, for his tender mercies are over all his works. God has ordered that, during part of every twenty-four hours, a weary, tired world shall, for a season, be steeped in the quietness of sleep. It is love that drops the veil over the sun, and darkens for a while the earth; while unnumbered flowers, as if tired through blooming during the day, shut up their lovely cups for the night, and go to sleep. God's songsters, that have been chirruping and singing all the day in the branches, need some rest for their little throttles, and God provides it. The birdies, wiser than man, understand God's signal in the sky, and they put their heads beneath their wings, and they sleep when God steeps nature in the quietness of night. And God has also arranged that, every seventh day, a weary world should have a break in the dreadful monotony of labour. Infinite love says, 'Once a week will I bathe a tired world in the bath of Sabbath rest, so shall she come forth fresh for her work on the morrow.' But God seems to argue that these rests that I have mentioned are only little siestas, and that nature needs a longer sleep; and so, when autumn comes, God begins to put the tired, and therefore fractious, child to rest. All the summer-time nature has been in high glee. She has been laughing and playing until she has grown tired; so God says to her, 'It is time to go to rest now.' And how long she is, often, in dropping to sleep. Autumn comes and throws its coverlet over the child, but some-times she flings it off, and there are two or three days of spasmodic summer. But God will have his way, and he hushes weary nature, until, at last, there is the deep sound sleep of the winter, in which nature rests in quietness until she awakes with the snowdrops and crocuses. Nature must have quietness, and God has provided it for her.

According to Jewish law, *the land* was to have its season of rest. In the 25th chapter of Leviticus, and the 2nd verse, there is a very notable passage: 'Speak unto the children of Israel, and say unto them, When ye come into the land which I give you, then shall the land keep a Sabbath unto the Lord. Six years thou shalt sow thy field, and six years thou shalt prune thy vineyard and gather in the fruit thereof. But the seventh year shall be a Sabbath of rest unto the land, a Sabbath for the Lord. Thou shalt neither sow thy field, nor prune thy vineyard.' Once in seven years all the land was to enjoy this quietness. Now, let a thousand years take the place of a day, for with the Lord one day is as a thousand years. God has promised another Sabbath rest. The six thousand week-days of the world are almost expiring, and he has promised to usher in, when they have gone, a Sabbatic rest, and God's millennium shall dawn. God teaches, all the way through nature, that rest is needed, and that quietness must prevail, and he has provided both alike.

But how is it with us? Man alone has broken God's law and so I find that sin, that arch-thief, has robbed us of quietness. This thief never took a more precious jewel than when he stole quietness from the world. Look abroad if you question whether I am correct or not. Where is quietness? Sin has so vitiated the taste of man that he does not even enjoy quietness, though he is wasting through lack of it. Night is turned into day, and society begins its life when all sane people go to bed. So completely has sin revolutionized everything, that God's season of quiet is turned into man's season of revelry. I find man growing sick of the quietness of the Sabbath, and denouncing it as 'horridly dull'. Oh, sir, have you no taste for quietness? Can you find no enjoyment in stillness? Have you become one of those that must hunt here and there, and run after this, and race after that, and have your whole life on a tension? Believe me, you are only giving a melancholy example of how sin vitiates the taste. The world is unable to rest because it is the world. The Hebrew word which is here translated 'quietness' is the word that is used by Isaiah where he says that the wicked cannot rest. The world is like the sea, never constant but in its restlessness. Look abroad on every hand, and where is there quietness? Do you find it in commercial life? You business men can answer that best. The only quiet is a quietness of trade that disquiets you. Is there quietness in the intellectual world? Where is the restfulness of the religious world? If I go into the social world, I find the very earth quaking beneath the feet. Revolution is in its throes. There is enough dynamite in society to rend it to pieces. Quietness? How few find it! Few find God, and it is *he* that giveth quietness.

Let me take you along another line of thought. If this text be true of a nation and of a man, it must also be true of that which lies between these two points, and therefore it will be true of a community. I desire gratefully to bear witness to God's praise that, as a church, we have experienced wonderfully the meaning of this text. 'He giveth quietness' might be engraved over the doorways of this tabernacle. When I look back for seven-and-twenty years, and think of all the characters, the temperaments, the dispositions, that have been brought together, I can see that there has been enough in our midst to rend us to pieces a hundred times over; but it is marvellous how God has kept this great host in peace and love. Never did a church give a more marvellous exhibition of this than was given in this place last Monday week. The perfect unanimity, the marvellous love, and the manifestation of abounding peace, were all too eloquent for words. How is it that, as a great company, we have thus been kept? Oh, look not to platform or to pew. The explanation of it is this, 'He giveth quietness.' 'When he giveth quietness, who then can make trouble? And when he hideth his face who then can behold him, whether it be done against a nation or against a man only?'

And this is not only true in the history of nations and in the history of communities, but *it is true in the history of the heart*. This is a history very little read. I do not think that many schoolmasters or schoolmistresses teach their children this; but there is no history more thrilling or more wondrous. When God gives quietness to a heart, nothing can give that heart trouble. Students of the word are aware that this verse is capable of a very remarkable rendering; and it is given in the Revised Version. 'When he giveth quietness, who then can condemn?' It is really the 8th of the Romans anticipated: 'It is God that justifieth. Who is he that condemneth?' The wonderful teaching of this verse is, when God gives quietness to a heart, who is going to condemn that man? When God gives peace to the contrite sinner, who is going to break that holy rest? 'Who, then, shall make trouble?' Shall the law? The law may thunder out its denunciations; but, if God has given my heart his quietness, it is a quietness that is *based on law*, and therefore is not afraid of law. Do you say, 'Conscience can make trouble'? Stay, if the peace which I have in my heart is the peace which God gives, then my conscience has been pacified by the blood of Jesus Christ. O conscience, thou canst make a hell within a human breast, but, if the blood of Jesus be sprinkled on thee, thy tones cannot affright. God has met the requirements of the law, and has pacified conscience, and the peace remains perfect. On the plain of Waterloo is a huge bronze lion, erected to commemorate the great victory. That bronze lion has an open mouth, and huge and awful are its fangs, and it seems to be snarling and growling over the battlefield and challenging anyone to come near. A friend of mine said that, when last he was there, he was very interested to observe that a bird had built its nest in the open-mouth of the lion, and that it had twined the little twigs and the soft downy stuff of which the nest was composed in and out of the great bronze teeth of the lion. They made a splendid foundation for the nest. There, in the open mouth, was a nest with the little fledglings in it, and he heard the chirp of the bird coming from the jaws of the lion. I thought, 'Ah, even so is it. I am not saved at the expense of the law. I am saved in accordance with the law, and I build my nest in the lion's mouth.' Afraid of God's law? Blessed be God, the law that terrified me as a sinner now gives me assurance as a saint. I build my nest in the lion's mouth, and I have the confidence of *righteous justification*. Now, if you have that, who is going to take it from you? If you have the peace of righteous justification, who is going to make trouble? I do not wonder if those of you who live on milk-and-water theology—no, there is no such thing: milk-and-water *neology*—I do not wonder if you find trouble; but the soul that knows what it is to be justified by the grace of God, through the finished work of Christ which perfectly honours the law, has its nest built in the lion's mouth, and sings for very joy, 'When he giveth quietness, who then can make trouble?'

But, if I am a believer, I have not only that quietness, but I have *the quietness of the Spirit's calmness*. The Holy Ghost smooths out the wrinkles of the soul. The Holy Ghost fills the spirit of man and gives a strange unearthly calm. You may dissipate the quiet of insensibility, but, oh, you cannot dissipate the quiet which is born of the Spirit. When he says, 'Peace be still', who is going to make the billows roll?

And there is also *the quietness and rest of satisfaction*. Everyone would know quietness if he had all that he wanted. If only a man be perfectly satisfied, what room is there for disquiet? Now, the saint has perfect satisfaction. Jesus Christ so perfectly satisfies him that, no matter what may happen, he is quiet. He has *the rest of fulness*. I have here in my hand a bottle of water. If I move it the water shakes and washes from right to left. Why? Because it is not full. If I fill the bottle right up, so that it will not hold another drop, and cork it, I may turn the bottle which way I will, but the water will not wash about. It is quiet because the bottle is full. God fills up his people. 'That my joy may be fulfilled in you.' 'When he giveth quietness, who then can make trouble?'

Is it not true of the believer that all the way through life God gives quietness of heart? I do not say quietness of circumstances. The Lord Jesus did not say, 'Let not your *homes* be troubled.' He said, 'Let not your heart be troubled.' It is not, 'Let not your circumstances be moved', but 'Let not your hearts be agitated.' And I do with my soul believe that God is able to keep a man in perfect quietness of mind, although there is nothing but tribulation round about. He makes himself to become the great breakwater. At a distance you would say, 'Dear me! that man must be swamped with trouble.' You see the billows rolling; you see the clouds of spray shooting up, and you say, 'He must be drowned.' Oh, no; what you see is the wave breaking on the breakwater. The man himself is in a quiet harbour, where there is perfect stillness. The breakwater meets all the force of the storm. So says Christ, 'In the world ye shall have tribulation. Crested wave after crested wave like ocean's racehorses, shall rush upon you. But in me ye shall have peace.' Lady Hope says that she noticed a guard on the Great Western Railway who had seven people speaking to him at once—a very uncomfortable experience. They were all pestering him with questions, and they all expected to be answered at once, and she was surprised at the calm way in which the guard answered each questioner. He did not lose his temper, and did not get flurried, and Lady Hope, after it was over, said to him, 'Guard, however did you keep so calm and so quiet with all those people pestering you as they were?' The guard, not knowing to whom he was speaking said, 'Ah madam, the peace of God which passeth all understanding does keep the heart and mind.' That guard on the Great Western Railway had discovered a secret that a good many of us have yet to learn. He had learned the meaning of that passage in the 4th of Philippians, where we are told that if by prayer and supplication with thanksgiving we make known our requests unto the Lord, the result shall be that the peace of God which passeth all understanding *shall* keep our hearts and minds. There shall be a quietness which none can break.

'Ah, dear Mr Brown', says somebody, 'it is all very well for you to talk like this; but you do not know how much I have lost this year. I am almost afraid to go through my books. As for my banking account, I am not sure that the bank will allow it to stand there much longer. I have been losing, losing, losing.' Well, sir, and suppose that you have a broken fortune all round about you this text shall still be true, 'When he giveth quietness, who then shall make trouble?' But says another, 'Ah, pastor, it is all very well but, do you know, I used to live without an ache or a pain, in the very buoyancy of health, and now it seems to me that my heart is not only undermined but likely soon to be shattered.' 'He giveth quietness. Who then shall make trouble?' I tell you that there are sick ones in the hospital today who know more about the quietness of God in their pain than some of us know in our health. Another says, 'But my home is desolated, its brightness has gone.' True, man, and yet does this text abide, 'When he giveth quietness who then can make trouble?' God can put a lamp into a dark room, and God can furnish an empty house, and God can put music into an otherwise silent abode. When he gives peace, none can break it. No slander, however cruel, no persecution, however fierce, no temptation, however searching.

Do you say, 'Why is this quietness unbreakable?' I will tell you. It is because this quietness comes through faith. Faith rests upon the word of God, and Jesus said, 'The scripture cannot be broken.' Let us work upwards. If the scripture cannot be broken, and my faith rests upon the scripture, and my quietness is the result of my so doing, then my quietness cannot be broken. Did I entertain one doubt about this Book being the word of God from beginning to end, I should not have an atom of quietness in my heart this morning; but when he who knows, and who was an expert in the matter of scripture, says that not a jot nor a tittle can fail, and that this word cannot be broken, I rest on that, and peace comes with the resting. God's love cannot be broken; his purposes cannot be broken; his covenant cannot be broken; and, whilst his covenant with Christ stands, quietness may be my portion.

Now, dear brother, do you possess this quietness that I have been talking about? Will you give the answer as before God? Is it in your heart? Remember that, if you have it not, you can neither grow, nor be fresh, nor make advance as a disciple, nor be of use as a servant. If you plant a geranium today, and move it tomorrow, and then shift it the day after, and then put it somewhere else the following week, I do not think that that geranium will be likely to grow. And I am certain that, unless I know the quietness which God gives, there will not be any growth. A restless, ever-moving spirit cannot develop in the things of God. How can I be made fresh? I am not going to apologize for the illustration that I am about to give, though perhaps it may seem rather simple. I have sometimes met God's saints that have reminded me of people who have been up all night. They have an 'up-all-night' look. Persons who have been up all night have a particular look of their own. They look more than sleepy. Their eyes are red, and they have a haggard appearance. All the juice seems to have been squeezed out of them, and there is no freshness whatever. They are like a dusty rag. I will tell you what they want. Not the doctor's medicine, but God's gift. What they need is to go into a room, pull the blind down, lie on the bed, and receive God's gift of sleep for some eight hours. Then look at them! All the bloodshot is out of their eyes, and the feverish look has gone. They are 'as fresh as a daisy'. Now, there is such a thing in spiritual life as getting an up-all-night, worn, and fagged feeling. If you try to talk for God, there is no unction about your speech; there is no power. But the quietness of my text is the balmy sleep that keeps the soul as fresh as the morning, and makes it a perpetual refreshment to others.

How are we to get it? Look at my text: 'When *he giveth* quietness.' Take it; it is God's gift; it is not your effort. You must tell all to God, though it nearly breaks your heart to make the confession. You will never have quietness so long as you keep a secret from God. Go and tell him all; tell him what a poor, wretched, selfish man you have been; tell him what a poor, hasty, bad-tempered woman you have been. Go and tell him what a failure you have been; and, *when you have told him all, believe all that he says, and then take all that he offers,* and you will find that he keeps his word, and that the peace which passeth all understanding does keep your heart and mind.

> We cannot understand why this is best;
> We tightly clasp His hand, and leave the rest.
> When He who knoweth all sends grief and woe,
> We can but trust, and say, 'He wills it so.'
> His love is mightier far than we can guess:
> His thoughts toward us are all tenderness.
> Then, though our hearts are sad, we still can pray,
> And He will make us glad in His own day.

'When he giveth quietness, who then can make trouble?' God give every beloved brother aud sister here this morning his own quietness, for Jesus's sake. Amen.

HIS GREAT LOVE[1]

His great love.
Ephesians 2:4.

IS great love is our great theme this morning, but, oh, how infinitely does the greatness of the theme transcend the slender abilities of the preacher: But this thought encourages him, that, let the preacher be whosoever he may, all are on one level here. All alike are powerless to rise to the height of the argument of the amazing theme: 'His great love.' No mere wealth of intellectual grasp avails here. Nay, nor does any Holy Ghost teaching or spiritual initiation fully avail, for, after the most profoundly taught man of God has dwelt upon 'His great love', he will be the very first to acknowledge that the subject lies infinitely beyond all that he has said, even though he may have been mightily helped by the Spirit of God. 'His great love.' Here is a greatness which so overawes and overwhelms that it belittles everything else, and yet the desire of our soul is in some measure to reach even to its dizzy height. May that which cannot possibly be fully expressed be yet, by the help of the Holy Ghost, so set forth that every one here shall leave with a truer conception of the greatness of God's love than he had when he entered the building.

'His great love.' This, you will see, is *the fountain-head* of the river of salvation. It is declared to be so here. In these words you have the eternal spring that supplies the whole of that river of salvation

---

[1] October 29, 1894, East London Tabernacle.

that makes glad the city of our God. How full, how deep, how clear, its tide. And yet the whole of that river, with all its endless silvery branches, is supplied from the mighty gushing spring of 'his great love'. If it is the fountain-head of all supply, you will see also from the context, that it is *the one mighty motive* for all. 'But God who is rich in mercy': there is the supply. But why is he rich in mercy? He is rich in mercy 'for his great love'. It is the great love that begets the rich mercy. The mighty motive that gives birth to all is infinite love. Come with me in thought, and gaze upon all the wondrous wheels that revolve in the great work of redemption, and then, as you gaze upon them, remember that the mighty motive power that moves all is this—'his great love'. There is no other argument for God saving us. There can be no other argument. Go back into the primary cause of all, and you will come to this, 'his great love'; and if presumptuously you ask, 'But what is the reason of that love? If his love be the original of all, what is the origin of the original? What gives birth to the great love?' my answer is that God loves us because he will; and I can give you no other explanation. God's love is sovereign love. The roots are in himself; therefore do the fruits abound toward us. Why does God save us? *He saves us in order to satisfy his love.* He loves us to satisfy his nature. 'God is love.' It is his love that craves for, plans, and works out, our eternal salvation. Love in itself is an invisible thing. It is simply an emotion of the heart; and an emotion is not that which can be beheld by itself. It can be seen only as it manifests itself. You cannot see love; you cannot handle love. Only as love reveals itself in action can you perceive it. And, as regards the love of God, you cannot even form an idea of its nature by a contemplation of your own emotions of love. Perhaps someone here is already searching his own heart with the hope of attaining to such an idea; but, when he has explored its depths, he will have a very poor standard by which to judge the great love of God. My poor, weak, imperfect, faulty emotion, which I call love, can never be the revelation of the great love of God. We are just shut up to the fact that we are absolutely dependent upon God's revelation for knowing what God's love is. Only as it has pleased him to reveal it to us can we possibly know it.

This morning I shall want you to look mainly at four points, and each point will have a separate text. We shall turn the flash-light of four or five passages upon our text, and from them show you, first, God's great love *manifested;* next, his great love *commended;* thirdly, his great love *measured;* and lastly, his great love *magnified.* You see our line of thought. It is that love, being an invisible emotion, can only be understood as it is revealed.

I.—First of all, note that God's GREAT LOVE IS MANIFESTED IN THE INCARNATION. You will find this in the 1st Epistle of John, the 4th chapter, and the 9th verse: 'In this was manifested the love of God toward us, because that God sent his only begotten Son into the world.' Note this word well, 'In this was *manifested* the love of God.' The invisible emotion of love was manifested in that God sent his only begotten Son. To understand this passage we must understand the meaning of 'manifest'. I thought that I would refer to the best dictionaries of the English language in order to see the definition of that word. 'Manifest' means to make evident, to make palpable, so that it can be taken hold of by the hand. We speak of a 'manufacture', which means something made by the hand, from the Latin *'manus'*. In the same way 'manifested' means brought into such a condition that it can be grasped by the hand. In other words, it is something made real. Or 'manifest' means to disclose, to display, to put beyond all doubt. Now read the passage thus: 'In this was displayed, in this was put beyond all doubt, in this was made palpable, the love of God, in that he sent his only begotten Son into the world.'

You will get, I think, a very striking light upon the word 'manifest' by turning to Acts 4:16, for, in the original, the same word is used. Peter and John had performed that marvel on the impotent man, and in the 16th verse we read that the members of the council said, 'What shall we do to these men, for that indeed a notable miracle has been done by them is *manifest* to all them that dwell in Jerusalem, and we cannot deny it.' The miracle was so manifest that they said, 'It is of no use to try to deny it.' You cannot deny that which is manifest. Now read the passage again. 'In this was manifest'—(that is, so displayed that it cannot be denied)—'the love of God.'

Once again. Let us throw another scripture light on the words, 'In this was manifested the love of God.' It is the very same word as that which is applied to our Lord's incarnation, for in the 1st Epistle of John, the 1st chapter, and the 1st and 2nd verses, we read, 'That which was from the beginning, which we have heard, which we have seen with our eyes, which we have looked upon, and our hands have handled, of the word of life, for the life was *manifested.*' Now, John, I can understand how it is that you have been able to see it, and hear it, and handle it, for the life has been manifested. So displayed was God in Christ that the invisible God was seen, heard, handled. Now, as God was manifested in Christ, so is the love of God manifested in the person of Christ. Christ says, 'He that hath seen me hath seen the Father.' Likewise also could he have said, 'He that hath seen me hath seen the great love of God.'

Oh, that the Spirit of the Lord would help us just now to rise to the great height of this declaration. Do you catch the thought? God's great love has visited the earth, and sojourned and lived on it. God's great love has been seen, heard, handled. It has been made so palpable that even human hands have been able to touch and feel the great love of God, while human eyes have gazed upon it, and human ears listened to its voice. There is the love of God *sleeping* in the person of that tiny infant that is pressed to the virgin mother's breast. Look again. There is the great love of God *toiling* as an artisan in the carpenter's shop. That one wiping the sweat from his brow, and with the shavings clinging to his gaberdine, is the incarnation of God's great love. Look a third time, and you see the love of God *preaching*,—the love of God as a God-sent prophet, declaring the truth, and exclaiming to the weary, 'Come unto me.' And now, bending over Jerusalem, with big tear-drops running down his cheeks, the love of God is *weeping*. Oh, have you ever looked at Christ really in this light as a perfect manifestation of the love of God?

Should we be spared for a few months we shall say that spring has come. What do we mean by spring? We have never seen the spirit of the spring. Spring itself is an invisible thing. How can I see the spring? I can only see it as it is manifested in buds that swell and burst, in the flowers that peep and open, in the rustle of the green leaves, and in the quickening of nature everywhere. In this I see and hear the spirit of the spring. In the very chatter of the birds I hear a testimony to this hidden force. I have not seen the spring itself but I have seen the spring manifested. So the love of God is in itself an invisible emotion, but I behold it in the tears of Christ, I hear it in the words of Christ, I see it in the person of Christ. In this was manifested God's great love, even that he sent his Son.

Can you not see now, in a moment, the utter folly of those persons who preach the love of God apart from Jesus Christ? Such preaching is worthless. I cannot know anything of the love of God save as he manifests it; and he has been pleased to manifest his love in that he sent Jesus Christ. Subtract Jesus Christ, and you wipe away the manifestation, and ask the people to behold the invisible. All the present talk about the love of the eternal Father, irrespective altogether of its manifestation in Jesus Christ, is a snare and a delusion, and not a gospel. God has said, 'Would you see my love? Look there. It is manifested in the person of my Son.'

II.—Now I have to flash a second light upon my text. You saw by my first text that God's great love is manifested in the incarnation. My second text shows that his GREAT LOVE IS COMMENDED BY THE DEATH OF CHRIST. You will find the words in the 5th chapter of Romans, and the 8th verse: 'But God *commendeth* his love toward us, in that, while we were yet sinners, Christ died for us.' The meaning of the word 'commend', literally translated, is to 'cause to stand together'; hence to confirm, to establish. God has confirmed his love to us, in that, while we were yet sinners, Christ died for us. God's love is manifested in the person of Christ, and then established by his death. Read the 7th verse of this 5th chapter, and you will see how striking is the argument which it contains. 'For scarcely for a righteous man will one die; yet peradventure for the good man someone would even dare to die' (RV). 'It is difficult to imagine it, but still', says the apostle, 'although for a righteous man—that is, an upright, honourable, but unloving man—no one would die, yet it is just within the range of possibility that perhaps for some dear, good, loving man, someone would die.' That is as high as human nature can get. To die for another is the greatest manifestation of love that can be given, but it is gravely questionable whether even for the best of men anyone could be found willing to give this supreme manifestation. 'But God commendeth his love toward us, in that, while we were yet sinners'—that is, neither righteous nor good—'Christ died for us.' *The supreme act of love is reached for the most unworthy.* Poor human nature can scarcely find one willing to die for the best; but God has commended his love in that he has reached the highest act of love in the laying down of his life, and he has done this for the very worst. That is how God commends his love.

But the very nature of the death enhances the love, for what says my text? 'God commendeth his love toward us, in that, while we were yet sinners, Christ died *for us.*' It was not simply a beautiful, painless, curseless death. It was a substitutionary, sacrificial death, which had the curse of Jehovah accompanying it; a death which made Christ cry, 'My God, My God, why hast thou forsaken me?'; a death not on softest bed, with every alleviation which love can suggest, but on a rough timber cross; a death in which every agony possible was compressed, and that death was all for us. Love, as we have been reminding you, is an invisible emotion, but it is manifested in the person of Jesus, and commended, confirmed, and gloriously established, by his atoning death for us upon the accursed tree. The manifestation reached its commendation there. The whole of Christ's life is a mountain range showing forth God's great love; but, when we come to Calvary, there shoots up from that mountain range a snow-capped peak so dazzling white, so awful in its height, that all the rest of the range seems dwarfed by comparison. Therefore let us learn the lesson that we cannot preach the love of God if we leave out the sacrifice of Christ. Oh, that it were possible to make one's words echo beyond this tabernacle into ten thousand deluded ears. Then would I cry aloud, 'You cannot preach the love of God if you leave out the substitutionary sacrifice. Your talk goes for nothing, for you leave the love of God without its commendation.' God's commendation of his love is this—and he can give no higher—that, while we were yet sinners, God, in the person of Christ, gave himself as a sacrifice for the lost.

III.—Our third point is HIS GREAT LOVE MEASURED. How can we measure this love? You get the answer in the 17th chapter of the Gospel of John, and the 23rd verse: 'I in them, and they in me, that they may be made perfect in one, and that the world may know that thou hast sent me, and hast *loved them as thou hast loved me.*'

Behold there the measure of God's love. God has loved us as he loved Christ. I can imagine some thoughtful hearer saying, 'But what is the good of giving us that measure? *The measure itself is immeasurable.*' That is just what I wanted to bring you to. We have an immeasurable standard given to us. What is God's love to us? It is just the same as God's love to Christ. But what is God's love to Christ? Immeasurable. Then what is God's love to us? Immeasurable. When we come to measure the city of love that lieth four square, an infinite measuring-rod is put into our hands. It is 'As thou hast loved me.' God's love to Christ was perfect; then God's love to me must be a perfect love. I hardly like to suggest the question, but can you conceive of the love of the Father to the Son being *capable of augmentation?* Can you conceive of the Father loving Christ a little more at one time than at another? It is almost. blasphemy even to suggest the thought. Can you venture to think of there being *any diminution* in the love which the Father has to the Son? You shrink back with horror, and say, 'God forbid!' Then Jesus tells us that God's love to us is something that cannot be augmented and something that cannot be diminished. Or, again, can you conceive of the Father's love to Christ ever being *alienated?* Oh, it were blasphemy to talk of it. 'As thou hast loved me', says Christ, 'so, Father, thou hast loved them.' There is the measure of 'his great love'. It is the same love as that which he has unto his Son.

> So dear, so very dear, to God,
> More dear I cannot be,
> For in the person of His Son
> *I am as dear as He.*

IV.—We have seen that God's great love is manifested in the incarnation, that it is commended in the death of Christ, and that it can be measured only by his love to his Son. Observe, lastly, that

HIS GREAT LOVE IS MAGNIFIED IN WHAT HE HAS DONE FOR US.
This is found in the 1st Epistle of John, the 3rd chapter, and the
1st verse. 'Behold'—here is something to be looked at—'Behold
what manner of love the Father hath bestowed upon us, that we
should be called the sons of God.' And then there ought to be
added the words found in the Revised Version, *and such we are.*'
The word 'manner' which occurs here is a very beautiful one. It
might he translated 'style'. 'Behold what style of love the Father
hath bestowed on us, that we should be called the sons of God.'
We have found that we are unable to measure God's great love,
because the only measuring-rod by which it can be gauged is itself
immeasurable; but we are able to judge somewhat of the style of
his love by what it has done for us. God is not content with simply
forgiving me. It does not satisfy his love just to cleanse me. God
does not rest in merely justifying me. His heart prompts him to
do something more for me than all this. Then in what further way
does his love show itself? Behold, it is God-like in its style. He
not only forgives and cleanses; he not only snatches from perdition, but he puts us right *into his own family.* That is what he does
for us. Behold what style of love is here. You may look until your
eyes grow dim with age, but the more you look the more you will
be amazed at this style of his great love. Not only does he save
me as a rebel, but he brings me into the King's house; and not
only does he bring me into the King's house, but he makes me the
King's son, and he says, 'Come, my child, and live with me.' That
beautiful parable of the prodigal son, so often made to teach error
because it is wrenched from its context, is intended to set forth the
reception which God gives to the soul when it comes to him. The
Shepherd, as Redeemer, has done his work in the first parable. The
Spirit, with the light and the broom, has done his work as set forth
in the second parable. The soul has been found and saved by the
Shepherd, and discovered by the Spirit, and now that soul goes to

the Father, in the third parable. What sort of reception is given? There is the young prodigal straight from the swine-trough—a stench, it may be, in the nostrils of decency. But the Father does not say, 'Let him go and take his dinner out in the kitchen among the servants.' Not at all. It is not, 'Rummage over the old clothes, and see whether you can find a worn-out coat, for the shabbiest will be good enough for him.' No, it is 'Bring forth the best robe and put it on him. Get a ring, and put it on the very finger that has been in the pigs' mash. And go and kill the fatted calf, and call all the household in; and let us eat, drink, and be merry.' And the old farm-house rang with melody, and the windows flashed with light, and the rooms shook with the dancing, because the prodigal had been welcomed home. That is Christ's own picture of how the love of God treats the rescued sinner. Here, methinks, I can in some measure understand his great love. Manifested in Christ, commended in the atonement, measured by his love to the Son, it is magnified in myself.

One thought, and I close. In the 5th chapter of Romans, and the 5th verse, we find what God does with that love. 'The love of God is *shed abroad in our heart* by the Holy Ghost.' We have seen its manifestation, its commendation, its measurement, and its magnification; and now we behold the communication of this wonderful love to our hearts. The love here mentioned is not my love to God; but God's love to me. And by what medium is this love shed abroad? By the only possible one—the Holy Ghost. It has been pointed out (I think by Godet) that the word translated 'shed abroad' literally signifies *'to be poured out of'*. The meaning, then, is that the love of God is poured out of God's heart into our heart by the Holy Ghost. Only the blessed Spirit who searches and sounds the depths of God knows what the love of God is, and he reveals the same by imparting himself. *By filling the heart with himself, he floods it with the love of God.*

Dear brother, is the great love of God shed abroad in your heart? Is the aroma of that love filling every chamber of your being? Blessed be his name, 'We have known and believed the love that God hath toward us.' Then my prayer for you and for myself is, 'The Lord direct our hearts into the love of God'; 'his great love', manifested and commended, measured and magnified, and shed abroad by the Holy Ghost.

> There are who sigh that no fond heart is theirs:
>> None love them best. Oh, vain and selfish sigh!
> Out of the bosom of His love He spares:
>> The Father spares the Son, for thee to die.
> For thee He died; for thee He lives again;
>> O'er thee He watches in His boundless reign.
>
> Thou art as much His care as if beside
>> Nor man nor angel lived in heaven or earth;
> Thus sunbeams pour alike their glorious tide
>> To light up worlds, or wake an insect's mirth:
> They shine and shine with unexhausted store;
>> *Thou art thy Saviour's darling:* seek no more.

IS THERE A HELL?[1]

What shall the end be of them that obey not the gospel of God?
1 Peter 4:17.

I am free to confess, dear friends, that I never came upon this platform with a greater sense of responsibility weighing upon me than I do this evening. I think I can in some measure take the language of the prophet as my own, and exclaim 'The burden of the Lord'. It is only the deep conviction that the subject demands an investigation which has induced me to select it as the subject of our evening's meditation. The subject is in itself so immense, the destinies involved so terrible and eternal, that in approaching the subject one seems to hear a voice saying, 'Take off thy shoes from off thy feet, for the place on which thou standest is holy ground.' The subject lies in the answer which Scripture gives to the question of the text, 'What shall the end be of them that obey not the gospel of God?—or in other words—What is the doom of those who die impenitent? Is there a hell or is there not?

The truths of God have suffered as severe a persecution as have ever the believers in them. No martyr burnt at Smithfield or tortured in the Inquisition of Spain, suffered worse treatment than has the word of God, for which he died. Texts have been broken upon the wheel of unsanctified reason and put upon the rack of atheistic philosophy until meanings and interpretations have been dragged from them that they never possessed, and were

---

[1] September 12, 1869, Stepney Green Tabernacle, London.

never intended to convey. Men, not content to take their plain and apparent teaching—that which has been for centuries so clearly stamped upon their brow that none thought of any other—now endeavour to show their superior spiritual knowledge, by declaring that the whole Christian church has for centuries been mistaken; and that it is for them to prove that the doctrines held by God's saints for over eighteen hundred years are nothing else than 'traditional prejudices'.

Whilst the attacks were confined to minor truths (if it is for us to call any truth a minor one) it was perhaps wisest for God's watchmen to take but little notice, and continue straight on the simple work of preaching the gospel; but waxing bolder, they now attempt to undermine the very foundations of the faith of the church. The blows are now aimed, not merely at the minarets of the temple of truth, but at the deepest laid stones of its basis. The very existence of hell itself is now called in question. That which we in our ignorance always thought beyond the shadow of a doubt is now declared not only to be doubtful, but merely a prejudice of man's, and something irreconcilable with the nature of God. Most certainly *if* this be true we have indeed been under a most grand delusion. When the psalmist said 'the wicked shall be turned into hell', we were simple enough to believe that he meant hell, but it appears he must have meant something altogether different from what we suppose by the word. Are we prepared, beloved, at once to give up the faith of our fathers, and adopt the new-fangled notions of would-be divines? I trust not. But in order to have our faith strengthened, let us with deepest humility, reverence and prayerfulness, try and find out the answer of Scripture to the awfully-momentous question of the text, 'What *shall* the end be of them that obey not the gospel of God?'

In order that the subject may have a close personal bearing upon us all, notice the persons concerning whose end the question is asked. It is not 'What shall be the end of the open and licentiously profligate?' Not 'What shall be the end of the profane swearer that belches out his blasphemous oaths?' Nor 'the end of him whose very life is a crying disgrace.' No such thing. Were it so, many might say, 'The matter has nothing to do with me, for I am neither the one nor the other.' No! the question is, What will be the end of those who, whatever other good qualities they may possess, yet die without having obeyed the invitations of the gospel?—what will be the end of those who have never complied with the command 'believe on the Son of God'? To put the question in a form that will give it a more tremendous interest—What will be the end or ultimate doom of that portion of this evening's congregation which dies without having rendered any obedience to the gospel of God?

May the Lord enable us to speak upon this theme in the right spirit and in the right way. It was that noble man of God, M'Cheyne, who, when a brother minister told him that on the previous Sabbath he had been preaching upon hell, asked, 'Were you able to preach it *with tenderness,* brother?' God is our witness that in such a spirit we desire to preach it tonight. If we seem to say hard and severe things, believe they are said in love. Love to your souls, which would rather wound than permit them to go chloroformed to perdition with the pernicious doubt of its existence. With heart full to overflowing then, and eyes directed to the Master for teaching, we will try and answer the question, 'What shall the end be of them that obey not the gospel of God?'

First, NOT ANNIHILATION. Doubtless many of you as well as myself have read with surprise some letters that have lately appeared in a widely circulated religious paper; letters written by men (one in particular) whose names are held in high repute by many. In these letters sentiments are expressed so perfectly contrary to all we have ever been led to believe, that they challenge attention. I will not attempt to quote from memory, but read you a few lines from the letter of one known by name to most. It is as follows—

> The dogma of eternal suffering is utterly unknown to Scripture and perfectly irreconcilable with the character of God: . . . immortality is to be found only in union with the Lord Jesus Christ. I entreat Christian men to lay aside traditional prejudices, and look this great question fairly in the face. The 'hell' of theology is the great weapon of infidelity, and I long to see this weapon wrested from its hands.

Now we may be mistaken, but it seems to us that these words teach as clearly as any words can, the annihilation of the sinner; if they mean not this, we are at a loss to know what they *do* mean. We have read them over and over again in the hope of coming to some other conclusion, but have been obliged time after time to come to the same decision. If there be no immortality apart from union to Christ (and there is no union to Christ apart from obedience to the gospel), then the ultimate end of them that obey not the gospel must be annihilation.

Let me here say before going into the particulars of what that punishment is, that *future punishment of some kind seems essential to the moral government of God.* To quote from President Edwards (to whom I acknowledge my indebtedness for many thoughts this evening), 'Unless there be such a state it will certainly follow, that God in fact maintains no moral government over the world of mankind. For otherwise it is apparent that there's no such thing as rewarding or punishing mankind, according to any visible rule, or, indeed, according to any order or method whatsoever.' Notice specially this sentence. 'There is nothing in God's disposals toward men *in this world,* to make his distributive justice and judicial equity visible, but all things are in the greatest confusion.' Take away future punishment and is it not so? The wicked prosper on every hand. Sin walks along triumphantly, while virtue is often pushed to the wall. The base and the mean succeed, whilst the true and the right often languish. The unscrupulous tradesman who sticks at no dirty trick in his trade, makes his fortune and retires; and the godly tradesman next door, after a manly struggle against his difficulties is obliged to succumb, a ruined man. The scales of God are not, and never were meant to be even on earth, though they are adjusted to a hair in eternity.

It was this very thing that was Asaph's difficulty, and this very explanation that removed it. Will all of you who have Bibles turn to the 73rd Psalm, and commencing from the 3rd verse, read for yourselves:

> I was envious at the foolish, when I saw the prosperity of the wicked, for there are no bands in their death; but their strength is firm. They are not in trouble as other men; neither are they plagued like other men. When I thought to know this, it was too painful for me.

There you have, beloved, Asaph's source of trouble, and many others have had it besides him; but see in the next verse what caused his murmurings to cease and convinced him of the equity of God:

> Until I went into the sanctuary of God, then I understood their end.

And that end thrown into the balances righted them. Yet again. There was once a godless wretch clothed in purple, who fared sumptuously every day, and lying at his gate was a godly beggar whose sores were licked by the rich man's dogs. Here is a mystery. Yes, but one soon solved. Affairs were righted after death. The rich man died and went to hell. The poor man died, and was carried by an angelic escort to Abraham's bosom, whilst God's perfect equity was taught the rich man, in those memorable words—'Son, remember that thou in *thy life time* receivedst thy good things, and likewise Lazarus evil things; but now he is comforted, and thou art tormented.'

In order that God's infinitely judicial equity may be manifested, a state of future punishment is indispensable. But the question is, *what is that punishment?* Is it merely a cessation of being, a want of immortality, or in other words annihilation? I venture to answer 'No'; for if it be so it lacks that which is certainly a necessity, in order to make it a punishment at all, viz.,—a knowledge of its infliction. That can be no punishment which I never feel and of which I am never conscious. It seems to me to stand to reason that the punishment of the sinner must be such as to make him see the connexion with his guilt, and make him learn that the threatenings of God cannot be despised with impunity. These lessons can never be learnt by annihilation. Moreover, the Scriptures declare if that the sinner 'shall drink of the wrath of the Almighty', which if it implies anything, implies that the wrath shall be actually tasted, which it never could be in an utter want of existence. Nay, in that same verse I think it states, 'he shall see his destruction', or in other words, the sinner shall behold his misery and doom, which would be a sheer impossibility if that doom were annihilation.

Another argument is that *the fact of there being various degrees in punishment makes it impossible for that punishment to be annihilation.*

Nothing is more clearly taught in the word than that all men receive not the same amount of punishment. Let me quote a few passages.

Looking upon the cities of Chorazin and Bethsaida, our Saviour said, 'It shall be more tolerable for Tyre and Sidon at the day of judgment than for you.' To Capernaum, the scene of his mightiest works, he declared 'it shall be more tolerable for the land of Sodom in the day of judgment than for thee'. He it was who pronounced the doom of him who knew his Lord's will, but did it not, to be greater than that of him who never knew it. It was he who turning upon those whited sepulchres—the Pharisees—who could pray all day in the streets, and prey all night on widows' houses, declared that they should receive the *greater* damnation, and the greater implies the less. But if annihilation be the sinner's doom, what room is there for any degrees whatsoever? I can no more be *less* than annihilated than I can be *more*. This theory at once puts all punishment upon a perfect equality.

All that is said about the sinner's doom shuts out the idea of annihilation. Concerning Judas, that wretched, double-dyed traitor, our Lord said, it would have been better for him 'if he had never been born'. Why so? Surely because he foresaw that the traitor's punishment was something so dreadful, that never to have seen the light would have been a boon. Had cessation of being been his punishment, there would have been no need for such a statement, for never having been born, and being annihilated, come to one and the same thing. Kindly turn with me to a few passages, and see if they do not bear upon their very face future torment rather than future nothingness. The first you will find in Luke 12, the 4th and 5th verses. Let us read them, they are our Master's words, 'And I say unto you, my friends, be not afraid of them that kill the body, and after that have no more that they can do. But I will forewarn you whom ye shall fear. Fear him, which, after he hath killed hath power to cast into hell. Yea, I say unto you, fear him.' Here there is certainly something more than death threatened; there is death *and hell*. Turn to Matthew 13, which we read at the commencement of this service. Read the 41st and 42nd verses. 'The Son of Man shall send forth his angels, and they shall gather out of his kingdom all things that offend, and them which do iniquity; and shall cast them into a furnace of fire; there shall be wailing and gnashing of teeth.' Can annihilation be compared to a furnace of fire, and can annihilated men be said to wail and gnash their teeth? Impossible. Yet once again refer to Mark 9 from the 43rd verse. 'And if thy hand offend thee, cut it off; it is better for thee to enter into life maimed, than having two hands to go into hell, into the fire that never shall be quenched; where their worm dieth not, and the fire is not quenched.' It is plain that here Christ meant something more than the grave by the word 'hell'. For the grave-worm *does* die, but *this one* never. In the grave is no fire, but in this hell there *is*.

The resurrection says, 'No annihilation.' That all will have to rise, whether saint or sinner, is certainly taught. For there to be any mistake about that seems impossible. Now if the sinner is to be annihilated, when is it to take place? Before the resurrection? Impossible. For how then is he to rise? After the resurrection? Then where has his soul been from the moment of death until the resurrection morn? Besides which, what is the sinner's doom after the resurrection? Turn to John 5, the 28th and 29th verses: 'The hour is coming in the which all that are in the graves shall hear his voice, and shall come forth; they that have done good unto the resurrection of life; and they that have done evil unto the resurrection of damnation.'

The doom of the sinner and the doom of the devil are identical. The verdict passed is 'Depart from me, ye cursed, into everlasting fire, prepared for the devil and his angels.' The master and the servants share one common woe. Is the devil's punishment annihilation? Most assuredly we find out to our cost it is not yet and that it never will be, Scripture sets beyond a shadow of a doubt, for it declares that he 'shall be tormented day and night, *for ever and ever*'.

Satan would leap for joy, and clash his chains in mad glee if he could look forward to such a termination of his torments. But his doom is for ever and ever, and the wicked are to share it.

Lastly, *the atonement is an argument for the existence of hell*. From what does my Saviour save me? Simply from cessation of being, or from a short residence in hell, to be followed by total forgetfulness of all its pains? The very idea is incompatible with the ransom price he paid. Gethsemane's bloody sweat—the bloodier scourging in Pilate's hall—and the awful death of Calvary—all seem to point to a punishment beyond description. If I believe (as I do) that Christ suffered in his own person the pangs and anguish I must otherwise have endured, tell me, what must they have been that forced from the quivering lips of incarnate love that terrific death-shriek, 'Eloi, Eloi, lama sabacthani?' 'My God, my God, why hast thou forsaken me?' O, take your stand, believer, at the foot of that cross, stained crimson with your Saviour's heart's-blood, look up into that face of anguish; listen to those deep-drawn sighs of misery; and then ask yourself, 'From what kind of a doom *must such* a sacrifice have rescued me?' What then shall be our answer to the question, 'What shall the end be of them that obey not the gospel of God?' We have only one to give, and that we utter with melting heart; it is 'hell', and that hell one of torment.

Having tried to prove that the punishment of the wicked will be no mere cessation of being, but actual torment, I now turn to my second answer to the text, namely:—

II. THAT IT WILL NOT BE MERELY A TEMPORARY PUNISHMENT. The generality of those who hold the view of immortality being only in union with Christ still believe that the sinner when he dies does enter an actual hell as described in Scripture, but that he only remains there a limited time, and is at last doomed to non-existence. Others there are who, though believing in the immortality of the soul apart from union with Christ, yet hold that after the sinner has endured for some period, either short or long, the terrors of hell, he will come from thence forgiven and purified, and join the ransomed throng in heaven. Without attempting to compare the merits or demerits of the two theories, I shall try and prove what both equally deny—the eternity of suffering. The most general argument brought against eternal punishment is that *it is opposed to the perfect justice of God*. 'The punishment', they say, 'being eternal must at last exceed the sin.' That, we reply, has yet to be proved, and if we can but show that the punishment is only proportionate to the sin, then the charge of injustice falls to the ground. In order to understand aright the nature of the sin, you must bear in mind the being against whom the sin is committed. It is against Jehovah, the infinite one; against one who is infinitely worthy of honour and worship, and against one to whom we are under infinite obligations. If then God and his gospel be infinitely worthy of obedience, they 'who obey not the gospel of God' are guilty of an infinite sin, and not a word can be said against the justice that visits an infinite sin with an infinite punishment. Do you find in *our* courts of justice that the length of the punishment is regulated by the length of time the offence took in being committed? The act of forgery or theft took but, perhaps, five minutes, and yet the punishment for that act may be transportation 'for the term of natural life' and who impugns the justice of the sentence?

'But', say others, *'God is infinitely merciful, and the very idea of eternal suffering is opposed to that attribute.'* It may be according to your idea of that mercy, and yet not against that mercy itself. Remember God is as just as he is merciful. His mercy provided the gospel; his mercy invited the sinner to obey it. His mercy stood waiting to save: but the sinner spurned his mercy offered, and declined 'to obey the gospel'. Then as he would not have the mercy he must have the justice. Justice never interfered with the sweet work of mercy and mercy can never interfere with the righteous acts of justice. God's mercy is not a mere passion over which he has no control, and which steps in to overturn the execution of his own righteous judgments. That misery and sorrow *are* compatible with God's being merciful can be seen in a hundred instances around us. Shall we say 'he has ceased to be merciful' because sometimes we hear of an awful colliery explosion in which hundreds are suffocated in a moment, and a whole neighbourhood plunged into grief? Does not infinite mercy look on, and yet stretch out no hand to save, when a whole ship's crew and crowds of passengers (as in the case of the *London*) sink in the wild waves?

That mercy *can* permit eternal suffering is proved by the fact that it does in the case of Satan and the rebel angels. Why should it permit it to be their doom and not ours? Is their sin greater than ours? Certainly not, there is only this difference, that they never rejected an offered Saviour, which the sinner has. Dispel the thought at once, believer, from your mind, that eternal punishment is opposed to the mercy of God.

There will be nothing in hell to refine or alter the sinner. Hell fire is no 'refiner's fire', to purge the dross away. Hell's torments are no 'fuller's soap', to cleanse the guilty soul. The sinner will be as great a sinner in hell as ever he was on earth. His hatred to God in hell will be as fierce as its fire. The very idea of improvement seems to me preposterous. Shall they without the means of grace become what they never did when they had them? They had Moses and the prophets, and they believed them not, and Scripture says that if that if that testimony be refused none other would ever be accepted. But in hell they will not even have these. The restraints also of earth will all be wanting, and sin will consequently be rampant. There will be no mother's tears, no godly father's entreaties, no ministry of love. All the barriers will be removed, and sin and hatred will roll through the infernal regions with unrestrained licence. He who was bad on earth will be worse in hell. In such a school as this think ye the sinner will learn to love his God and obey his gospel?

There is nothing in the word about hell torments having a termination.—Think not although we preach it, we delight in the thought. Could we hold out a hope that those who are now lost should ever escape from their torments, believe us we would do so with joy. But we search in vain for any ground for such a hope. Scripture holds out none, and therefore we dare not. Listen to the solemn words of inspiration and see if thou canst extract the shadow of a hope from them that hell is not eternal torment. 'Who among us shall dwell with the devouring fire? who among us shall dwell with *everlasting* burnings?' 'He will burn up the chaff with *unquenchable* fire.' 'The smoke of their torment ascendeth up for *ever and ever.*' 'These shall go away into *everlasting* punishment.' The same word is used to describe the duration of misery as is employed to describe the duration of bliss. Let one mean anything else than 'for ever', and the other does also. If it be possible for sinners to leave hell, it is equally possible for the saints to lose heaven. The verdict of Scripture is that the torment of the lost shall last for ever and ever, for ever and ever.

I would now occupy the few minutes that remain, in trying to apply these solemn truths to your heart. Be not deceived, sinner, about your future doom by the sophistry of the present day. I entreat you by the value of your own soul, tread under foot these wretched theories, which like opium, will lull you into a deadly sleep, only to awake in hell. It will be no consolation when there to remember that when on earth you doubted its existence—and when by awful experience you have learnt that hell is eternal, you will gain no comfort from the thought that you had always doubted it. Awake! Awake!! Awake!!! sinner, to thy danger. Hell is no ugly dream to be laughed at in the morning. It is a dread reality. It is no mere wretched scare-crow placed in Scripture to frighten children—no mere stock theme for the minister when all else fails him. It is the *certain* end of every sinner that dies in his sins. If indeed this be the case, then how momentous is the question, 'Am I saved?' Poor, careless, thoughtless one, come in here this evening you scarce know why—'Flee from the wrath to come.' Worldly pleasure seeker—cold professor, 'Flee from the wrath to come.' O sinners all, I implore you by the reality and eternity of hell to 'Flee from the wrath to come.' Do you say, 'Where?' I answer, To Christ.

Hide in the cleft of that 'Rock of ages', and thou art safe. As a lost sinner, as one who deserves eternal wrath, cast thy whole soul upon Christ and thou art secure. Trust him only, trust him wholly, trust him now, and thou shalt be eternally saved.

The Lord have mercy upon all this great company, and grant that none may ever find out by experience that there is a hell and that an eternal one. God grant it may be so, for Jesus' sake. Amen.

A ROUGH NIGHT AT SANDOWN[1]

Hitherto shalt thou come but no further,
and here shall thy proud waves be stayed.
Job 38:11.

THE night was a wild one on the southern shore of the Isle of Wight. Throughout the day the wind had been blowing with increasing strength, and, as evening came on, the sea rose mightily, so that when the darkness settled down there was a fair storm blowing. The moon struggled through the tattered clouds, for the scud was flying fast, and looked, with all its ragged edges, as if it had been suddenly torn from the black canopy of heaven by the giant hand of the storm. The fitful moonbeams fell upon a wild, tumbling, roaring, waste of waters. It was nigh high tide. We came out in front of our house and stood in the balcony watching the seething mass of water. It was a fine sight. The waves curled and broke upon the sea wall. Hurled back, they only returned to meet the next advancing wave, and then in a wild embrace the two together thundered on, and so over and over again. Far away were to be seen, in the moonlight, line after line of advancing billows. They looked like chargers rushing on against that wall, and each one seemed to hiss to its fellow, 'I will back you up.' Endless reinforcements seemed to be coming towards the shore. There was but a roadway with a narrow parade between us and the deep, and it sounded almost like presumption to say, 'Well, it is time to go to

---

[1] November 6, 1892, East London Tabernacle.

bed now.' What? Go to rest with destruction so near? Talk about calmly sleeping when, within a few yards, there is power enough to sweep everything away? Yet we said, 'Better go to rest now', for, taking out our watch and looking at the hour, we saw that it was high tide. 'It will not come any further', we remarked. No sooner had we uttered these words than they started this train of thought: What perfect faith in the law of nature does this sentence set forth. I dare to stand within a few yards of a roaring sea like this, and calmly suggest that it is time to go to rest, because it has reached its highest point and there will be nothing more to see. What faith in the law of the tide! Yes, behind those crested waves there was a power mightier than the storm, unseen, but wondrously real. Driven by those winds, the waves, like mad chargers, may leap and rush, but there is an unseen hand holding them, and saying, 'Thus far. No further. It is high tide. It is time to go back.' The sea cannot go beyond the line of decree. The Lord has said, 'Here shall thy proud waves be stayed.' No sooner had we said, 'It cannot come any further; it is time for the tide to turn', than it flashed through our mind, 'But suppose that it should *forget* to turn. It is all very well to talk like this and be so calm, but suppose that it should not turn, and that for the next six hours, instead of receding, it should still advance. Where wouldst thou be, and where thy abode, and where all thy loved ones?' But then we remembered, 'But this law is as certain in its action as the rising and setting of the sun.'

The others went to rest, but I remained for some time gazing out upon that wild surging sea. I know not how long I stood, but, as I gazed upon it, it preached to me; and, as I looked at it, it seemed to assume different forms. I want it now to preach to you, as I tell you as far as I can what I saw in that raging sea trying to get beyond the barrier that God had set, and yet finding that the eternal word is true, 'Thus far, no further.' God has a 'Here' at which the wildest waves must stop. As I looked I saw, first, *hell's forces restrained.* Then the scene changed, and I beheld *temptations limited*. And then a cough upstairs reminded our heart of *sorrows measured*. And then, lastly, as I looked out, I saw *apostasy arrested*.

Let me try to give you these different lessons of a stormy night.

I.—First, we have HELL'S FORCES RESTRAINED. Now, I know that Satan in his personality, Satan in his craft, Satan in his power, Satan in his wrath, is very far from being a reality even to a great many professing Christians. I know that the spirit-world is all too little thought of, and the world that we can see is to us ten thousand times more real than the world which we cannot see, though, in my heart of hearts, I believe that there is a spirit-world, not thousands of miles away, but all round about us, and as real as the world of men and women which we see. We pass in and out among spirits good and bad. They are round about us on every hand.

But that foaming sea spoke to me, not of the gentle ministry of the unfallen angels, but of the awful, damning ministry of Satan and his followers. I said just now that Satan is all too little of a reality with most of us, and yet, mark you, if the Bible be true, Satan is the most dreadful reality conceivable. I ask you to listen for a moment to words in which this truth is better put than I can express it on the spur of the moment: 'The question of Satan's personality is one relating to the credibility of the Scriptures. The existence of the devil is so clearly taught in the Bible, so necessary a part of the revealed word, so legible on its very face, and so thoroughly interwoven with all its utterances, that to doubt it is to doubt the authenticity of the Bible itself. The entire system of revelation stands or falls with the personality of Satan, not that he is essential to truth, but that the very verity of the record concerning him is essential to God's honour and our hope. This fact has worked itself out in history.' Let me say for a moment, in parenthesis, mark and see whether this next sentence is not true of today: 'In all ages of the church, unbelief in this doctrine has been marked by a corresponding unbelief in the Scriptures. The man who can reject a doctrine so fully revealed as this, will find no difficulty in rejecting all if it ever suits him to do so.' So long as we accept this Bible as a revelation from God, we are bound to accept this awful, mysterious truth—(and here I quote from memory)— 'that there is a being of fearful might and power who is wicked, always wicked, totally wicked, incurably wicked; a being who is a stranger absolutely to all love, all pity, all goodness; a being who is the embodiment of all malignity, the concentration of all wrong, the essence of all vice; a being who has no one bright spot in his black character; a being who, if he could, would quench every sun that shines, extinguish every star that twinkles, blight every flower that blooms, and turn every song that rises from consecrated lips into a lewd lascivious song; a being who, if he could, would turn heaven itself into hell. He is one whose heart is hate, whose mind is revenge, and whose life is an eternal damnation.' And this weird, inscrutable awful being, we are told, is the master of uncounted legions who serve their captain with an unswerving fidelity such as an earthly monarch never knows. At his beck and call are spirits that are lying, seducing, unclean, and murderous; and these forces of hell never cease to surge and roll on God's fair earth. Without pause or let, hell seeks to swamp, damage, and damn the works of God. I say not that the storm is always equally high. It is not so. I believe that there are times when hell's power is greater than at others. Beyond all question it was so when the Son of Man walked this earth. Oh, how the ocean boiled then! It seemed as if the word had gone forth through all the hosts of perdition, 'Fight neither with small nor great but with the King only.' None of us can ever tell what Christ passed through in personal combat with Satan.

Now, mark, if you are going to make a semi-joke of the devil, if you are going to speak of Satan as simply a name for something that is impersonal, you are doing an awful wrong to your Lord. If you can only prove your point, you prove too much, for you prove that Christ himself was a dupe. I find the Saviour, when he stood foot to foot in the wilderness, saying distinctly, 'Get thee hence, Satan.' I never find our Lord explaining away demoniacal possession as it is fashionable to do now. Jesus came to reveal truth. Jesus came to clear the world of superstition. If the poor creatures whom he healed simply had epilepsy or fits, our Lord knew it; and yet he never uttered a word to clear away the common superstition. Indeed, he endorsed the superstition of the day, for he said, 'Come out of him, *thou* unclean spirit.' We say with all reverence that in such a case our Lord added the weight of his personal testimony to a popular fallacy. But he knew, and he saw *demon power* working on every hand. When he is arrested in the garden, what does he say? Not only, 'The hour is come', but he adds, 'and the power of darkness.' The tide of hell reached its highest point at Calvary; and, as I gazed from the balcony upon the boiling waters beneath, I seemed to see the scene.

Behold Jesus there upon that tree. How do the billows beat upon that breast! How do they roar upon him! He is enveloped. He is drenched with the spray. We hear in the darkness, 'My God, My God, why hast thou forsaken me?' and my heart asks, 'Will the tide never turn?' and I think I hear a voice saying, 'The tide has reached its highest point. It can go no further now.' He lies there dead in the tomb. But look ye. On the third morning he comes forth in resurrection beauty. Ah, Satan, how art thou defeated! God said by that tomb, '*Thus far*, no further.' He said at that tomb, '*Here* shall thy proud waves be stayed.' Having no personal Christ on earth to contend with, Satan now devotes all his power to Christ's people, and he is seeking ever to swamp the church. Christ said, 'Upon *this* rock will I build my church, and the gates of hell shall not prevail against it.' Jesus knew very well that the gates of hell would ever be belching forth their animosity and power against the church. At your leisure read the 6th chapter of the Ephesians. The Holy Ghost there says that we wrestle not against flesh and blood, but against the principalities, against the powers, against the world of rulers of this darkness, and against wicked spirits in high places. O brethren and sisters, round about each one of us there is a roaring tide of hellish hatred. There is enough to make each one ask, 'Can I ever be kept? Must I not be swept away by this irresistible flood?' Thank God that there is a 'Thus far', for, listen: Christ said to Peter, 'Satan hath desired to have thee that he may sift thee as wheat, but I have prayed for thee.' O thou blessed living Christ, we look to thee. Fling back the advancing tide, and, by thy power, the very weakest saint shall be more than a match for hell. Come, dear soul, though you may be belted with hell's power, there is a 'Thus far and no further.' A mightier power than the mighty one holds back the tide of hell. 'Here shall thy proud waves be stayed.'

II.— The scene changed, and, as I looked out on the sea, I beheld TEMPTATIONS LIMITED. This is a branch of our previous head, and yet it is quite distinct from it. The one is the objective fact: this is the subjective experience. Satan may set the waves rolling, but there would be very little weight in them apart from the aid of my own sinful nature. If there were only an outside hell there would be but little danger. There is, alas! an inside nature that is corrupt. I daresay that I shall be speaking to some who will not understand much of what I am saying. For years there may be little more than the ordinary swellings of temptation. I think that, generally speaking, the young convert knows but little of the wild scene which I want to portray. He knows something of being tried by the ordinary temptations of daily life, but nothing else. But there will come the day when *the wind blows from the right quarter to make a heavy sea.* Everything depends upon the quarter from which the gale comes. The wind may be blowing never so strongly from the west, but you will have it calm in the bay of Sandown. That which sends the thundering billows on the shore at Black Gang will raise no sea at Sandown. So every one of us has his right—or rather wrong—quarter; and here may be the reason why some have never yet known any awful temptation, that which fills a brother's soul with a boiling ocean of spiritual agony does not affect you. But wait. There will be a time when the wind will be dead on shore for you. Some particular temptation will awake you to the fact that you have within you a capacity for sinning of which you never dreamed. I think that it was Martin Luther who said that no man could be a good preacher without having had much temptation. Oh, what degrees of temptation there are! I can say before God that I think I have known more temptation this one year than I have known in any five that have gone by. Did you ever know, man, what it is not only for the wind to be in the right quarter, but to have a high spring tide at the same time? What a sea runs then! You can look out and see not only one billow, but another billow behind it, and another behind that, and another behind that; temptations physical, temptations mental, temptations social, one rolling after another. And then, when, in the power of God, you have hurled away the first one, it only goes back to meet the next, and the two together leap upon you. You know then what it is to be in the condition which John Bunyan described when he said that he knew not which was his own voice and which was the voice of the tempter. You are only conscious of a roar of temptation in your ears; and you sometimes ask the question (I am sure that I have asked it often), 'Can I stand? Must not the sea wall give way? Can it for ever fling back these surges?' And then faith pulls out her watch and says, 'It is high tide now. It cannot come any further.'

Turn with me to a passage or two, ye tempted ones. You will find them sweet to your soul. Read the 13th verse of the 10th chapter of the First Epistle to the Corinthians. It is God's 'Thus far.' 'There hath no temptation taken you but such as is common to man; but God is faithful, who will not suffer you to be tempted above that ye are able, but will with the temptation also make a way to escape, that ye may be able to bear it.' It is 'Thus far and no further.' The God of decrees has his high-water mark for temptation. He says, *Here* shall thy proud waves be stayed.' I think that I see one of you (ah, there you are) just marking that verse down, and you say, 'I will have a look at that again when I get home. What, is that true—that God is faithful, and will not suffer me to be tempted above what I am able? Come on, then, ye black billows, and in the name of God I defy you all.' But do you want something else to help you? Then turn to the 2nd chapter of Hebrews and the eighteenth verse. There is a sea wall. 'For in that he himself hath suffered being tempted, he is able to succour them that are tempted.' Then the 15th verse of the 4th chapter: 'We have not a high priest which cannot be touched with the feeling of our infirmities, but was in all points tempted like as we are, yet without sin. Let us, therefore, come boldly to the throne of grace that we may obtain mercy and find grace to help in time of need.' Does unbelief say, 'But oh! if the tide should forget to turn?' God is faithful. The tide has never forgotten to turn yet in the channel; and never yet was God less faithful in the working out of spiritual law than of natural. You may look therefore upon hell's waters surging within your own soul, and, whilst you deplore them, yet say, 'The God of the storm has said, "Thus far and no further."'

III.—Perhaps I may come nearer to some of you in the next point. As I looked, the scene changed again, and those wild waters were neither hell nor temptation, but they were sorrows; and I saw in them SORROWS MEASURED. Have you had trouble long continued? It is not a mere day of trouble that tries you so much; it is not even a week. But I am speaking to some of you who are able to look back long, long months, and there has been nothing but trouble, trouble, trouble. The constant washing of water will wear away even a stone, and perhaps some of you are beginning to think, 'I cannot stand it, and, as far as I can see, I perceive that there are other troubles coming.' At Sandown I not only saw the waves that curled over in the moonlight on the shore, but I could see out in the Channel those big hills of water that were coming in. And you, looking out into the future, can say, 'Why, I can see other troubles advancing. There are troubles in the family, troubles financial, troubles physical, each one following to join its fellow! No sooner does one trouble roll back from me than it joins another rolling towards me.' You have come into this Tabernacle this morning about as down and depressed as mortal man can be. The spray of life's troubles has been washing over life's parade. You are drenched right through with it; and unbelief says, 'Everything will go at last.' Stay a moment. Do you know that you are not the first man who has said so? Read that story of Job again. See how the billows came upon him one after another. I am not surprised that Job was ready to curse the very day that he was born, and yet, when I come to the last chapter, I find that he was made a better man than ever he was before. 'And the Lord turned the captivity of Job.' It was, 'Thus far and no further.' Remember David, again, when he said, in the 42nd Psalm, 'All thy waves and thy billows are gone over me.' But what does David say afterwards? 'For the Lord will command his loving-kindness in the day-time, and in the night his song shall be with me.' But I think that the most exquisitely beautiful illustration is in the 22nd Psalm. You know it well, do you not? Read right away from the 1st verse till you get down to the 21st. 'My God, my God, why hast thou forsaken me?' That is the key-note. It is the outcry of an agonized heart; but when you come to the 25th verse, what a change. The one who said, 'Why hast thou forsaken me?' says, 'My praise shall be of thee in the great congregation.' Jesus Christ found that there is a high-water mark in sorrow. It is, 'Thus far, but no further.' Behind the billows there is God. Behind the storm that I saw there was a tide; and, thank God, behind our troubles there is an eternal decree, and at the back of our sorrows there is eternal love. Only trust him. God says, *Here* shall thy proud waves be stayed.' I want to emphasize that word 'here'. Where? In the matter of trouble I think it is *just where faith has been perfectly tried.* There will the waves be stayed. God is glorified in the trial of our faith. You have talked a good deal about believing. Now God is going to make you show to other people what a reality there is in it.

'Here shall thy proud waves be stayed.' That is, *just where you have learnt the lesson which you need to learn.* You have naturally a proud spirit and a nasty temper. God means to keep you in the college of sorrow until you have learned there to be humble and gentle and forbearing and tender. Then when you have learnt those lessons God will say, 'Here shall the proud waves of thy sorrow be stayed.' 'Here', where we have *learned to trust God solely; 'here', where we learn to bow with delight before the uncontrolled and uncontrollable will of God.* Look up, brother. It may be that the lesson is nearly learnt. It may be that already the angel-watch is saying, 'It is just high tide with that man. The water will rise no further.'

IV.—Lastly, I looked out, and in that scene I saw APOSTASY ARRESTED. The sight that presents itself to the eyes of spiritually taught men today is something appalling. Look abroad which way you will, there is a surging sea of infidelity; the wind has been blowing very strongly from Germany for some years. Oh, what mighty blasts of scepticism have come across, and what a sea is now rolling! How the waters thunder! As I looked I seemed to see billow after billow of 'higher criticism' sweeping in. Oh, how they broke upon this sea wall, the Bible! And I noted how the men who ought to have been preachers of the truth were themselves its critics, and the men who ought to be leading their congregations into faith in God were busy making infidels. And I heard the shout, 'Genesis is rocking. It will soon be down. Exodus is reeling. Leviticus is giving way. Deuteronomy is all but swept away. David and Goliath are but a parable. The story of Jonah is ridiculous, and condemned by reason.' I listened, and I heard the scoffers say, 'We will clear all the Old Testament off before long.' I noticed that the billows, though they were flung back, returned in strength; and I thought, 'O God, if that Old Testament goes, I am done for. If thy Book is swept away I have not a foothold of hope for time or eternity.' But a voice said, 'Thou canst go to rest. There is no real danger whatever. It is just about high tide now. The waters cannot come any further, for the Son of God is going to be revealed soon in flaming fire, taking vengeance upon them that believe not the gospel of God.' Oh, when he shall come then will the Lord rebuke the apostasy of the day. Then shall men see in the returning Christ that every jot and every tittle of this Book is God's. It has stood the storm, and it will, for God's decree is sure. Faith hears the voice of God saying to all the infidel criticism of the day. 'Thus far. Your higher criticism has gone as far as I can allow it to go. Here shall its waves be stayed.'

I know not which part of the subject will suit you best, but whether you have regard to hell's forces, or inbred temptations, or earth's sorrows, or Christendom's apostasy, you may say, 'It is about high tide. It cannot go further.' These are the thoughts that flitted through my mind as, in the moonlight, I looked out upon a raging sea that could not pass God's decree. May God bless them to us all for his name's sake. Amen.

A VOICE FROM POMPEII[1]

And turning the cities of Sodom and Gomorrha into ashes,
condemned them with an overthrow, making them an
ensample unto those that after should live ungodly.
2 Peter 2:6.

I KNOW that in selecting my theme for this evening I am venturing to swim against the tide of public taste. I doubt not that, in many quarters, the sermon of tonight will be severely criticized, and by not a few regarded as a proof that I am irreclaimable and incapable of advancing with modern thought, Every age has had its popular heresy. For a while it has run like wildfire, and then gradually died out to give place to another. Any casual reader of so-called Christian literature must know the distinctive feature of this nineteenth century. There has arisen in the midst of the church an anti-Christ which is known by the name of 'modern thought', at whose altars tens of thousands are bowing the knee, and offering their devotion. There is a horrid malaria abroad—a malaria breeding doubt and scepticism, and giving birth to wholesale practical infidelity. Surely the gospel of the present day might be rendered—'He that doubteth shall be saved, and he that believeth shall be counted a fool.' All things are now being called into question, and the work of the modern critic is either to destroy or tone down, or annotate the word God, until, were our fathers to rise from the grave, they would find it difficult to recognize it as

---

[1] February 24, 1878, East London Tabernacle.

the same old book on which they lived, and on whose truths they dared to die. The eternal covenant of God is torn up with a glib remark and a smile of contempt by some boy-censor. The threatenings of God are having all the thunder taken out of them; and now let any one venture to say that he believes in such doctrines as the sovereign grace of God, an atoning sacrifice, and a doom of unspeakable horror awaiting the man who dies unconverted, and if he is not derided he will at least be looked upon with contemptuous pity.

Now, the fiercest onslaught has been made upon the doctrine of God's severity against sin, and the reason why I have selected this topic this evening is that, somehow or another the evil is finding its way into all the homes of our church members. Papers—and specially one—which profess to be Christian, prostitute their influence, week by week, in bringing before their readers all sorts of new-fangled notions, and thinly veiled blasphemy. I do not marvel that the doctrine of eternal punishment has been the subject of fiercest attack. It is only natural that man should desire to believe that he can live in sin with comparative impunity. I wonder not that the natural man says, 'Only prove to us that there is no perdition, and you shall be the preacher of our choice.' Such teaching is sure to be popular.

There is also an immense amount of cant about the 'universal fatherhood' of God. We are told that God is so good, so kind, so indulgent, that he cannot possibly visit a sinner's sin with the dire doom that Scripture language declares.

Now, I want, this evening to take you right away from the enervating air of the valley of modern thought, up into the bracing atmosphere of Peter's words. I want them to blow upon you, clear and strong and crisp as the air we have felt coming off the glacier. And, young men, as I am preaching specially to you, I say that, if you are worthy of the name, you will never mind being asked to look a fact straight in the face. If we be wrong, then at some future time show us so; but I think you will see that there is a need-be for us to dwell upon the theme. Suppose there be no such hell as we have been led to believe, then I am as well off when I die as any. But if, on the other hand, there be, where then is the derider of it? If it be a mistake, yet it has been a blessed one, for it has often times inflamed our zeal to try and bring men to Christ. But O sirs, if it be no mistake and hell have all the horrors our fathers believed, I beseech you fall not into such incredible folly as to be damned in order to find out its truth.

Now, observe that Peter in this chapter is just dealing with this very thing. There were many false teachers abroad and he says in the 3rd verse, 'They shall with feigned words make merchandize of you, whose judgment now of a long time lingereth not.' And to show that God has a judgment for sinners, he adduces three examples. Let me read the verses to you. You will find the first illustration of the fact in the 4th verse, 'For if God spared not the angels that sinned, but cast them down to hell, and delivered them into chains of darkness, to be reserved unto judgment.' Now comes the second. 'And spared not the old world, but, saved Noah, the eighth person, a preacher of righteousness, bringing in the flood upon the world of the ungodly, and—(for a third example)—'turning the cities of Sodom and Gomorrha into ashes, condemned them with an overthrow, making them an ensample unto those that after should live ungodly.' Then learn this—and you get it in the 9th verse—'The Lord knoweth how to deliver the godly out of temptations, and to reserve the unjust unto the day of judgment to be punished.'

Putting all we desire to say into one sentence, it is this: it is not our work to say what God ought to be or what he should do, but to find out what he has done, assured that his performing an action is proof of its justice. Down, puny reason! Wilt thou dare to say that, if God acts in this way or that, he is unjust? *Has* God so acted? If so, it must be right. God's action is its own guarantee of holiness.

Now, you will see that in our text we have shown us, first, that God's severity on sin is an awful fact; and then secondly, that this particular act of severity, namely, the destruction of the cities of the plain, is to be an ensample for all ages unto those who live ungodly.

I. Now let us to our first point, namely, that our text shows that GOD'S SEVERITY ON SIN IS AN AWFUL FACT.

I would seek to force this thought home because I am persuaded that, unless I can make you realize it, all the invitations of the gospel will be of little worth to you. Unless a man believes that there is something to flee from, it is a waste of time to tell him to flee. Unless a man believes there is a doom to escape, it is folly, if not impertinence, to keep saying to him, 'Escape for thy life.'

Now let us see whether the God of Abraham, Isaac, Jacob and Elijah, is the sort of God that modern thought gives us—a God who has been well described as a sort of effeminate incarnation of shallow benevolence. I venture to say that the God I read about in the Old Testament is no more like the God of modem thought than he is like the heathen deities of mythology. Let us, then, dwell on these three facts which Peter brings forward in order to show that God has severity on sin and sinners.

The first is the *vengeance which he executed on the sinning angels.* You have this in the 4th verse,—'For if God spared not the angels that sinned, but cast them down to hell.' I have often marvelled that those who are so ready to accuse God of want of love when the perdition of men is mentioned, have not seen that they have greater cause to arraign him at their bar for having cast the angels headlong into hell. If it be unjust and unkind to deal out eternal punishment to fallen men, how is it that they are silent about the doom of the fallen angels? God made bright spirits, capable of standing, yet free to fall; and some did fall, and there was war in heaven, and a third part of the stars of heaven were swept into eternal darkness, and, as we read here, hurled down to hell and 'delivered into chains of darkness, to be reserved unto judgment'. Young men, can you not see that every argument which can be employed against the ultimate punishment of men applies with equal force against the punishment of the sinful angels? Am I told, as we are repeatedly, that there is such a nobility about man, such a natural grandeur, that it is almost impossible to imagine that God can ever consign so glorious and intellectual a being to perdition! I reply, What is man, after all, compared with the angels and the archangels who have received their doom? Nobler in being, far, were those sons of the morning, pure spirits who stood before the eternal throne of God and sang his praises, and mightier still in intellect. Yet when they sinned did the nobility of their nature save them from the hell that awaited them? Am I told, 'Oh, but, surely, there can not be eternal punishment because it would disarrange God's beautiful universe? It would be a discordant note in the great realm.' I reply, The angels lived nearer God than man; and yet when they sinned, heaven itself shall be put into confusion, but they shall be turned out. When I see the sinning angels falling over heaven's brink into hell, I see something before which my spirit stands appalled, but something which makes me say, 'The God of the angels, and the God I worship, is an awful God when his anger is aroused.'

Peter then passes on, you will see, to the second illustration which is in the 5th verse,—'and spared not the whole world but saved Noah'. Now here the destruction was more complete. In the former case a glorious company of untold legions remained to sing their sovereign's praises, but now God speaks the word, and the foundations of the great deep are broken up. How many are saved? 'A few, that is, eight souls.' Come, Mr Modern Thinker—you who are so shocked at the idea of God ever pouring out his wrath on any—how do you account for this? Does this look like 'universal fatherhood'? Does this look like an indulgent father who knows nothing of righteous indignation against sin? It has been computed that the population of the world at that time was as great as now, owing to the longevity of the race, and yet the waters rose until the few—the eight—who rode in that ark were the sole remnant of a world that God had made. Come, open your ears and hear the shrieks of the drowning; hear the cries of the strong swimmer in his last agony, and account for it, if you can, on any other ground than that God is a hater of sin,—that when the accursed thing reaches a climax, he pours his wrath upon it—ay, though doing so destroys a world he fashioned.

Then we come to the third illustration, and I think you will see that they become stronger and yet more fearful. There were eight saved from the flood, but in the case of the cities of the plain only four were rescued, and out of the four one of them was turned into a pillar of salt, because she dared to look back. I wish I had the power to paint in words the scene which this text presents. When going lately among some of the loveliest villages and towns that lie round about Naples, under the shadow of Vesuvius, I thought I had an idea of what these cities of the plain must have appeared like—exquisite for their beauty, charming for situation; and yet, as old Matthew Henry well remarks, it is very rare to find God's pity where there is much of God's plenty. Generally speaking, the fairest spots on earth are the places where sin is most rife, and iniquity most rampant, as if to give the lie to the statement that nature leads to nature's God. Now, the sin of the cities of the plain had waxed to such an extent that God's indignation burned and he rained down a fire from heaven. Now, Mr Modern Thinker, you who are so shocked at anything that is dreadful, you who, I have no doubt, will go home from this tabernacle and say that the sermon was hardly fit for polite ears—how do you account for this? Does this look like 'universal fatherhood'? Behold yon black cloud gathering over the city! Listen to the hissing of that hail of fire. Mark that pitiless sleet sweeping down across the plain! Come, sir, it may be that some of the flashes that devour the city may open your eyes to an awful fact. Do you hear the crackling of the timbers? Hark to those piteous cries and shrieks! It is fearful! Ay, and, mark you, even to this hour it remains the witness of God's hatred of sin, for those plains were blasted with a barrenness that shall last till the end of time. Walk by the shores of the Dead Sea, where once those cities stood. Death reigns! No fish glide in its deep, no flowers bloom upon the shore; and the silent voice of that Dead Sea is this—'Turning the cities of Sodom and Gomorrha into ashes, condemned them with an overthrow, making them an ensample unto those that after should live ungodly.'

Now these are the three instances Peter brings forward; but do you suppose that they are the only three? Far from it. I will, however, but mention others, as time presses. How about the death of the first born in Egypt? Why do not those who are so ready to charge God with being cruel accuse him of harshness in relation to Egypt? I suppose that in Egypt there were more people than there are in London tonight, and yet in every house the first born was found dead, and from end to end of Egypt's land a great wail of grief went up. Does that look like 'universal fatherhood'?

Go a step farther. We all joy with Israel when it passes through the Red Sea. In spirit we clap our hands with Miriam as she strikes her timbrel. It was a glorious deliverance for Israel. But how about the other side? Was it very glorious for Pharaoh and all his hosts? We joy with the Israelites, but let us remember the fact that their salvation meant the destruction of all the chivalry of Egypt. Look yet, again, farther on in history. Do you see Sennacherib's host covering all the land? Need I tell you how

The angel of death spread his wings on the blast
And breathed in the face of the foe as he passed,
And the eyes of the sleepers waxed deadly and chill
And their breasts but once heaved and for ever grew still.

Go look into those silent tents; lift up those trumpets that have never been blown, handle those spears that have never been placed in rest; twang the bow that has never sent the arrow, and then account for the scene of death, if you can, on any other ground than that our God has a hatred against sin, and will, when it pleases him, strike the sinner to the dust. But you turn round and say, 'Ay, Mr Brown, but you forget that all these examples are in the Old Testament. We are not living in Old Testament days.' Then come with me to the New. It is now customary to describe the views of future punishment held by most of us as 'medieval', and to declare that our ideas are mainly gleaned from what monks wrote and said, and from pictures to be found in old galleries. I suppose I have seen about as many of the old masters in the galleries of Europe as most, but I must acknowledge I have never yet seen any picture from hand of medieval artist half so dreadful as some of the descriptions that fell from our Lord's lips. 'Medieval' is it, to speak about weeping and wailing and gnashing of teeth? These words came not from the lips of any mortal man. They fell from the same lips that said, 'Come unto me, all ye that labour and are heavy laden, and I will give you rest.' Neither Paul, nor Peter, nor any of the apostles, ever uttered such words as leaped from the lips of the Man of Sorrows. Christ's descriptions of hell are the most fearful that we have. It is the lips of infinite love that speak of being cut asunder, and about burning with the fire that is never quenched.

One other thought, and I conclude this point. To my mind, at least, the most awful proof of the divine severity against sin is to be found in the fact of the atonement. I have no doubt there are many here who not only remember, but, with the speaker, revere the memory of Henry Ollerenshaw, who used to labour in Bethnal Green. If ever there was a man of God in the east of London it was he. I remember well some years back, when the new views, as they are called, concerning the doom of the wicked were getting popular, that he said to me, 'Mark if with them the views of men concerning the atonement are not altered. When one goes the other will go with it.' And what is the fact? Find those who most deride the idea of an awful doom awaiting the sinner, and you will find those who rob the death of Christ of its sacrificial element. It is the logical sequence. If there was nothing much to save me from, it was almost superfluous for an incarnate God to die upon the tree. But, O brethren, if you want to gauge the deep horrors of the lost, you must guage them by the cross of Christ. It is his groans, his tears, his cries, that tell best what hell means. Thy breaking heart, Lord Jesus,—thy flowing blood,—thy death-cry of 'My God, my God, why hast thou forsaken me?'—these are the things that say to me more than all the cities of the plain, 'There is an awful judgment to come upon the sinner for his sins.' I trust that this fact is believed by all of you. God give it power! There is an awful doom for every man and woman in this sanctuary who dies impenitent rejecting the offer of the gospel of God.

II. Now, then, let us look at the next point. THIS PARTICULAR ACT OF SEVERITY MENTIONED IN OUR TEXT, IS TO BE AN ENSAMPLE FOR ALL AGES. If those of you who have Bibles will look at them you will see that it says, 'making them'—that is the cities of the plain—'an ensample unto those that after should live ungodly.' Then this is not to be shelved as a bit of past history. We are not to put the destruction of Sodom and Gomorrha on one side, and say, 'Oh, that will keep as an interesting relic of the past.' It is not to be treated as something with which we have nothing to do. 'No, says Peter, 'you look at it, for God intended it throughout all ages to be an ensample unto the ungodly.'

Just three weeks ago I was staying in that most beautiful but most depraved of cities, Naples, and, looking across its charming bay, I could see, just in front of our window, Mount Vesuvius. I need hardly say that there the sky was not simply clear or blue. It was such a dazzling blue as we poor unfortunate Britishers know little, if anything, about. As I gazed upon that mountain it seemed to me as if it were painted on ivory. Everything about it was so softened. The smoke that came from the mountain was pearly white. It rose in slow folds, fold over fold, fold over fold, and before the gentle breeze it stretched away for miles until lost in the dim distance. It really seemed more like the white pennon of peace flying from the crater's mouth, than anything else. And there, all up the sides of Vesuvius, were the little white cottages of the peasants. And under its shadow were smiling villages, and it seemed almost impossible to believe that Vesuvius could do any harm. I was almost inclined to think of Vesuvius as modern thinkers dream of God—that surely all the old fire has burned out. Still, there was some smoke rising which showed me that, though at that time no burning lava was pouring out upon its iron-bound flanks, *yet it could do it again.* Three weeks ago tomorrow I took a drive out, and I thought I would go and see this innocent-looking mountain. Still the smoke came away in white folds, and, as we neared it, the driver pointing to the foundations of some house, and speaking in Italian, made us understand that those houses were built on *lava.* Then, after all, this mountain can not be quite so harmless as it looks. And, by and by, we found that the road on either side was lined with lava, and now our carriage wheels rattled over the lava which had once poured down the mountain side. There, a little to the right, was Herculaneum once buried; and a little farther on we entered Pompeii. I wish I could make you see it, as I beheld it. I think you would understand the text better then. I suppose most of you are aware that it was in the year 79 A.D. that this strange city of the dead was covered, and that for nearly eighteen centuries it has been buried, and only one third of it at the present time excavated. We walked along its silent streets, and there we could see the rut which the wheels of the chariots had made as they rattled on their noisy way. We went into the silent houses on either side of the streets. Where were the owners? There were none there to refuse us entrance. We walked into the houses; we looked at the frescoes on the walls, some of them as fresh as if painted only yesterday. You must remember that it was not covered with burning lava, as is popularly supposed. That would have destroyed the city: but the cinders fell until the whole city was covered over. Then over the cinders there flowed a torrent of boiling mud which cooled and caked, and then over that there went the burning lava; and this again became like iron, so that there was the city hermetically sealed up, and, for 1,700 years, the world forgot that there was such a place as Pompeii. But we not only saw streets covered with the marks of chariot wheels, and houses with their frescoes. There were other sights sadder far. There were the relics of the past. There I saw the marble table, still standing in the garden as it was left that afternoon; and there was a bottle with the oil still in it; and there was the loaf half eaten. Yes, but what is that lying there? It is the body of a woman with her face in her hand, seeking to avoid the cinders that were falling. And you can stand there and look upon her, still lying as she cast herself down centuries back. I walked in and out those empty houses in this city of the dead, and I thought of the text, 'turning the cities of Sodom and Gomorrha into ashes, he condemned them with an overthrow'. Sudden was the destruction. There was the bread in the oven which was never taken out by the baker, and the wine was still in the bottle on which the date of the vintage was clearly written. In the house of Diomed which you enter almost first, there, down in the cellar, were discovered seventeen skeletons, all of women, and we saw the marks of their bodies where they huddled on the ground amongst the wine flasks that were yet down there. In a backroom in a house in the street of Abundance, there was found, lying in a heap of rubbish, a man with outstretched hands and clutched fingers, and there, close by, the diggers brought up four hundred pieces of silver, and jewels, and brooches. The miser was caught as he was counting his hoard; the harlot was arrested in her house of shame; the prisoner was suffocated in his cell, and the sentry as he stood at the gateway. Now, can you not imagine that those men and women of Pompeii thought that the day of judgment had come? A darkness that might be felt swathed the city. The earth rumbled; then the sea became tortured; and giant waves rolled up upon the trembling shore; and over all there were the lurid flashes from the crater of Vesuvius, while masses of blazing rock went hissing through the air, and the shrieks of the terrified people rose until death triumphed and stilled the clamour.

As I stood in lonely Pompeii, looking at Vesuvius, the mountain did not appear quite so innocent. It seemed to me, as I stood there, that I heard Vesuvius speak. And the mountain muttered these words,—'I can do it again! I can do it again!' O sirs, believe me, there is a day coming compared with which all we have described is devoid of terror. I mean this world's *last* day. And then will men be caught careless, as they were then.

O sinner, just for one minute, in conclusion, I want you to look at the actions of God in the past, just in the same way as I looked at what Vesuvius *had* done. I could not believe that there was no fearful power for destruction in the mountain, when I walked those empty streets of Pompeii. If any modern thinker had come to me at the time, and said, 'You know, Mr Brown, it is all a delusion. It is a medieval idea that Vesuvius has any lava in it. It is all a mistake to think that Vesuvius ever can destroy. It is always quiet, as you see it.' I think I should have taken him by the arm and said, 'Look, sir, do you count me a born fool? How about Pompeii? If there be no destructive power in Vesuvius, how about Herculaneum? What mean these heaps of lava on which the villages now stand? What mean these ruins? And Vesuvius can do it yet again.'

My brethren and sisters, go back and see what God has done. When God smites Judah it is that Israel should take warning, and he who hurled the angels from heaven to hell, and drowned the world, and destroyed Sodom and Gomorrha, has power still to smite. Oh, do not rouse my God to anger. Will you count his long-suffering to be slackness? and because he still lengthens out the time of grace will you presume on it? 'Escape for thy life.'

I have finished, and, as an old preacher once said, 'Now may God begin.' I feel that, though we have tried to preach to you earnestly, our language has been but cold and faint. Young men, I do not suppose I shall ever see you all again. It is impossible. But as surely as you are sitting in those pews there is a day coming in which you will find every word we have uttered to be true. There is a day coming in which the heavens shall pass away with a great noise, and the earth shall melt with fervent heat, and the trumpet of the archangel shall wax louder and louder; and if you die rejecting Christ you will find yourself, in spite of all that modern thinkers say, doomed to eternal perdition. Fly, then, to Christ, I beseech you. Trust him and he will save you this evening. Rest on his atoning sacrifice, and all sin shall be forgiven you. Go now, and presume no more on God's longsuffering. FLEE FROM THE WRATH TO COME! God add his blessing, for Christ's sake. Amen.

A PARDONING GOD[1]

*Who is a God like unto thee, that pardoneth iniquity, and passeth by
the transgression of the remnant of his heritage?*
Micah 7:18.

NO God like Israel's God—this was the joyous boast of
patriarch, psalmist, and all the prophets. Not only was it
rung into the ears of the chosen people, that the 'Lord
thy God is One Lord', but that their God was incomparable in
himself and all his actions. With what triumphant joy does Moses
utter his song and extol his God before the assembled congregation of Israel. How defiant does the song become, as glorying in
his Rock, he challenges all others to show its equal, and exclaims
'their rock is not as our Rock, even our enemies themselves being
judges'. Well did Elijah, that prophet of fire, maintain the same
when on Carmel's mount he dared all the prophets of Baal to the
test; when before an assembled host he vindicated the honour of
his God, and made the conscience-stricken crowd declare, 'The
LORD, he is the God—the LORD, he is the God.' The psalmist bids
his harp sound forth the same bold strain, as he sings, 'Wherefore
should the heathen say, where is now their God?' And then lashing
their idols with bitter sarcasm, continues, 'They have mouths, but
they speak not: eyes have they, but they see not: they have ears, but
they hear not: noses have they but they smell not: they have hands,
but they handle not: feet have they, but they walk not; neither

[1] May 28, 1871, Stepney Green Tabernacle.

161

speak they through their throat. They that make them are like unto them; so is every one that trusteth in them.' Grandly does Jehovah throw down the gauntlet through his servant Isaiah, and challenge all comparison. 'To whom then will ye liken me, or shall I be equal? saith the Holy One.' 'Thus saith the LORD the King of Israel, and his redeemer the LORD of hosts; I am the first, and I am the last; Is there a God beside me? yea, there is no God; I know not any.' God laughs to scorn all rivals. Idols, the work of men's hands, he spurneth. Jehovah shareth not his glories with another. Alone he is God, and incomparable are all his actions. It is happy work to boast in the Lord. Good is it for the soul to get out of itself its petty cares and trials, and revel in what its God is. This holy boasting is an atmosphere that strengthens while it rests—it prepares the heart to endure suffering with patience, and makes it bold for any enterprise. He who has a little God will always be a small saint; but in proportion as we understand the grandeur of our God, will our spiritual manhood grow strong. Everything about our God is great and worthy of himself. Every attribute is that attribute in fullest perfection. Everything our God does is done in a God-like manner. All he is—all he has—all he does, is beyond compare. Is he wise? Yea, he is the 'only wise God'. Is he potent? Yea, something more, for 'the Lord God *omni*potent reigneth.' Is he holy? Yea, the Holy One—him before whom the angels veil their faces and cry, 'Holy—*Holy*—HOLY.' Thrice must the word be repeated to set forth the holiness of him they praise. When his mercy is the theme, the holy writers seem as if they felt all language far too poor to describe its matchless worth, and so they heap words upon words, and thus in every verse of a whole psalm it is declared that 'His mercy endureth for ever.' He is the God, 'merciful'—or *full* of mercy, and all his mercies are '*tender* mercies'; and his kindnesses '*loving* kindnesses'. But most transcendent is he in his pardons. Here indeed the incomparable God shines forth in glory all his own. His pardons, like himself, are infinite, and know no bounds or limit. Well may we sing in triumph

> Who is a pardoning God like Thee?
> Or who has grace so rich and free?

My purpose this evening is, by the Lord's help to set forth before you the all-excelling nature of our God's forgiveness. This we shall try and do by asking six questions, each question like our text, challenging comparison.

I. WHO PARDONS AT SUCH A COST? Earthly pardons are cheap luxuries. Although often hard to get and difficult to give, yet most cost but the *sacrifice of a little personal feeling*. Let that go, and it is easy to forgive. I can easily imagine there are two here this evening who have long been severed in their friendship. Both feel a reconciliation ought to have taken place before this, 'But', they say, if spoken to on the subject, 'it is impossible.' Why? The simple reason is that neither is prepared to pay his share of the cost of a pardon, and that amounts to the sacrifice of a little personal pique, and a good deal of foolish pride. Neither likes to be the first to offer his hand. Both are waiting for each other, and so a miserable estrangement is carried on through weary months and years, because neither will exchange pride for pardon. O 'tis a thousand pities that when pardons are so cheap, they yet remain so scarce! Turn now to the pardon of our God and see if it be not an incomparable one for cost. Before God could forgive a sinner in accordance with his infinite holiness and perfect justice think what had to be done, sacrificed, and suffered. Measure God's desire to pardon by the obstacles his pardoning love overcame, and then you can form some idea of its intensity. No little sacrifice of feeling—no small surrender of pride would have availed here; something infinitely greater must be surrendered, and the sacrifice must be that of a

Son. God has fathomed his love and pity in one text, 'God *so* loved the world, that he gave his only begotten Son, that whosoever believeth in him should not perish, but have everlasting life.' That little word 'so' contains more than heaven or earth can describe. In it is the heart of God—in it is the depth of pardoning love. O think for a minute what that pardon cost that now makes your soul to sing for joy. You received it freely enough because another paid the price; but what was that price? It cost the Father the gift of his beloved Son—he who from eternity had dwelt in his bosom, must be surrendered and become incarnate. It cost the Son a price no lip can tell—no heart conceive. Do you see him tied to yonder pillar—mark you that awful scourge as it falls again and again upon his quivering flesh; do you note how deep the thongs cut, drawing blood at every stroke? Your pardon cost *that*. 'By his stripes we are healed.' Follow him in that weary walk to Calvary—linger by him as fever courses through his veins, whilst head and hands and feet all drip with gore—stay by him until his sacred head falls upon the breast, and his great heart breaks with anguish, and then looking up into that white countenance, say, 'My pardon cost him that.' Yes, no pardon could ever have come to guilty man had not an atonement been made that satisfied justice, honoured the law and magnified the holiness of God. Sweet work is it to trace the silver stream of forgiving love; and mark how it *would* flow on until it reached the sinner, yea, even though it flowed along the channel of a Saviour's wounds. Contrast, beloved, this evening the poor cheap pardons of man, often withheld because he will not sacrifice his foolish feelings or his paltry pride, with the rich costly pardons of our God, given at the price of his own Son—given through the agonies of Gethsemane and Golgotha. Contrast them until you sing with tearful joy.

Truly the poet is right when he says that the tenderest hearts have limits to their mercy. The most loving may have his compassion put to a test that shall prove the best of human love is but human love at best. With the generality however, the limit of forgiveness is soon reached. Many are the crimes marked down by men as 'unpardonable'. All Europe seems to agree in putting the wretched assassins and incendiaries of Paris beyond the pale of mercy or hope for pardon. Their hands are too red with blood—their outrages too gross and vile. But behold God, and wonder at his pardoning love!! Man has revolted against him—murdered his servants—lighted his church with the fires of martyrdom—laughed to scorn and derided his Book, and even crucified his own Son, and yet he says to such red-handed rebels, 'Come now and let us reason together; though your sins be as scarlet, they shall be as white as snow; though they be red like crimson, they shall be as wool.'

No sinner has ever yet been lost because his sins were too great for pardon. God's power and willingness to forgive, go beyond—yea, infinitely beyond—the greatest lengths of sin into which any desperate sinner has dared to run. Go bring me the vilest wretch that breathes the air of heaven—out of depravity bring me the most depraved—one on whose head is accumulated the guilt of every sin, and every sin in its most aggravated and malignant form—one who has vice written in every line of his sin-stamped countenance and hell's hatred in his heart; and I venture to say to such a one: 'There is mercy sufficient for thee and God's pardoning love reaches a deeper depth than thine iniquity.' Men are not damned because their sins surpass mercy, but because they refuse to accept it when offered. God's pardoning mercy is like the waters of the Red Sea when it rolled upon the Egyptian host; the captains and the charioteers were as much overwhelmed as the common footmen. The impetuous tide knew no distinction, it drowned Pharaoh with as much ease as the horses in his chariot; it swept in triumph over all alike. The great sins and the mighty sins are as easily drowned in the blood of Jesus, as those, which in our ignorance, we call but 'failings'. The depths of pardon cover them; they sink into the bottom as a stone; the sea covers them, they sink as lead in its mighty waters. O blessed deluge of forgiving mercy, surely this second question has stirred our hearts to highest gratitude, and put on every lip the adoring challenge—

Who is a pardoning God like Thee?
Or who has grace so rich and free?

II. WHO PARDONS SO WILLINGLY? It is almost difficult to decide which calls for loudest praise, the pardon or the way in which the pardon is bestowed. Not only is God incomparable in the forgivenesses he has, but also in the way he gives them. Human pardons arc generally spoilt in the mode of bestowal. The bloom of their beauty is lost by the hot hand that holds them so long before it parts with them. Too often man's pardon is only the result of long pleading. It never gushed forth towards the guilty one with holy alacrity, but was wrung out by many an argument and plea; then when it came, how ungracious was it in its language. Who, among us, has not known what it is to be forgiven in such a way that we felt more miserable after the pardon than before, and inwardly resolved we would never ask another from the man? Henry Ward Beecher has well said: 'There is an ugly kind of forgiveness in this world—a kind of hedgehog forgiveness, shot out like quills. Men take one who has offended them and set him down before the blow-pipe of their indignation, and scorch him, and burn his fault into him, and when they have kneaded him with their fiery fists, then they forgive him.' How different the manner of our God— how infinitely higher in this matter are his ways than our ways. I will show you an illustration or two of *how* the Lord forgives. Our Saviour is sitting at meat in the house of Simon the Pharisee, when a woman comes timidly to the door. The woman is too well known, her shame has been her living. She is a sinner—a woman of the town. Respectable morality will

> Make a wide sweep,
> Lest she wander too nigh.

She is fallen, and sanctimonious Phariseeism would lose its caste if it was weak enough to pity. Something tells this poor creature that Jesus may be ventured nigh; perhaps she has marked a look of deep compassion on his face as she has passed him in the streets, and that look has broken her heart;—at all events she comes to where he is, and bending over his feet upon the couch, big tears begin to fall. The bold look of the past has gone; she can but sob as she remembers it. Her tears wet those blessed feet she has come to anoint with ointment; so stooping down, she uses her long tresses to wipe them. The host at the head of the table looks on with scorn. He seems to have known the woman well, and says within himself, 'If he were a prophet he would have known who and what manner of woman this is that toucheth him.' Jesus perceives his thoughts, rebukes him, and then turning to the weeping sinner, says, 'Thy sins are forgiven; go in peace.' O the exquisite tenderness of our Lord in giving that guilty soul its pardon.

Yet again. The scribes and Pharisees bring unto him one day a woman taken in adultery. Here is, if anything, a greater sinner than the last. They demand that she should be stoned to death and ask his approval of the sentence. Appearing to be occupied in writing on the ground, he only for a moment looks up to say, 'He that is without sin, let him first cast a stone at her.' Convicted in their own consciences, they leave one by one, until only the woman remains. Jesus looks up again from the ground, and says to that guilty wife, 'Hath no man condemned thee?' And she said, 'No man, Lord.' 'Neither do I condemn thee; *go and sin no more.*' Could anything be more delicately done? Could reproof and pardon be more sweetly blended? Would you yet know, dear friends, how God forgives? Then take his own picture in the parable of the prodigal son, and there in every line you will behold the beauty of his pardon. In the father who sees the prodigal 'afar off', who 'has compassion', who 'runs', who 'kisses', who interrupts even the confession of guilt, and puts on the best robe at once; in all these things I behold my God who is *ready* to forgive,' and am compelled to sing

Who is a pardoning God like Thee?
Or who has grace so rich and free?

III. WHO PARDONS SO FREQUENTLY? On this point there can be no question. No difference of opinion. The stock of man's pardons is very soon exhausted: I have no doubt Peter thought he displayed marvellous magnanimity when he said to the Lord, 'How oft shall my brother sin against me, and I forgive him; till seven times?' Seven times seemed to him a great many, but how few and small they looked after the Saviour's answer. 'I say not unto thee until seven times; but until seventy times seven.' How much greater was the divine idea of pardon than the human. Peter and Christ both consulted their own hearts, but how different the response. But he who tells us to forgive our brother seventy times seven, forgives his brethren seventy million times seven, and more than that. We notice when we do forgive. Never is there a minute when our God is not forgiving. His pardoning love runs parallel with our erring life. I marvel not that Newton said, 'I am downright staggered at the exceeding riches of his grace. How Christ can go on pardoning day after day, hour after hour!!! Sometimes I feel almost afraid to ask for a fresh pardon for very shame.' Who has not felt the same? The very multitude of God's pardons overwhelms. It would tire out any angel to write down all the pardons that God bestows on one of his children. Dear friend, if indeed you be a Christian, then rejoice in the thought that you are ever pardoned. True is it, even unto you, 'The blood of Jesus Christ cleanseth us from all sin.' O, how precious is that present tense—'cleanseth'—keeps on cleansing, never ceasing in its purifying work. Being reconciled unto God, the friendship is ever maintained—sins forgiven as soon as committed—wrongs pardoned every day—guilt purged by precious blood every moment. O bear me witness, saints of God, that his willingness to forgive has often amazed you although you knew it well—over and over again have you returned unto him after seasons of backsliding, until you felt ashamed to go again—you felt he could never forgive you any more, it was almost presumption on your part to ask for it; but at last you were obliged to seek his face, you could stay away no longer. With many a tear you told him how again you had fallen into the very sin that had been forgiven a thousand times, and how you felt you were no more worthy to be called his son. How did he receive you? Never can you forget how he ran to meet you and, as if this was the first offence, hastened to give the kiss of forgiveness lest your heart should break with sorrow. Then did you indeed sing:

> Who is a pardoning God like Thee?
> Or who has grace so rich and free?

IV. WHO PARDONS SO COMPLETELY? There is much that goes by the name of forgiveness that is no true pardon at all. The tongue may declare that all is forgiven and forgotten, but let some fresh little difference arise, and all the past has a resurrection—old wrongs that have been buried for years, rise from their graves, all the more hideous for their partial burial. Forgiving love had never made clean work of it. The remembrance of the past still rankled in the breast, it required but a touch to remove the outer skin and reveal the festering wound beneath, or, to use another illustration, wrath's fire had never been put quite out, it had just smouldered for years, and a new wrong stirred the slumbering embers and made the old flames break out again. Not so is it with the pardon of our God. It is as real in its nature as comprehensive in its embrace—it is as true as oft repeated. God never brings old scores up again, or taunts with the past whilst he forgives the present. When he says 'forgiven', we are forgiven, and the sins he buries in the grave of pardoning love never live or are seen again. The grave is too deep for hell to find them.

Have you ever, beloved, noticed the different terms employed in Scripture to set forth the forgiveness of our God? They are well worthy of study. Words and illustrations more expressive of completeness could not be found. I will mention one or two. Not only are they declared to be 'covered', but 'washed' away. 'He hath washed us from our sins in his own blood.' However perfectly anything may be covered, it yet *exists*, therefore the more expressive term of washing is employed. When a stain has been removed by purging, it is something more than hidden, it is *clean gone*, so entirely that the same can never be restored. A fresh one may take its place, but the old one is no more. Our previous question showed that the fresh one shares the fate of the old. As if 'washing' were not sufficiently forcible, a stronger word is also used: 'As for our transgressions, thou shalt purge them away', and again, 'When he had by himself *purged* our sins, he sat down on the right hand of the Majesty on high.' Washing and purging imply thorough work. Another beautiful emblem is that of 'blotting' them out. Just as the sun not only shines through the cloud but dissipates it—blots it out of existence and leaves nothing but the blue firmament over head, so says God, 'I have *blotted out* as a thick cloud thy transgressions, and as a cloud thy sins.' 'I, even I, am he that blotteth out thy transgressions for mine own sake, and will not *remember* thy sins.' Our sins when pardoned are as the cloud that melts in the air—gone. They are also declared to be 'removed', and that to an infinite distance: 'As far as the east is from the west, so far hath he removed our transgressions from us.' Who shall say where the east commences or where the west terminates? The distance is boundless. Yet as far as the furthest east is from the remotest west, so far has pardoning love taken our sins from us. They are not nigh thee, believer, they have been carried by thy scape-goat into a land uninhabited; so far that even the eye of God perceives them not. Yet one more illustration and I think the loveliest of them all. You will find it in the chapter from which the text is taken and the 19th verse. 'Thou wilt cast all their sins into *the depths of the sea.*' Notice here two beauties. First the number of sins that God takes away, '*all* their sins.' Not one is left to tell the tale. Observe, secondly, where all the sins are cast: 'In the depths of the sea.' Not in any river lest like Kishon it should run dry and reveal the hidden crime. Not in the foam of the waves that break along the beach, lest when the tide went down they should be left high dry upon the shore. But 'in the depths'; far out to sea, where the waters cover the face of the deep. There God drops his people's sins. They are out of sight—eternally hidden—not only forgiven but forgotten—wondrous love!

> Who is a pardoning God like Thee?
> Or who has grace so rich and free?

V. WHOSE PARDON IS SO FULL OF GRACE? Only a word or so on this division. However sweet human pardon may be, there is nothing gracious in it. There is not one reason why we should *not* forgive, there are millions why we should. Needing forgiveness ourselves of man, 'tis but our duty to forgive. But why should God forgive us? What reasons can there be but those found in his own gracious purposes why he should pardon fallen man. The roots of pardoning love are in his own heart, and therefore the fruits appear on us. It is Archbishop Whately who says, 'It is a remark-able fact that the words in all European languages which express forgiveness or pardon, all imply *free gift.*' Here indeed our God stands forth incomparable, for 'Who has grace so rich and free?'

VI. Whose pardon but his subdues the sin? Most beautiful is the teaching of that sentence in the following verse to our text. He who pardons our iniquities subdues them as well. The fond parent may forgive his child over and over again, and yet die of a broken heart through seeing that the more frequently he forgives, the more reckless does his son become. He has the love to pardon, but not the power to subdue the sin. Blessed be God, he has both. Whilst he forgives the result, he heals the cause. God subdues our iniquities *by* forgiving them. It is a great mistake to imagine that a consciousness of pardon will lead to an indifference about sin. Love is a mightier motive power than fear, and gratitude for forgiveness will make the soul hate sin far more than a dread of lacking pardon. It is when we enjoy in the fullest measure the sweets of pardon felt, that we abhor our sins with deepest detestation. Is it not, dear child of God, a joyful thought, that whilst infinite love keeps on pardoning our ever recurring sins, infinite power is at the same time bringing our wayward hearts more and more under control? God is gradually putting our iniquities beneath his feet and still pardoning them as they rise.

I will now conclude with a sentence or so of application. Believer, rejoice! rejoice!! rejoice!!! You are a traitor if you do not sing. The past is forgiven—the present is being forgiven—the future will be forgiven. You are surrounded by pardons, and they line the road to heaven's gate. O triumph in your God tonight—let your soul make her boast in the Lord, and sing of pardon bought with blood.

Sinner, has this verse no word of hope to you? It has. It is all hope. Whilst it stands part of inspired Writ thou never needst despair. Do you say, 'But there is no sinner like me'? Granted, and there is no God like our pardoning God. Let an incomparable sinner and an incomparable Saviour meet tonight. Thou shalt find his pardons are even greater and more numerous than thy crimes. I have read of a most hardened sinner who was condemned to death in the town of Ayr. It pleased the Lord, however, to save his soul whilst in prison, and so full was his assurance of pardoning mercy, that when he came to the place of execution, he could not help crying out to the people, 'Oh, he is a great forgiver! He *is a great forgiver.'* The Lord have mercy on you, my hearer, and then with us you will exclaim—

> Who is a pardoning God like Thee?
> Or who has grace so rich and free?

GRACE AND GLORY[1]

For the LORD God is a sun and shield: the LORD will give grace and
glory: no good thing will he withhold from them that walk uprightly.
O LORD of hosts, blessed is the man that trusteth in thee.
Psalm 84:11, 12.

W E were very wishful, on this our last season of worship with you for a little while, to have something to
pass on to you that should be so full and so sweet,
that the savour of it should abide even until our return from those
holy fields of Palestine: and in prayer we sought such a theme,
and it seemed to us that these words came in answer—'grace and
glory'. We were somewhat startled at the answer to our prayer:
we asked for something full—and can you imagine anything that
is not included in this little sentence 'grace and glory'? We asked
for something that might be sweet—I know not which of the two
words after all is the sweetest; there is all the delicacy of the hon-
eycomb in both 'grace' and 'glory'. We asked for something that
should abide—I know not how this verse can ever be forgotten,
because every hour of every day I shall need the grace—there is the
reminder, and every hour of every day I ought to be longing for the
glory—'grace and glory'.

But we found what we have so often discovered before: that
however beautiful a passage may seem to be isolated, it always
gains when you take it in connection with its context, and if for

[1] January 7, 1906, Chatsworth Road Chapel, West Norwood, London.

a few moments you look at the setting of this verse you will see that it becomes more wonderful still. This 84th Psalm is in itself a marvel, it is unique. Dr Elder Cumming in his work on this Psalm says that there is no other record in Scripture to compare with it as a record of holy sentiment; it is what a heart feels; from the first verse to the last in a most beautiful sense it is sentimental, it is the soul's deep feeling towards God; the man from the first verse to the close really struggles to find words in which to express all that God is to him.

This wonderful song is divided by two 'Selahs', they are musical pauses, and they are intended to make us mark the words immediately preceding them. You get the first in the 4th verse: 'Blessed are they that dwell in thy house, they will be still praising thee. Selah'—pause here, and think of the abiding continuing joy of the one who dwells in Jehovah's presence. You get the second dividing Selah after the 8th verse: 'Oh LORD God of hosts, hear my prayer; give ear, O God of Jacob. Selah.' Ah! that is beautiful—Jacob, not Israel; not the God of the heavens—not the God of the arch-angels—not the God of seraphim and cherubim, but the God of Jacob—a very imperfect character, a poor weak man, faulty almost at every step. And yet God allows himself to be known by us as the God of Jacob. When I read of him as the God of Abraham I am not always sure that I can claim him, for I lack faith; but the God of Jacob I feel can be the God of your pastor. The God of a poor weak Jacob who so often fell—I do not wonder that the Holy Ghost puts a musical pause after that statement.

Then you will see that with the two 'Selahs' there are three ben-edictions pronounced in this wonderful Psalm. In the 4th verse: 'Blessed are they that dwell in thy house.' In the 5th verse: 'Blessed is the man whose strength is in thee.' And in the last verse: 'O LORD of hosts, blessed is the man that trusteth in thee.'

Now, in the verse which we have selected, you have a constellation of words beginning with the letter 'G', and I want you to note these very specially. As I read the 11th verse I find that 'God gives grace and glory, and no good thing will be withheld.' 'God," 'giving', 'grace', 'glory', 'good'. Here is an infinite fulness, and if by simple faith I am only able to lay my hand upon all this and appropriate it, how rich I shall be.

Let us look into this wonderful passage for a few moments. You have, you will see, the donor, then the donation, and then the big extra. You have the donor—'the Lord God our sun and shield'; you then have his donation—'the Lord will give grace and glory', then you have the magnificent extra—'no good thing will he withhold'. If you can conceive of anything that is not included in the two terms 'grace' and 'glory', and if it is good for you, you may be certain you will have that. He guarantees the grace, he promises the glory, and then he throws in as an extra every good thing.

Let us try and gaze upon *the Donor,* and oh what a task lies before us. Have you ever noticed how through this Psalm the sweet singer takes title after title to set forth the glory of God? In the 1st verse it is 'Lord of hosts', it is 'living God' in the 2nd verse, it is 'my King' in the third verse, it is *Elohim*—'God', in the 7th verse, it is 'Lord God of hosts' in the 8th verse, it is 'God our shield' in the 9th verse, it is 'my God' in the 10th verse, and it is 'Lord of hosts', in the last verse. So that you have a most extraordinary combination of God's sweetest and grandest titles. But the one in our verse, how amazing! 'The Lord God is a sun.' I wonder when David used that illustration for the first time—for it has never been used in Scripture before. God has never been directly termed 'Sun' before—did even David dream what an illustration he was using! I imagine not. The Holy Ghost allowed him to use a metaphor which the Spirit knew ages afterwards would mean infinitely more than David could conceive. A sun—why, this is a blazing text, 'The LORD God is a sun.' Have you ever tried to look at it?—you become half blinded as you look. If it means anything it means this, THAT GOD IS AN INFINITY OF BLESSING. AN INFINITY OF BLESSING! Let me try for a moment to illustrate this. No one can say what are the secret supplies, and what the measurement of the heat and warmth and light pouring out of that sun and have been pouring out all these ages—and as far as we know without any sign of diminution whatever.

But an American astronomer has in a very original and suggestive way given us some faint conception; he says, 'In our State of Pennsylvania we have the richest coal-fields in the world. Underlying the whole State of Pennsylvania there is coal,—enough coal to supply every fire in the whole of the United States of America for over one thousand years.' That is the supply of the coal-fields at Pennsylvania alone. 'Now', says the astronomer, 'imagine for a moment, that the solar heat of the sun ceases, and there is to be an equivalent for it, imagine that it were possible to transport the coal of Pennsylvania into that great furnace up there. How long would it last in order that the sun, that great furnace, might give the same heat that it is giving out now day by day?' And the astronomer puts it in the form of a query; he says, 'Would it last a year? Would it last a month—all the coal-fields of Pennsylvania, would it last a month? No. Would it last a week? No. Would it last a day? No. Would it last an hour? No, Would it last a minute? No. *It would not last the one-thousandth part of a second!* Were all the coal-fields of Pennsylvania hurled into that great furnace, in one-thousandth part of a second all would be consumed.' And yet this wondrous sun pours out its rays with undiminished heat. Oh, the mystery of it! Beneath the corona of the sun there is what is called the chromosphere, and for want of a better term I will call it 'an ocean of fire', and that ocean of fire is between six and nine thousand miles deep—twice as deep, that ocean of fire, as the Atlantic is broad; and from that ocean of fire there leaps up what, for want of a better term we describe as flames, at the rate of one hundred and fifty miles a second; these flames leap up to the height of one hundred thousand miles, hang over the Sun perhaps for a few hours or a few days, and then drop in fiery sparks back again into the furnace. One such eruption as that would be enough in one hour to render the whole of this earth what Pompeii is today under an eruption of Mount Vesuvius. Were this world to fall into the sun it would simply be annihilated and evaporate before it even touched its flames—like a snow-flake falling on a red hot iron-bar.

All that lies in this text—God is a sun. And there is more than that. Everything on earth that lives, moves, circulates, is a child of the sun. There is not a flower that is not born of the sun. You could not live without the sun. The very colour on your cheek tonight you may thank the sun for. The sun blows in the wind, the sun flows in the river; it is the sun's mighty hands that lift the ocean up, and puts it in the form of snow and glacier upon the tops of the Alps. Were the sun's rays withheld for three weeks the whole of this earth would be death and desolation. And, led of the Holy Ghost, David, who knew not these wondrous things, says: 'The LORD God is a sun.' That is, he is to the believing soul; he is to a redeemed church everything that the sun is to the solar system—the centre, the light, the holding power, the living power, the all in all.

'The LORD God is a sun', and then he adds, 'and shield'. One writer beautifully says: 'This is a counterpoise blessing.' We could not bear the first blessing if we had not the second: the very fact that God is the sun necessitates that he should also be a shield. How could I live in that uncreated light—may I say it with reverence—I need God to shield me from God; I need God to be my shield in order that I may dare to know him as my Sun. And how beautiful it is to observe that in this shield we have Jesus in the Psalm.

It does not say that God will hold a shield over me, but that he himself will be the shield. In the 9th verse David says, 'Behold, O God our shield', and yet in the text he says, 'the LORD God is a shield'. What is the explanation of that? Why, that Jesus Christ, who is God, is my shield, and that I am in him; and it is only as I am in him that I can dwell before those eternal burnings. Hidden away in Christ in God: he is in both sun and shield.

So much for the glorious Donor. Now *what does he give?* 'The LORD God will give grace and glory.' I think grace is about the grandest word in Scripture: omitting the name of our adorable Master, where will you find one word to equal grace? When dear Moody was converted out in America, he began to study the Scriptures—all converted people do—and he came across this word *grace,* and when first that word laid hold of him—I had it from his own lips—he said he was so amazed, so captured by it, that for three days he thought of nothing else, and talked of nothing else; he went from house to house to his different friends, and said: 'Have you heard of the grace of God?' Have you ever heard of the grace of God?' We get so used to these things that we do not realise the marvel. What is grace? You say 'Love'. No, it is more than that; it is love to the unlovely; it is love to the unlovable; it is love that has no reason whatever save in itself for being where it is; it is that which has its springs in God's own heart, and so the fruit appears on us. He gives grace—undeserved love. And observe the order: the grace comes first; it is not, 'He gives glory and grace.' Ah, that is how some of you would like it. I will guarantee that even this wet night there are people here who would like to have the glory, only they do not care about having the grace first. Oh, if they could only just get to heaven without any grace it would be delightful. But God won't give number two until number one has been received. He gives grace and glory; and a moment's thought will show you how absolutely imperative it is that this order should be kept. How can I receive glory if I have not first received grace? I should not be fit for it. Can you imagine a glorified sinner—I mean a man who has not been saved from his sins and yet is glorified? A glorified drunkard reeling in heaven! A glorified sensualist there! Why, the angels would shrink back from him in horror, and the man himself, though in heaven, would have a hell within his own soul. He must be renewed in nature or else how could he enjoy the glory. Do you enjoy spiritual things? When you hear it announced that there is going to be a gathering for prayer and praise, do you feel that it is such an attraction that you must be there, or would you rather go to some silly sing-song; which do you like best? Supposing God were to take you to heaven as you are now, you would feel that you were a fish out of water; there would be nothing in harmony between yourself and your surroundings. If I do not love the sanctuary on earth I am sure I shall not love the sanctuary in heaven; if I do not find joy in worship down here it would be an eternal perdition to have eternal worship up there. Man's nature must be renewed, and grace must do its work before glory can come. It is first the grace and then the glory.

And what is the meaning of that glory? I do not know—I cannot imagine—I could tell better after I had been a few months in heaven. We read these words, and we become so accustomed to them that perhaps we hardly pause to ask what do they really mean? There was a poor member of this Church, a dear girl that we lost sight of for two years; we had news of her only the week before last; she died in a poor agricultural labourer's cottage, down in Essex, and as she died she spake of Jesus, and her face was radiant with the light of coming glory. The labourer was so poor that he has to collect five shillings to put a little plate upon the girl's coffin. But were that poor girl to come back to earth and stand on this platform she would be able to tell you more of the meaning of the glory than all the theologians and all the preachers and all the writers on the earth today; you have to be there to know the meaning. We may talk of its brightness and sing of its music—but what must it be to be there? Glory; it means something for the spirit, something for the mind, something for the body. It is something for the spirit, for there is absolute freedom from all sin. I cannot conceive of it; I have been a sinner ever since I was born, and sin seems ingrained in me, but I can just get a glimmering of this— that if I were perfectly free from sin I should step into a heaven at once. There is something for the mind; all our mental limitations will be dropped, as we saw last Sunday, now we only know in part. Didn't you feel, as we were talking a little while ago about the wonders of the sun, how little we know? All our knowledge is only a modified form of ignorance. But then I shall know even as also I am known. Oh, God has wonderful treats for us mentally. And then glory means more than rest; it means more than happiness; the idea of the word glory is this—exultation, joy, triumph. Do you see that General as he comes home in triumph from a successful campaign; the waving of banners, the blare of trumpets, the shouts of the multitude, the waving of handkerchiefs, there is delirium, there is triumph and ecstasy. And all that lies in this word. There will be the palm branches, there will be harps; these things symbolise something. Oh, it is hard to keep patient with some people who say, 'Do you believe that there will be a literal harp and a literal palm branch?' I do not care whether there is or not. But *they stand for something:* the harp means something, the palm branch means something, the shout of triumph means something, and in heaven it will be the glory of victory. Satan under our feet; sickness, death, temptation—all these for ever over, there will be glory in the air. There is something for the spirit, something for the mind, and there is something for the body, for I read in the First Corinthians, 15th chapter, and the 43rd verse—and it is true of your body if you are a believer, and mine—'it is sown in dishonour; it is raised in glory'. I know not how, but by the wonderful working of him who feeds the furnace of the sun, he is going to turn this body even into the perfect image of Christ's body in the glory. It is 'grace and glory'—there is the order. Only please do not leave out the conjunction. It is 'grace *and* glory'. How often at a railway station you have seen something like this:—there is a railway porter down on the lines standing by the side of a carriage and you see him pick up that big iron chain, there is another part of the train being backed on, and as it comes you see him put the link over and then fasten those two chains on either side: one carriage cannot go without the other now, they are linked into oneness. That is what the word *'and'* is; it is a CONjunction 'grace and glory', and all hell's powers cannot separate these two. There is no glory, mark you, without grace, and I thank God the reverse is true. Where there is grace there must be glory. Grace is glory in the bud, but glory is this—grace in full bloom and thou canst not have the glory, man, without the grace, but if thou hast received the grace thank God thou art coupled to glory, and no power that hell knows can snap that coupling.

In conclusion. *All this is given.* It is 'the LORD will GIVE grace and glory', not barter it—not exchange it—not sell it; he gives it: he bestows salvation as a free gift from beginning to end. And then here is the climax—the finale, 'And no good thing will he withhold from them that walk uprightly.' That is, if you can conceive of anything that is really good for you which is not covered by the two words 'grace and glory', God will give you that. Then says someone, 'Why am I not a richer Christian? How is it that I am not a happier, stronger, more buoyant, more demonstrative, more glorious Christian?' I will tell you why: you have not noticed the word 'withhold'. It does not say, He will GIVE every good thing: it says, He will not WITHHOLD. Have you gone to take it? I know he will give grace and glory, but there are ten thousand other little extras that I want in order to make my life here happy, peaceful, useful, and a blessing to others, and God says, 'For these extras you are to come and ask me. I will not withhold them, but you must ask me.' Why are you poor spiritually? Because you are not applying for the extra, you 'do not ask, you do not seek.' God has pledged his word that he will not withhold anything good, only he will decide what that is.

The benediction that is pronounced then is 'Blessed is the man that trusteth in thee.' I should think he was. The man who can look up and say 'Jehovah is my sun, I live in his light: Jehovah Jesus is my shield. I live in him, he is round about me, the LORD God giveth me grace, and he has coupled that on to glory, and he has pledged his word that every good thing I need I have only to ask for and he will not withhold it'—that man can only pronounce one verdict, and it comes from the depth of his soul, it is

'BLESSED IS THE MAN THAT TRUSTS THIS GLORIOUS GOD.'

HIGGAION[1]

The LORD is known by the judgment which he executeth; the wicked is snared his own hands. Higgaion.—[Margin, 'Meditation'.]
Psalm 9:16.

YOU who worship here regularly will, I know, bear me witness that my general theme is the love of God—his compassion towards the fallen, and his willingness to save the vilest. The themes we love to dwell on are the all-glorious sufficiency of the atonement, and the unutterable love of that heart that broke with anguish on Calvary's cross. We most frequently have the flageolet of mercy's invitation to our lips, and most love to make our harp strings vibrate—as we sweep our hands across them—with the melody of dying love. But there are seasons for all things, and there are times for everything; and sometimes the day dawns when the preacher would be false to himself and false to his people if he did not declare to them the other side of the subject. Yea, I know not how he could answer for it at the last, or how his garments could be clear of the blood of souls, if he never put down the flageolet invitation, and lifted up the war trumpet to his lips, trusting to God to awaken a thousand echoes of alarm in as many hearts. If he would be true to himself, to his people, and to his God, he must sometimes make the strings of his harp tremulously vibrate to the mournful notes of a judgment to come. It behoves him sometimes to declare that the Lord is known not only by his

[1] August 17, 1873, East London Tabernacle.

matchless mercy, but by the judgment which he executeth; and
if it is right for him to say 'Come' it is as right for him to thunder 'Higgaion'—'Meditate on the threatened judgments of an offended Jehovah.' In our experience we have found that God uses
all kinds of instrumentality for the ingathering of souls. Whilst
there are numbers allured by mercy's music, there are almost as
many driven into the arms of heaven by the alarm bells of wrath
to come. As there is a diversity in the operations of the Spirit, so
is there a diversity of instrumentality, and we are bound to employ
all means, yea, to 'become all things to all men, if by any means we
may save some'.

The burden of our heart is the unsaved portion of this night's
concourse, and that which makes the burden the heavier is the
remembrance that 'The Lord is known by the judgment which
he executeth'—that 'the wicked is snared in the work of his own
hands.' O sinner, I pray you have a 'Higgaion' this evening. If you
have never been serious before be serious now, if but for forty minutes. If you never think of heaven or hell again, give me for a short
time not only your ears but your attention as I say to you 'Higgaion'; meditate, dare to look the fact in the face that Jehovah hath
said he is known by the judgment which he executeth.

I shall want then, first of all, *to speak to you about the truth that is
here stated,* and then, secondly *to cry 'Higgaion' concerning it.*

First of all then let me try and state the truth of
the text. The truth is that the Lord makes himself known by his
judgments; that is, that not only is the character of God discernible
in the gentle mercy that he showers down on every hand, but that
the same character is as distinctly set forth in his sterner actions.

There is a fashion in theology as well as in everything else, and
the fashionable thing at the present day seems to be to depreciate
entirely divine justice and pooh pooh the idea of God possessing

such a prerogative as vengeance. The fashionable thing now is to let all the sterner lines of Jehovah's character evaporate until nothing is left but a dreamy misty thing called 'universal fatherhood'; and I suppose a more treacherous dangerous falsehood than this has never been launched by the father of all lies. It is just because this thing is so abroad and finding its way everywhere, that we want to clear our souls in your case and to say 'the LORD is known by the judgments which he executeth'.

Let us then look at what God's thoughts in relation to sin are as demonstrated in his judgments, and I am inclined to think that we shall find there are far sterner traits in Jehovah's character than these prophets of molluscous theology imagine, we shall see that although his love to the sinner is wonderful indeed, there is dire wrath for him that refuses to accept the mercy offered through the atoning sacrifice of Christ.

Let us then have a look at God as he has made himself known by his judgments.

What ages have passed since first man fell. What centuries have rolled by since God first pronounced the threatened judgment on sin. Now, if God's hatred to sin were anything less then intense there would surely have been a mitigation of the sentence before this. If I can show you that although ages have rolled by since man fell, yet God's threatened punishments are as real and tremendous now as ever, I think I shall have shown you that God's hatred to sin is something terrible beyond all description. One judgment was that the earth should bring forth briars and thorns to scourge the labourer after bread. Now surely if there were unmixed mercy on the part of God—if there were this universal commiseration at the expense of his own justice and truthfulness, such a light and additional part of the curse must have been altered before this. But what is the state of the case? The earth tonight brings forth her briars and her tangled thickets. To this day the earth suffers for sin's sake, and 'the whole creation groaneth and travaileth in pain together until now'. There was a solemn judgment pronounced in the ears of Eve, the first mother. Has that become obsolete? 'In sorrow shalt thou bring forth children.' You may say that had we taste we should not even refer to so delicate a subject. But we answer that we have to prove our point, not conciliate hypercritical hearers. Has there been any mitigation of this? Are mothers' sorrows less than they were? Even in the common sorrow of motherhood I see a tremendous proof that God will not lessen one atom of the threat he pronounced. 'In the day that thou eatest thereof thou shalt surely die.' Has death become a thing of the past? Is not this world fast becoming a huge cemetery? Has the scythe of the mower become less sharp? Has he put his sickle on one side? Are not men dying now as regularly as when Cain and his children gave up the ghost? They are; and the cemeteries on every hand, and the bells that toll, tell me that God is known by the judgment which he executeth. He must be besotted, indeed, who, having eyes and using them, can see aught else than fearful proofs on every hand that whilst God is love he is also inflexible in his justice.

But let us take up this book, and see what God's character is, as revealed by his judgments here, and I think I shall be able to show that there is something in the character of God very different to that which is so universally represented now.

Let us proceed to review the days of Noah. The world had become exceedingly sinful, its crimes cried to heaven; then did the great fountains of the deep break up. Do you see how the black clouds gather? Do you hear the piteous pelting of the storm as it comes down? Do you mark the waters, how they rise? The hills are covered. Do you see the mad fight, the desperate struggle for the highest part of the mountain-peak? Can your eye see those corpses floating far and wide on every hand? Think you of the time when a billow swept round and round the world without a mountain crag to break on. From the awful silence of a drowning world there breaks upon mine ear, 'The LORD is known by the judgment which he executeth'; and in that judgment I see something far sterner and more awful and terrible than universal fatherhood. Those cold billows say to me that it is a dreadful thing to fall into the hands of an angry God; and a drowned world tells me that he who dares to war against God wars against one who has a thousand weapons in his hand, and says 'Vengeance is mine, I will repay, saith the Lord.'

Come later on. There are cities full of iniquity. They burn with lust unnatural, so God decrees that they shall burn with unnatural fire. Do you see the sulphurous torrent as it pours down on those cities of the plain? Do you hear the crackling of the timbers, and the shrieks of the men, and the women and the children? Do you remember that woeful sentence, 'The smoke of the country went up as the smoke of a furnace'? I see no universal fatherhood there. 'The LORD is known by the judgment which he executeth', and the sea of death in the Holy Land still bears its testimony to the fact that God abhors the sin, and hath judgments for sinners. 'The LORD is known by the judgment which he executeth.' Israel, not satisfied with the bread that comes from heaven, lust after flesh and, forgetting all previous mercies, insult their God by murmuring and longing after Egypt; they cry for meat and they have it, but while it is still between their teeth, the wrath comes down upon them, and a great plague sweeps through the camp; graves are dug by hundreds and the rebels flung into them, and the place is called Kibroth-hattaavah, that is, the graves of lust. Go walk ye among those numerous graves, and remember that in every one there lies a sinner smitten down by the hand of God in the very midst of his iniquity, and then talk to me, if you can, about a God that is weakly merciful and will in no wise punish any. 'The LORD is known by the judgments which he executeth', and let every man woman and child in this Tabernacle tonight say 'Higgaion', and meditate on the tremendous truth. Korah, Dathan and Abiram insult God through his servant Moses. 'Stand back, stand back', cries a warning voice, 'back every one of you', and all Israel stands grouped at a distance around those tents. Mark you the wives and the children of Korah, Dathan and Abiram are there and their household goods and their cattle, besides. Do you see the earth yawn as down its horrid throat households, wives, children, tents, cattle, furniture, all are swallowed as in a living grave, whilst Israel terrified flees at their cry? The LORD is known by the judgments which he executeth. Therefore let all the world give ear, and take to heart.

But after all these instances are only in the retail; there is a wholesale judgment I must call to mind. Do you remember how it is said concerning the people of Israel that out of the entire multitude that went out of Egypt only two entered the Holy Land—Caleb the son of Jephunneh and Joshua the son of Nun? Where are the hosts? Where are the people that Moses and Aaron numbered in the wilderness of Sinai? Their carcasses are lying in the wilderness as the Lord threatened, and I stand aghast at this stupendous judgment. Here is a people brought out of Egypt with high hand, and God smites all the chivalry of Egypt for their sakes, and yet as the fruits of rebellion only two out of the hundreds of thousands enter the Holy Land. Let the carcasses in the wilderness declare, 'The LORD is known by the judgment which he executeth', and let every heart here give the echo—'Higgaion', pause, meditate. And yet I feel that up to the present I have only been showing you God's hatred of sin as it gleams. I have yet to show you the lurid light of its glare.

I have only given you the milder specimens of God's wrath—not the most terrible. Oh, would that the Holy Ghost might give power to our lips for a few moments to tell you how God has once in boundless degree shown his abhorrence of sin!! I ask you to come with me now, not to the wilderness, but to a place called Calvary. I want you to gather together on that little spot just outside the city, and see such a sight as Moses never saw when he beheld the bush burning. I want you to see on Calvary the Lord making himself known by the judgment which he executeth. Who is that upon the tree in agonies and blood? The answer is, Jehovah's Son! What, his loved Son? Yes, his loved and only Son. But mark his agony. Do you see that white face, furrowed deep, turned up to heaven? Hear you that cry that seems to pierce the clouds, 'My God, my God, why hast thou forsaken, me?' Why? O friends, 'the LORD is known by the judgment which he executeth; and when he looked at the adorable Jesus he saw in him not only his own Son, but the sinner's substitute. He saw on him my accursed sins, he saw yours also; and oh, awful truth, although the substitute was his own Son, he would not, he could not spare the blow. That heaving breast was made the sheath of the sword of his justice. God must undeify himself before he can wink at sin or fail in the execution of his threatened wrath against iniquity. He must cease to be the Holy One before mercy can ride rough-shod over equity and truth. But righteousness and mercy, truth and peace all meet in the atoning sacrifice. 'The LORD is known by his judgment which he executeth.' Above all, by his judgment of sin at Calvary. Oh, am I speaking to any who imagine sin a trifle? I pray you measure sin by the woes of Christ. If you think that iniquity is but a small thing, understand that iniquity can only be understood as it is measured by the agonies of a dying God. Probe those wounds—fathom that depth of anguish if you can. Tell me how hot the fire burned within that loving heart; and when you have told me that, you have told me how much God hates sin. Whilst Calvary is the most matchless exhibition of mercy, it is the most terrific exhibition of holy wrath. In one and the same person, and at one and the same time there is illimitable love to the sinner and there is illimitable hatred to his sin. Go to Calvary, not to Sinai, to learn how much God abhorreth this accursed thing.

Ah; but I think I can hear one of you saying, 'We agree with you thus far; but have there been any such declarations of hatred to sin since that time? Remember, we are living in the New Testament days—in another dispensation. Does God make himself known by his judgments now?' Well, let us come to a later time than the death of Christ. Behold Herod taking to himself praise that he has no right to, and insulting heaven by allowing himself to be called a god. There he lies eaten up of worms, smitten and blasted in a moment. That putrid mass of corruption, from which the courtiers shrink with horror, says, 'The LORD is known by the judgments which he executeth. Higgaion. Meditate.' 'Ah', you say, 'that is an exceptional case. Herod was a king, so God noticed him more than if he had been a private individual.' Indeed! Then listen. Ananias tells a lie—he falls a corpse. Sapphira, his wife, endorses the lie, and the young men returning from carrying him out, are just in time to bear away her body. What think you of that? 'The LORD is known by the judgment which he executeth. Higgaion.' And had we time (which we have not) it would be easy to show you that there is rather more judgment even now on earth than some people like to believe. You would find it rather difficult to find persecutors that have died happy in their beds, or men that have imbrued their hands in innocent blood but have had dire retribution fall on their own heads. Many a monster has had a foretaste of his coming perdition. Do you still doubt the existence of any present judgment whereby the Lord is known? Then have one other tremendous proof—THERE IS A HELL TONIGHT. Its fires have not gone out nor burned down. Oh, will you doubt God's vengeance against sin when there is a hell burning at this moment? Will you call in question Jehovah's wrath when at the very moment I am warning you there are souls suffering it? Ah, you may turn away in scorn and say, 'That is the hack subject when preachers are hard-up and know not what to talk about.' Say what you like—God knows the thought is an agony to me—but there the fact remains. There is a hell *somewhere* tonight, and that hell ought to say to every soul in this Tabernacle, 'Higgaion', 'meditate'; 'The LORD is known by the judgment which he executeth.'

Observe, too, that these judgments are wonderfully just, for the text says, 'The wicked is snared in the work of his own hands.' The sinner after all, ruins himself, and the vile man becomes his own executioner. This is even true on earth. The drunkard burns his entrails and maddens his brains. The prodigal beggars himself until he envies the swine he feeds. As for the vicious, we won't talk of the dire judgments they bring on themselves; but if in this company there are found licentious young men, or an abandoned sisterhood, I say to you, 'The wicked is snared in the work of his own hands.' 'Higgaion', both of you. No one can break through any of God's hedges but that an adder is sure to sting him; and he who hurls his sins against God, shall find them come down on his own head like a thunderbolt. But oh, beloved, how awfully true is it that the sinner is snared in the work of his own hands in *eternity!* There is one place where the justice of God in punishment is never called in question. There *is* a place where no whisper has ever yet been heard against the righteousness of divine anger, and that place is hell. It is believed in there. The rich man may lift up his eyes in torment but I do not find that he calls in question the justice of his doom. Every sinner damns himself; and in hell men and women acknowledge the they are reaping the righteous fruits of their own sowing. 'Higgaion! Meditate!'

This brings us, you see, to the close of this subject. I have tried to state the truth of the text. If it is unpalatable to any of you, remember it that it is not *my* truth; it is *God's*. If it seems dreadfully strong to some of you, bear in mind it is the Holy Ghost that has put it there, not the preacher. Therefore 'Higgaion.'

II. We have now, in our second and closing place, simply to CRY OUT ONE WORD, AND THAT WORD 'HIGGAION!' When the psalmist wrote this verse, and reached the words 'The wicked shall be snared in the work of his own hands', he seemed to be overpowered at the terror of the thought, and so put a full stop and wrote in the word 'Higgaion', as much as to say, 'O my soul, meditate on the tremendous truth my hand has penned, and let all who read the same meditate.' And then after 'Higgaion' he puts 'Selah'. He would have there to be a solemn pause. Oh, I would that there could be just one moment's solemn pause in our meeting tonight. Would that there could be a Selah, an Higgaion! Friends, shall there be? I put it to you. 'The LORD is known by the judgment which he executeth; and the wicked shall be snared in the work of his own hands.'

Now let us just for a moment meditate on that. Let there be a solemn Higgaion, and let every heart ask itself the question, 'How do I stand in reference to this tremendous truth?' I shall now for a minute or two call out Higgaion to a few different people. And the first I shall call it out to is *the saint*. O saint of God, Higgaion! It is for you to meditate on this solemn fact—the threatened judgment of God against sin. First of all let the minister have his Higgaion. Oh, what a grand thing it would be for this land of ours if every minister went into his pulpit under the power of a text like this! Higgaion! Yes, let the preacher remember that nicely turned sentences are, after all, poor things for perishing souls. Higgaion! Yes, let the minister understand that his congregation must be either damned or saved, and that the Lord is known by the judgment which he executeth. Do not think I am speaking to others and not to myself. God knows that I am condemning myself wholesale tonight. If I realized this truth more, do you think I should be preaching with a dry eye, as I am tonight? If I said 'Higgaion' to my soul, as I ought, do you think I could look upon you without anguish? Friends, I tell you solemnly in the sight of God, I sometimes feel more when I don't see you than when I do. I don't know why, but I suppose the excitement of standing here takes off the edge of the thought. God is my witness, I have my Higgaion sometimes, and when I meditate on these pews full and these aisles full, I am ready to exclaim, 'O Lord, it is more than heart can bear.' I tell you, sirs, we have had our Higgaion, and we have meditated on your doom; and the idea of this Tabernacle being a mere channel to hell to any of you, has wrung tonight's sermon from our soul. We would that this text had more power over us, and that we might be clear of the blood of every one of you. And Sunday school teachers, let the Higgaion come to your soul. You are entrusted with those young immortals. Do you believe the truth that God's wrath is out against sin? Oh, if you do, you will not be content with going through a mere formal routine of lessons. You will travail in birth that these little ones may be saved. But to come nearer home. Parents, I want you to have a Higgaion tonight. Do you ever meditate on the possibility of a child of yours being damned? Have you ever really dared to entertain such contemplation? Then I ask you in the name of God, *'What are you doing for the conversion of your children?'* Brother, what are you doing for that unsaved sister? Sister, are you seeking the salvation of that brother? Higgaion, all of you, meditate on the truth that 'God is known by the judgment which he executeth.' May the Higgaion come with power upon the heart of every saint, until we each know what it is to plead with souls, as if we saw the waves of eternal wrath coming nearer every moment to the objects of our love.

But, perhaps, there may be in this throng a bitter scoffer. I know not, but likely enough there are some here who glory in their hatred of all that belongs to Christ. Ah, sir, you lead your godly wife a rare time of it, and you are not ashamed to boast of your deeds!! Bitter are the scoffs that come from your lips, and cruel the words that cut her soul. *Higgaion!!!* There is a time coming when all your scoffing will be taken out of you. There is a day yet to dawn when even your brazen face shall turn ashy white. There is a moment yet to tick when you will tremble before an insulted God. I know you will laugh at all we have said tonight, and make merry at our expense. I have no doubt you will crack your jokes over the sermon at your supper table. But even in your laughter may the awful word 'Higgaion' rise like a spirit from the deep, and stand before you. O, meditate, sinner, and remember that there is a God in heaven, and he is known by the judgment that he executeth.

Poor thoughtless pleasure-seekers—and I know we have plenty here—I want to give you also this word. I see you putting the cup of sparkling dissipation to your lips, but before you drink it, I wish to drop something in—it is only one word—'Haggaion.' Let that fall into your cup of pleasure, and I think it will spoil its taste. If you can be merry, remembering the judgments of God, you are a strange being. O, poor sinner, you who are leading a butterfly life, and entirely thoughtless about eternity, won't you listen, as I say 'Higgaion'? Will you meditate just for a moment, and work out this problem? Is it worth while being damned for a little frothy pleasure on earth, and are the frivolities of time worth the woes of hell? Some of you will be off to the theatre tomorrow; well, I pray that amidst the glare and the glitter of that soul trap, a word may ring right round the place and in your ears, and that word be 'Higgaion.' Ah, if but one flash from the pit were seen, how would it extinguish all the footlights, as far as you were concerned. Some of you will be off next Tuesday to your Foresters' Fête, and you will be swept along on the tide of your wild mirth—Higgaion!! Remember this, amidst all your boisterous laughter, that the truth remains untouched, 'The LORD is known by the judgment which he executeth.'

But, alas, there are some who are just stupidly indifferent, and I suppose we have as many of those here as of any sort—people who do not seem ever to trouble themselves about eternity at all: not pleasure-seekers or God-seekers either, content just to jog on without a thought either way. It struck me that this word might serve as a kind of bombshell to drop down under your window, and I wish it would explode and wake you up out of your stupid lethargy. Thou indifferent one, HIGGAION!! Will not the thought of the judgment to come rouse thee from thy slumber; or are you so dead asleep that even the roar of perdition shall fail to awake you? Sleeper, awake! Higgaion!!

And you, money-maker, who have got every atom of your heart and soul in your business, look at your sovereigns and see if there is not a word tonight stamped on them, and that word 'Higgaion?' How many of them will you take with you when you die? How many of your bank notes are you going to cram into your coffin with you? 'What shall it profit a man if he gain the whole world and lose his own soul?' Do you think you can cash a cheque in hell or buy your freedom from perdition by your gold? Your money will perish with you. 'Higgaion!'

And, lastly, I would speak to some of you here who have been impressed. I know you have. I have seen the tear in your eye, and I have marked the way you have listened. Well, dear friend, remember that impression is not conversion, and the mere shedding of a tear is not coming to Christ, nor is the feeling uncomfortable under a sermon, a change of heart. To the most impressed I say, 'Higgaion.' Now may you hear the sound of the tide of the water of condemnation as it comes running after you with race-horse speed, gaining ground every moment. O God, come and arouse the lethargic tonight! Come and wake the sleepers now, and let there be a Higgaion in every heart. Do you say 'When shall we meditate? When shall we look these facts in the face?' I have but one answer to give. *Now! Now!* Tomorrow may be too late. There are many having their Higgaion in hell. They meditate, now it is too late, over invitations that they refused and warnings that they scoffed. Ah friends, I am afraid there are some of you who will meditate there upon this sermon. God forbid it. Oh, that you would meditate now—now while mercy holds out her golden sceptre—now whilst long-suffering keeps back the thunder-bolt:—now while God says 'Come'—now before hell embraces you—now while the bosom of Christ is open to welcome you—now while God's children pray for you. HIGGAION! When? Oh, this moment! The rush of time says 'Now!' And the song of the angels says 'Now!' And every ransomed heart that is here tonight says 'Now!' Methinks even Jehovah, looking from his eternal throne, says 'Now!' And— deep hollow toned, there comes from the pit the word 'Now!' Oh, may God either draw you or drive you; but if you forget every word we have uttered, let the text be engraven as in brass upon your soul—'The LORD is known by the judgment which he executeth. The wicked is snared in the work of his own hands.' May God give the Higgaion, for his name's sake.—AMEN.

A BLAZE OF DIAMONDS[1]

*But the God of all grace, who hath called us unto his eternal glory by
Christ Jesus, after that ye have suffered a while, make you
perfect, stablish, strengthen, settle you. To him be glory
and dominion for ever and ever. Amen.*

1 Peter 5:10, 11.

OUR first experience in reading this verse is amazement
that borders on bewilderment. The whole is a perfect
blaze of diamonds, and the very brightness serves to
shroud the glory, for there is such a thing, as Milton expresses it,
as being 'dark through insufferable light'. There is such a combination of splendours here that the mental eye is almost dazed at
the first reading, so that one cannot immediately distinguish the
actual teaching. You have such marvellous words coming one upon
another, each word so full, so bright, so splendid, that you are well
nigh lost in the whirl. Keep your eyes upon the verse, and see what
words we have: 'God', 'all grace', 'called', 'eternal glory', 'Christ
Jesus', 'dominion for ever'. And, as if these were not enough, we
find also perfection thrown in as well: 'make you perfect'. And
these marvellous words, each bright with all the splendour of
deity, daze us all the more because of their contrast to that which
has gone before in the previous verses; for, read a few lines back,
and what are the words that meet you in those verses from the
7th to the 9th? 'Your adversary, the devil', 'a roaring lion', 'seeking

---

[1] No date, East London Tabernacle.

whom he may devour', 'whom resist'. And then we find 'suffer-ings' added. Put the two groupings of words side by side. Can you imagine anything more startling in the way of contrast? 'The devil', 'a roaring lion', 'suffering', 'adversary', 'God', 'grace', 'eternal glory', 'perfection'. Yes, it is on black velvet that this diamond pendant hangs, and the diamonds flash all the more brightly because of the exceeding darkness of the background. But now, having taken a glance at it, our eyes are more accustomed to the brilliance, so we will try to place the words. Up to this moment, perhaps, this text has been to some of you, as it was to me in studying it—a perfect shower of meteors—a cluster of bright flashing words. Now we will seek to put the words in order, and link them together.

And observe here that, though this text reads as a prayer, *it is really a promise,* and so it appears in the Revised Version. Instead of the first word being 'but', it should be 'and'. *'And* the God of all grace, who hath called us unto his eternal glory by Christ Jesus, after that ye have suffered a while'—now read—'shall himself perfect, stablish, strengthen, settle you.' It is not something that Peter asks for, but which, perhaps, may be denied, but it is the solemn promise of the Holy Ghost given through Peter that, though I have to meet the roaring devil, though I have daily to combat the power of hell that would devour and swallow me up, yet the God of all grace shall himself perfect, strengthen, and stablish me. In the previous verses the Holy Ghost has been telling us what *we* have to do. Now he tells us what *God* has promised to do, and, oh, brothers and sisters, what a marvellous difference this makes! We must never separate the things that God has joined together. If God says in one line, 'Work out your own salvation with fear and trembling', he says in the next, 'for it is God that worketh in you'. And so, if here I am told that I am to be sober and vigilant, and that I am to stand foot to foot with the adversary and resist a roaring devil, and I say, 'How can it be? It is more than I can do', he who bids me do it tells me what he will do: 'And he himself shall perfect, strengthen, and stablish you.' The words, you see, are beginning to fall into order. We are now getting the outline of this diamond pendant.

But there is one important point which I question whether many of you have seen, because in nine cases out of ten that sentence, 'after that ye have suffered a while', is linked with the last clause of the verse, whereas it belongs to the first; and if you look you will see what a difference it makes. People generally pause at the word 'Christ Jesus', and then they read, 'after ye have suffered a while make you perfect, stablish, strengthen you'. Indeed, then that last clause tells us, does it, of heaven's work, that after my sufferings are over the Lord is going to perfect me, and that it is in heaven that he is going to stablish and strengthen me? But, the moment that you put that little middle clause, 'after that ye have suffered a while', in its right place, the diamond pendant is seen clearly in all its exquisite symmetry and beauty. It is this: the God of all grace who hath called us, after that we have suffered a while, to his eternal glory, will himself, whilst we are suffering—during this little interval that lies between the grace and the glory—so sanctify the suffering, that it shall perfect, stablish, strengthen, settle us. The sufferings come between the grace and the glory. One hardly likes to use such a homely illustration, but I might almost call it 'heaven's sandwich'. There is grace: then there is a thin slice of suffering: then there is glory on the top of it. The God of all grace has called us to eternal glory, but between the call and the eternal glory there is just a little while of suffering; but during that little while of suffering the saint is not to be a loser, for the God of all grace shall perfect, stablish, strengthen, settle him. Though, when we commenced, we were almost blinded by the brilliancy of the text, I think that now we can make out clearly its outline and its setting.

Let us go into the subject a little. First of all we have to meditate on *the God of grace;* and, when we have done that, we must go a step further, and observe that he is *a God who calls unto his eternal glory*. And, when we have reached that point, we shall have to note, in conclusion, that *this God of grace allows a little interval of suffering before the glory*, and that this little interval, though full of painfulness, is also full of blessedness, for it leads to perfecting, stablishing, and strengthening.

I.—Who shall rise to the height of this first expression, 'THE GOD OF ALL GRACE'? What is intended by it? Something far more than a gracious God. It does not mean that God is gracious in his tendency, or simply gracious by his nature, but that he himself is the reservoir, the home, the source, the supply, of grace in all its manifestations. 'All grace'; that is all the grace that I need between these two points, the point where God finds me steeped in sin and dead in iniquity, and that point of eternal glory that he has sworn by himself he will bring me to. How much grace I need between these two! *He is the God of all the grace that I need from hell's mouth up to heaven's throne.* The streams of grace are many: the fountain head is one. He is 'the God of all grace'. Every sparkling rivulet, every flowing tributary, of grace springs from him. Need I recapitulate them to you? Divine choice with all its inscrutable mysteries. Redemption accomplished at Calvary's hill on a bloodstained cross by a dying Christ. Redemption? Ay, justification also in all its wondrous harmony between mercy and perfect equity. Justification? Yes, and regeneration too with its heaven-born purity, and its new-created tendencies within the soul. All these are covered by the word 'grace'. These things are only different manifestations of one and the same sublime attribute. But, when I mention these, I have only just touched the spray of the wave. There are deeps that lie beneath in this expression, 'the God of all grace', for it contains *all the graces* which the soul must possess before it can enter eternal glory.

I think that any child here could mention most of those graces that are absolutely requisite for entrance into the eternal glory. Most certainly there must be the grace of *repentance*. How can a man who repents not be saved? But God is the God of all grace. My sob for Christ comes from God himself. The very tear for sin is not an earth-born thing. It is heaven's own pearl that is strung upon the human eyelash. The cry of 'God be merciful to me' is a cry that comes down from heaven before ever it can break from my lip. 'The God of all grace.' But repentance must ever be followed by *faith*. I do not weep myself to Christ. I appropriate Christ by faith. But whence this grace of faith? It is the gift of God. Then there are other graces yet to be manifested. 'Faith worketh by *love*.' But love is born of God, for God is love, and if I love him it is because he first loved me. He is the God of all my graces. But no man can see the Lord apart from *holiness*. Without holiness shall no man enter into the glory. How am I to be holy? How can this poor, sin-stained, sin-ingrained man become holy? And the answer is that it is the Spirit of the Lord that worketh holiness; and so, whilst he is the God of all manifestations of grace, he is the God of all the graces that I possess.

But I have hardly begun yet with this enumeration. This text covers much more, for it includes *all the supplies of grace* that are needed along the road. It is a weary road: I need refreshing grace. It is a sorrowing path, because it is a sinful one: I need comforting grace. As a wandering sheep prone to go astray, I need restoring grace. Being weak as a babe, I need upholding grace. What do I not need? And yet, precious thought, everything that I, as a saint, can need from the moment of my new birth to that ecstatic instant when I stand before his eternal glory, without spot or wrinkle, lies centred in God. He is 'the God of all grace'. Do you not see, therefore, that God does not send his people unarmed into the battle? The word of command is not 'Go and fight the roaring devil, and get on as best you can.' If God tells me to fight the devil, he says, 'I will find all grace for you to do it.' If he says to me, 'Go meet an adversary that could devour you in a moment, and would', he also says, 'But I am able to perfect you, strengthen you, stablish you. I am the God of all grace.'

II.—I think that we may now leave this first point, although we have only just skimmed its surface. THIS GOD OF ALL GRACE CALLS US TO ETERNAL GLORY. Let us read the sentence slowly, that we may understand it: 'Who hath called us'—(it should be 'who hath called you')—'unto his eternal glory by Christ Jesus', or, as it should be rendered, '*in* Christ'.

Let us begin at the beginning. He has called you. Need I say that the call here is not the call that is ringing from this platform this morning? It is not intended to describe the call that comes from any preacher's lips. It is not the call of God's world-wide mercy to a fallen race. The call that is intended here is, as Archbishop Leighton beautifully puts it, that call which goes deeper than the ear, touches the heart within, throws open the door, and admits the Christ. And consequently you will find that the word 'called' becomes the title of the true Christian. Look at the references on this subject at your leisure. If you turn to the 1st chapter of Romans, you will find the saints there described as 'called of Christ Jesus'. In Romans 8:28, we read, 'All things work together for good to them that love God.' Who are they? 'The called according to his purpose.' It is a Scripture name for the saint. A man of God is one who has been called. But how is he called? It is 'unto his eternal glory *in* Christ'; not simply, mark you, for Christ's sake. That is true, but it is not the truth here taught. He has called us to eternal glory *in Christ*. He called Christ into glory, and, when he called Christ into glory, he called me, because I am in Christ. The call that I receive is a call that sounds in the Son's ear. It is a call 'to his glory'. Jesus looked up and said, 'Father, I will that they also whom thou hast given me be with me where I am, that they may behold my glory.' Where God calls the head he calls all the members. And the call to eternal glory is the call that comes to us by virtue of our oneness with the Lord Jesus Christ. We share his blessedness.

For a moment pause here. Do you see what this teaches? There is no getting to eternal glory apart from Christ. God does not call anyone to eternal glory except 'in Christ'. If any of you are hoping to enter into eternal glory by virtue of the 'universal fatherhood', you will find that it will drop you into perdition. The only call unto eternal glory is in Christ. It is as a member of his body that I share his glory. Heaven is his. I have no merits, but he deserves all. He deserves everything that the eternal Father can give him. And so Christ says, 'I will that my redeemed share with me that glory which is mine.' It is 'the called in Christ Jesus'.

And what is the call to? To glory. I must confess that I looked at that word until I could not see it for the tears that came into my eyes. 'Called unto glory.' Glory? What have I to do with glory? I seem altogether out of court for glory. Glory? Glory for me? You might as well speak about putting a king's crown on a sweep's head. What connection can there be between me and glory? But, my brethren, because it seems too good for us to receive we must not think that it is too good for God to give. The call is to glory, *and to nothing short of it*. I know not whether I am speaking this morning to some dear Arminian friends who rather delight in the thought that you may start on the road to glory, and then be left in the middle of it to perish. Do you see that this call is not a call merely to start for glory? It is a call to glory. It is not a call to two-thirds of the road. It is a call to eternal glory. Thirty odd years ago I listened, and I heard the call of God, and, oh, it called me into such sorrow for sin; but I found that the call did not end there, for when I had reached conviction of sin I found that God was still calling me. The call came from further away, and I went on, until I came to 'a place called Calvary', and I thought, 'Surely, the call has come from here.' But after I had looked and gazed upon Christ and entered into peace, I found that the call still sounded far ahead. It had brought me to Calvary, but it came from beyond there. It came from the throne in the glory. And then I found that when God called me as a sinner he did not call me simply to repent or to believe. He called me unto his eternal glory, and that is the purpose of his call. Are you downcast this morning? Are you depressed in spirit? Why, God is calling you unto his eternal glory. Shame on us that we are ever anything else than rejoicing. We have a call to glory, and nothing less. Yes, but hitherto we have only been fluttering round this word 'glory'. What do you understand by it? Does he say, 'He has called us unto glory'? No, it does not say that. It says, 'He has called us unto HIS glory.' What is his glory? Moses said, 'Show me thy glory', and Jehovah said, 'I will cause my goodness to pass before thee.' Then, do you not see, God's glory is his holiness; and if I am called unto his glory I am—amazing thought—called unto infinite and perfect holiness. Oh, heaven would not be heaven if there were a stain of sin upon one of the golden pavements. Heaven would not be heaven if there were a thought of sin passing through the brain. Heaven would not be heaven if there were a moment of defilement there. He has called us unto HIS glory, the glory of his perfect holiness, that glory which overwhelms archangels as they sing, 'Holy, holy, holy, Lord God of hosts.' But God's glory is himself. There is nothing more glorious about his glory than himself. The only way in which God can glorify himself is to reveal himself. He is his own glory, and when the shekinah light burned of old in the tabernacle, the glory of the Lord appeared. It was the out-flashing of God. And so, when God calls you to his glory, he calls you to himself. He says, 'Come up, poor weary blood-washed sinner. Come up into my embrace; come and live in my bosom.

Let the everlasting burnings of Jehovah be thy couch. Come lave thy spirit in the eternal blaze of deity. Come, be at home with me.' It is a call unto his glory. It is a call to dwell in his immediate presence. It is a call to pass into his light, for God is light. But can you tell me all that the word 'glory' covers? In the ordinary acceptation of the word you say of a departed saint, 'Ah, he has gone to glory', and what does 'glory' mean? That one word 'glory' includes all the angels, cherubim and seraphim; it includes all the harps of heaven; it covers all joy, all blessing, all bliss. God has called us unto his eternal *glory*. But this is only the beginning of the theme. We have left untouched one infinite word. He says that he has called us unto his *eternal* glory. You have to put the word eternal into the scale. It is not a call for an age or for a millennium. It is his eternal glory. Oh, fools that we are to weep our eyes out over earth's sorrows, and to grumble our spirits into wretchedness because of a passing moment of care! It is eternal glory. The spirit sinks before the very word. When myriads upon myriads of ages have passed, we shall be only in the infancy of glory then; and when a myriad myriad ages more have gone we shall be no further advanced. It is simply endless. This is what God means to do for you. He means to bring you into his own eternal glory.

III.—And now our third point is that HE ALLOWS A LITTLE INTERVAL OF SUFFERING WHICH IS ITSELF FULL OF BLESSING. Ah, we too often want to leave that bit out, 'after that ye have suffered a while'. The call comes, but the glory does not come immediately after the call. I remember that, when I found peace thirty odd years ago, I wished that the Lord would take me to glory then and there. Yes, the birds of Paradise all want to fly off at once into their nests. But God says, 'No, I have called you unto my eternal glory.' The glory is quite safe. You shall have it, but it shall come to you 'after that you have suffered a while'. Then, brothers and sisters, carry away this thought, that *the suffering is part of the call, as well as the glory*. It is not a haphazard thing that comes in. It is all part of the plan. When God calls you to glory, he calls you to come to glory through a little while of suffering. How this takes away all the bitterness and acidity of one's sorrows. Does it not? I know that some of you are weighted with care. Humanly speaking it would be far easier to weep than to sing; but how this transforms all grief. It is no chance work. It is part of the road to the eternal glory. It is just as much included in the plan as all the rest.

And then, you see, it says that it is only a *little* while. 'After that ye have suffered a little.' So it is in the Revised Version. Really the word 'while' is not there. It is 'after ye have suffered a little'; and you, can choose, if you like, whether it means degree or duration. 'After ye have suffered a little.' Why, the heaviest sorrow is but little if you compare it with the weight of glory. Or, if you take it to mean duration, what a little while the suffering lasts if you put it alongside of his eternal glory!

You say, 'But why can I not go to heaven at once? Why should there be this interlude of suffering between the grace and the glory?' The answer is found in the last line of our text. He himself will 'make you perfect, stablish, strengthen, settle you'. He will do it through this little interval of suffering. He will perfect you. Now, do not run away with the idea that I am preaching 'perfection'; and yet I am. But what sort of perfection? You have to understand the word. People often take a word and run away with it, just as a trout catches hold of a fly and gets hooked, and is not very much advantaged thereby. You may snap hold of this word 'perfect', and run away, and say, 'Ah, then I may expect to be perfect whilst I am on earth.' Of course you may; only the word here translated 'perfect' means 'to repair'. It is precisely the same word that you find when you read that the disciples were mending their nets, and it means to finish, or to put into repair. You will find that when

Paul writes to the Thessalonians he says, 'That I may perfect that which is lacking in your faith.' There is a little bit of a rent in it and I just want to come and mend that little hole. Ah, there is nothing about us that is not imperfect. There are many little rents in us, and the Lord allows us to go through this little while of suffering so that he may repair the imperfections. *Bad as you are, brother, you would be worse if you had less trouble.* There is not here, today, a child of God who is not the richer and the holier for the little while of suffering. God passes his children through the interlude of suffering to repair the imperfect.

The next word is 'stablish', and that implies fixity. Oh, we are very prone to fluctuation. I know that some of you shift like a weathercock from one doctrine to another. There are some of you here who have at present so little stability that you come and hear the Word of God expounded here in the morning, and then run away to hear something quite the opposite in the evening, and manage somehow to enjoy them both. Well, God loves his children a great deal too well to allow them always to remain shifty and unstable; and so he passes them through this little while of suffering, and they gradually get more and more stablished and fixed in faith and holy resolve. Trouble weights men in a very blessed sense. I know that it grievously weights the heart. But *sometimes nothing but a heavy heart will give weight to a character,* and so God says, 'I cannot let that light and frivolous child remain like a piece of thistledown floating at the dictation of every breath of air. I must pass him through a little while of suffering.' That is stablishing.

The word 'settle' does not appear in the Revised. The last word there is 'strengthen', and the meaning of the word is 'made powerful to resist attack'. There is the devil. He is roaring. More than that: he has mighty paws and terrible claws. And who among us can enter into the lists with him? You fight the devil, man? Do not ever make a joke about the devil. The man that jokes about the devil has the devil nearer to him than he imagines. Do you think you can resist the great adversary? Never! But the Lord steps in, and says, 'If I bid you meet the roaring lion, I will pass you through a little season of suffering which shall repair and stablish you, and put spiritual thews and sinews into you, so that in my strength you may overcome.'

Brethren, what then is left for us to do other than to say with Peter, 'To him be glory and dominion for ever'? Where else can we place the glory? It is cut completely from under our feet, for God is the God of all the grace that we possess. He calls us to his own eternal glory. Then if I am saved from sin and called to eternal bliss, all that I can do during 'the little while' is to look up and say, 'Unto him be all the praise and dominion, age upon age, throughout all eternity. Amen and amen.'

UNTO HIM BE GLORY[1]

*Unto him be glory in the church by Christ Jesus
throughout all ages, world without end. Amen.*
Ephesians 3:21.

OUR text is the divine climax of a doxology which is itself the crown of the most stupendous prayer ever uttered even by that prince amongst pleaders, the Apostle Paul. Keeping your eye upon the passage, you will observe that from the 14th verse we are led upward as by an Alpine guide. We ascend from height to height, and the ever-growing glory of the view overawes and overwhelms us. At last we stand upon the dizzy eminence of that 19th verse, 'Filled with all the fulness of God.' From that altitude we look down upon the previous petitions as upon lower mountain ranges which are dwarfed now by the exceeding height on which we stand; and yet each one of those petitions, when viewed from the base of the prayer, seemed to tower above us like a Himalayan peak. Would you know the exceeding height of our text, it is necessary to go down into the valley, and allow this Alpine guide to take us up stage by stage. We commence at the 16th verse, and he leads us up to the first range. 'That he would grant you, according to the riches of his glory, to be strengthened with might by his Spirit in the inner man.' O Paul, thou hast pioneered us to a wondrous position here! What fresh breezes blow over this mountain top, 'Strengthened with

[1] January 1, 1888, East London Tabernacle.

might by the Spirit in the inner man.' What a view the soul gains from this elevation! But our guide points upwards, and mounts to a yet higher stage, 'That Christ may dwell in your hearts by faith.' He prays that I may know the habitual residence of Jesus Christ within my soul. I can now look down upon the first mountain range, though at the commencement of my ascent that seemed to be a dizzy height. But still the apostle says, 'Follow me higher yet: comprehending the breadth, and length, and depth, and height and knowing the love of Christ which passeth knowledge.' My guide has now taken me up into the blue ether itself. I feel that I am already in sky-land. Oh, the purity of the air that is breathed on this height, an apprehension of all the love of Christ to me, in its height, and depth, and length and breadth! Whilst enraptured, I look around upon the out-spreading scene, he says, 'Higher yet!' and he leads me to another range, which towers overhead—'Filled with all the fulness of God.' From this point all the other requests, each one of which seemed to be a mountain in itself, become dwarfed into lowly hills. But I see that there is still towering high above me one remaining peak, and it rears its awful head so high that even the height on which I stand seems as nothing. It is that glittering peak of the 20th verse. Shall we attempt its ascent? We may surely do so if Paul, as guide, will only lead the way. We start from 'Filled with all the fulness of God', and we ascend to 'Now unto him that is able to do more than we ask.' Ah, I have asked God that I might be filled with all the fulness, and now he is able to do more than I ask. But have I gained the summit? My guide says, 'No; up to a yet higher stage: able to do more than we ask or think.' I can think more than I can ask, and God can do more than I can think. This is an awful height, but still the apostle says, 'Up; you have not reached the summit yet, for he is able to do *abundantly* more than we ask or think.' Oh, apostle of the Lord Jesus Christ, is not this the topmost pinnacle—'abundantly more than we ask or think'? 'No', he replies; 'there is a higher peak still. He is able to do exceeding abundantly—not only abundantly, but exceeding abundantly above what we ask or think.' Is this the climax? 'No, there is one other pinnacle. He is able to do not only abundantly, and not only exceeding abundantly, more than we ask or think, but exceeding abundantly above all we ask or think. He is able to do not only above one or two thoughts, but above all my highest thoughts. Now we stand on the very topmost peak of this stupendous prayer—a prayer crowned by this doxology, and, standing on the heaven-high summit, we shout with the apostle, 'Unto him be glory in the church by Christ Jesus throughout all ages, world without end. Amen.'

We have selected this closing verse of the 3rd of Ephesians as the motto for the church for 1888, because it contains all that is worth living for, all that is worth labouring for, all that is worth suffering for, and all that is worth dying for. 'Unto him be glory.' As the Lord liveth, I know of nothing that is worthy of life with all its powers, life with all its activities, and life with all its sufferings, save this—'Unto him be glory.' He who lives for less than this lives for that which is unworthy of his manhood and his God.

Let us note, then, that we have here, first the melody: 'Unto him be glory.' Then, the harp that is to sound it forth—the church. And then, the duration of its echoes. How long shall the strings vibrate this melody? 'Throughout all generations, world without end.' And our soul adds, 'Amen.'

Let us, then, note that we have first *the melody:* 'Unto him be glory.' Being a note of praise it necessarily has 'him' for its theme. Rapturous melody can only be employed concerning God. When the saint takes up his music book and begins to sing—when the soul inspired of God begins to pour out rapturous expressions of praise, there is no need to ask, 'Of whom does he sing?' If a child of God praises he must praise God, for God only deserves to be praised; and the saint feels that in the matter of adoration he is shut up unto his God. The *Miserere* belongs unto us, for unto us belong shame and confusion of face, for we have sinned. But the *Gloria in Excelsis* of the child of God must have God himself for its theme. Believer, have you not often realized this? All song is taken out of your mouth unless God be the subject of it. Can you sing about yourself? Have you one high-sounding note for your own attainments? Have you one adoring sentence for your own achievements? Rather, do you not feel that, when you turn to yourself, the saddest dirge that music can convey is the most appropriate? But when the timbrels are taken up, and when the joyous notes of praise are heard, it 'goes without saying' that it is unto him the praise ascends. All the birds of praise fly upwards. When they are allowed to escape from the cage of a saint's mouth they never wheel low to and fro over earth, but they always beat their way straight up at once—'Unto him, unto him, unto him.' Praise knows no other direction than an upward flight.

For a moment give me your careful attention, and you will observe that it is absolutely necessary that the saint's praise should be 'unto him'. If it were not so he would be *out of harmony with the whole of nature*. Before man existed nature sang this song, though in a lower key. Before ever man raised his voice to God in adoration, nature broke the silence. There is a voice that goes forth even from inanimate creation, and it is 'unto him', for 'the heavens declare the glory of God, and the firmament showeth his handiwork. Day unto day uttereth speech.' And the burden of the speech of nature is, 'Praise be unto him.' With a splendid touch of poetry the psalmist says, 'Praise him, ye stars of light'; and it needs no very vivid imagination to conceive the stars sending back the answer, 'David, you need not tell us to do that. We cannot do anything else. As we walk in our courses we celebrate him. There is not a point of light in God's heaven which does not glitter to his glory.' In the Psalms again we are told that the trees of the forest clap their hands, and the hills rejoice and leap for very joy before the Lord. Old ocean is not silent. A deep diapason note comes from her awful mouth, for the waves roar out their doxology to him. Those thundering, foaming, rolling masses with their shaggy manes praise Jehovah. Were not the saint to have him as the matter of his song, he would be positively lower in his praise than nature. He would be a discordant string in God's great harp. If he praises, it must be unto him.

And yet, again, if the saint's song were not unto him it would *clash with the songs of heaven.* You know the songs which the angels sing. They gave earth a rehearsal on that first Christmas morning and their song awoke the echoes and made the welkin ring with 'Glory to God in the highest! On earth peace, good will to men.' If I say not, 'Unto him be glory', my song clashes with the melodies of the angels, for they know no glory save glory unto God. Seraphim and cherubim continually do cry, 'Holy, holy, holy, Lord God of Sabaoth.' The redeemed raise their note, and what is that? Listen! 'Unto him.' That is the key-note—'Unto him that loved us and washed us from our sins in his own blood, and made us kings and priests unto God and his Father—unto him be glory.' Yes, there is a sweet necessity that the melody of the saint's song should be 'Unto him.' Oh, may God give us such loving hearts, such consecrated souls, such sanctified tongues, that the note of our every-day life shall be, 'Unto him.' There is the melody.

Now, I want you very specially to note *the harp that is to sound forth this melody.* 'Unto him be glory *in the church.'*

There is a very notable alteration in the Revised Version. I do not purpose dwelling on it, but I like in all things to be fair to the word of God, and therefore I remind you that this passage may be read, 'Unto him be glory in the church *and in* Christ Jesus.' Ah, yes, in him the glory of God is perfect. To carry out our metaphor, *Jesus is the one perfect harp* that sounds forth the glory of God, without one string being a fraction out of tune. Jesus is himself the chief singer in the glory, for we are told in the 22nd Psalm that he says, 'My praise shall be of thee. In the midst of the congregation will I praise thee.' Jesus Christ praises the Father perfectly.

But praise is to be *in the church,* as well as in Christ Jesus. Let me ask you this question: If God does not receive a tribute of glory from the church, where shall he look for it? If the church yields not a revenue of praise unto God, what harvest-field shall he reap? The world pays God no rent, no matter how he may lavish his kindness upon earth. The natural man gives him no return. There is a deep conspiracy on earth to withhold from the Lord of the Manor the rental of glory due unto his holy name. But the redeemed of the Lord must not, cannot, remain silent. If our lips are dumb, whose lips shall be vocal? The church is God's family, and who shall speak well of the Father if not the sons and the daughters? Where can the Father expect to receive a tribute of praise if not from the lips of his own children? To change the metaphor, is not the church his own vineyard? Does not he say concerning the church, 'A vineyard of red wine. I, the Lord, do keep it. I will water it every moment. Lest any hurt it I will keep it night and day'? He has dug about it, and walled it, and put up a tower in it. Has he not a right to seek fruit for his toil? If he find none from his vineyard, shall he look to the desert for it? O church of God, thy Lord and Master has a right to expect that his praise shall ring in sweetest strains from every string his grace has put in tune. Art thou not his own blood-bought? If the church, which he has purchased with his blood, sings not 'Unto him be glory', how guilty is the silence! The church is his temple, and every living stone in that temple may well shout, 'Glory unto him who hath reared his sanctuary of stones cut out of nature's quarry!' As David sings in his 29th Psalm, 'And in his temple doth every one speak of his glory', or, as it is beautifully rendered in the

Revised Version, 'In his temple everything saith, Glory.'

But it is much easier to deal in generalities than to make a home application. My deepest wish, therefore, is to get as close as possible to your heart and my own, whilst I dwell, for a few moments, on the thought that, as part of the one church, *we must raise the strain.* We must see to it, beloved, that our portion of the church is not barren in this respect. What shall it profit us that all the rest of the church raises the anthem, 'Unto him be glory', if there be silence so far as the church in this Tabernacle is concerned? My soul longs with an unutterable longing that this should become the only one matter about which there is a jealousy in our borders—Who shall praise him most? Who shall sink lowest that he may be exalted? Oh, brothers and sisters, I beseech you as pastor, as friend, as brother, and, I trust, as teacher sent of God, to let everything else be reckoned by you as trivial and as unworthy of your thought and time, compared with this. Is God being glorified in our midst? Is there ascending unto him from the sanctuary a perpetual song of praise? I imagine for a moment that no member in the two thousand of us has any other ambition, any other wish, or any other aim, than this, 'Unto him be glory.' Would it not be at once the death of all self-seeking? Oh what a revolution there would be! How all petty jealousies would die out before this one overmastering ambition! It would save us from all clashing one with another. Think of every member of this church aiming at nothing, caring for nothing, praying for nothing, and troubled about nothing, but that the Lord should be glorified in this church. I do not think that there would be then any fear of A running up against B, or of C clashing with D, or of D getting in the way of E. Like the seraphim Ezekiel saw, born in the fire-cloud and them-selves a flame, we should go every one straight forward. Whither the Spirit was to go they went, and they turned not when they went. No clashing, no confusion, no hindering one another. They were all flying to one goal, which was the glory of their God. Oh, if the day might come when every member of this church should be eaten up with a passion for the glory of God in our midst, every little bickering would die, every scheme for self-exaltation would be swamped, and brother would grip brother's hand and say, 'Let God alone be magnified.' One would not say to the other, 'I think I have more right to that position than you have.' No, but all would cry, 'Unto him be glory.' The Lord hasten the day!

How is God glorified in the church? The great honour of Israel was that the Lord made that nation the custodian of the oracles of God. When Paul asks the question, 'What advantage then hath the Jew?' he answers, 'Much every way, chiefly because that unto them were committed the oracles of God.' The high privilege of the church of God today is the stewardship of the truth. Then, if I pray, 'Unto him be glory in the church', I am virtually praying the Lord to maintain truth in the borders of the church; for, if the truth of God be not kept inviolate and held in sacred reverence, there is no glory in the church. If the day should ever come (which God forbid!) that there should be a gospel preached on this platform which has not a clear unmistakable blood mark upon it—if the day should ever come in the which a reference to the word of God should not be considered by this church a satisfactory argument or proof—if the day should ever dawn in the which the word of God was tampered with and moulded and altered, though this place might be filled as it is filled tonight, and though the world might say, 'Behold, a great success', yet 'Ichabod' would be written upon its walls. Unto him be glory in the church *by fidelity unto the truth.*

Yes, and the glory of God in the church lies also *in the conversion of souls.* He is more glorified in the conversion of a little boy than in the creation of a world. It is impossible for me to pray honestly, 'Unto him be glory in the church', unless I desire above everything that sinners should be saved. Fellow church-members, hold, with a grip that nothing can relax, the truth that no church is prosperous where conversions do not abound. If God is to be magnified and glorified in the church, there must be a constant succession of converts coming forward and saying, 'I am the Lord's.' Oh, if conversions are wanting, the glory of the church has departed! 'Unto him be glory.' Yes, in the salvation of the drunkard. 'Unto him be glory.' Yes, in the reclamation of the fallen. 'Unto him be glory.' Yes in the tears of the penitent, in the sobs of the contrite, and in the fresh joy of the young convert. All this is included in the aspiration for God's glory.

'Unto him be glory.' Yes, *by whatever instrumentality*. We are not on right ground, brethren and sisters, unless we are prepared to say this. There is a tendency for us to put it thus: 'Unto him be glory by me in the church.' Or, perhaps, loving and devoted church-members may be tempted to look towards the pastor, and say, 'Unto him be glory in the church by our pastor.' No, no; there must be no restrictions. 'Unto him be glory by any instrumentality which the Lord may be pleased to use.' Unto him be glory, whoever may be the chosen vessel. 'Unto him be glory', whoever may be laid low. 'Unto him be glory' at all cost, all hazard, all pain, all suffering, for his glory is cheap at any cost.

I want you, brethren and sisters, before God to know no other ambition concerning the work of God in this Tabernacle than this. I pray you, forget yourselves; forget me. Let no loving association, or years of service, or bonds of affection that may have entwined about us, warp the prayer. It is, 'Unto him be glory.' Lord, choose thy own way, thy own method, thy own instrumentality. Put us aside, or bid us remain, but unto him be glory, and our soul shall be content. This I think is the very essence of Paul's exclamation.

In conclusion. *How long are the echoes of this melody to last?* Is it to be only during the evening of the first Sunday of a new year? Only to the end of a week or of a month? Listen: 'Unto him be glory in the church by Christ Jesus, throughout'—as it should be literally rendered—'all the generations of the age of the ages.'

Do you catch the thought? It is that this magnificent ascription, 'Unto him be glory', is to go rolling on from generation to generation. It means that our children shall sing it when our lips are silent. It means that the son shall take up the song where the father broke it off. It means that the daughter shall continue the song at the note following that which died away on the mother's lip. So shall it be from generation unto generation, until Jesus comes; and then unto him shall be glory in that day when he shall appear and his saints shall be caught up to meet him. In that day when the ransomed dust shall be quickened, and shall come out of its long imprisonment to enjoy the blessings of the first resurrection; in that day when he shall come to be admired in his saints and in all them that believe; in that day when with his iron rod he lays low all rebels and asserts his divine sovereignty; in that day when heaven and earth is set on a blaze; in that day when there is a new heaven and a new earth, the song shall still be ringing, 'Unto him be glory!' In that day when he shall have delivered up unto the Father the key of government, in that eternal day that knows no change, rolling ceaselessly down the ages and gathering volume as it rolls, where shall still be heard the solemn anthem of tonight, 'Unto him be glory.'

Brethren and sisters, we have been singing tonight a song that is never to die out! This is a thought which makes my soul burn with joy. When we sang at the commencement of the service the glowing hymn, 'All hail the power of Jesu's name', we sang a song that shall never tone down into silence. When we sang just now, 'Come, saints, and adore Him, come bow at His feet', we only sang the first bar of an anthem that is to roll on for ever, throughout all ages, world without end.

Do you marvel that the apostle said 'Amen'? Our hearts add

their 'Amen' to his. God grant that among the eternal choristers who maintain this undying song, there may be found all of you who are present in this Tabernacle this night, with your sons and your daughter, for Jesu's sake! Amen.

THE HEART'S CRY AFTER GOD[1]

My heart and my flesh crieth out for the living God.
Psalm 84:2.

IT is a matter of very little consequence who penned this psalm, or at what exact date it was written. It is enough for us that it is a psalm which has set forth the desires of God's people in all ages, and it is a sweet song which the saint specially loves to sing when the day of worship has come round again. It is pre-eminently the Lord's Day psalm—the hymn that well becomes the multitude assembled for worship. But, with regards to the writer, we may remark that although no name is given, yet the psalm is so Davidic (to coin a word) that you feel David must have been the penman. There is a peculiar ring about the composition which betrays the authorship of the sweet singer of Israel; and, as a well-known commentator on the Psalms has said, 'It smells of the mountain heather, and the lone places of the wilderness where King David must have often lodged during his many wars.' One can feel that it is written by a man of God who has not seen the inside of the sanctuary for some little while. Through stress of circumstances he has been a fugitive from his home—maybe from his native land; and as he rests on mountain side, or sits in quiet glen, he begins to think of the time when he went up with the multitude that kept holy day, until he breaks out in the fervent exclamation, 'How amiable are thy tabernacles, O Lord of hosts!' It is not a question

[1] March 30, 1879, East London Tabernacle.

asked; it is an exclamation made. 'How amiable!'—beyond all description—outside the poet's power to tell. The sanctuary is just one of the many mercies the worth of which is never known until they are lost. I suppose there is nothing which you or I have on earth which is fully prized until taken away for a season. Then our eves are opened to see how large a portion of our life it occupied, and how great an amount of our happiness was yielded by it. There are worshipping with us this morning some who now find the sanctuary a dearer place than they ever imagined possible. During the weeks you were laid aside, sir; during those weary days when you thought of the company going up to the Lord's house, and sighed because you were not able to join them, did you not come to the conclusion that, after all, there was a charm about public worship, a delight in the songs of the multitude, and an exquisite pleasure in the gathering together of the hosts of the Lord's ransomed company, beyond what you had ever previously imagined? The whole of this psalm is the uttered desire of a soul for public worship, and, as the psalmist muses upon the matter, his language burns, and he goes as far as it is possible for man to go, for he begins to envy the very sparrows their privilege. I think I see the royal writer. There he is, an exile from home, for a while camping out, and he thinks, 'I wish I were a bird! Here am I, governor of the land, and yet I cannot go up to the tabernacle; but lo, there is not a sparrow but can fly into the holy place.' And then he remembers how he has even seen the swallows make their nests under the eaves of the altar, and he covets their quiet and holy abode. 'Oh, blessed are they that dwell in thy house! Blessed are those who keep the doors, yea, the menials who sweep out the sacred courts, and those who light the candles of the sanctuary!'

If you look into the psalm, you will see that it would be impossible for him to use stronger language than he does to express his desire, for in the second verse, from which we have selected our text, he says, 'My soul *longeth*'. The word in the original is stronger than that. The literal translation would, perhaps, be more after this sort: 'My soul hath grown pale. It is ready to faint away for the courts of the Lord.' Just as intense desire will eat into the strength of our manhood, and put a premature paleness upon the cheek, and earlier furrows on the brow, 'so', says the psalmist, 'my soul is literally pining away to be found once more with the Lord's people'. As if that were not enough, he adds, 'Yea, even fainteth'; and the idea there is 'consumed' with desire. And then he goes one step further, 'My heart and my flesh crieth out for the living God.' They can contain their desires no longer, and so my tongue maketh this wilderness to echo with my call. I cry until these rugged mountains send back the sorrowful notes of my voice. 'My heart and my flesh crieth out for the living God.' You will see that, after all, the psalmist reaches the climax of desire, not when he speaks of the sanctuary, but of God himself. 'My heart and my flesh crieth out'—not for the tabernacle—not for the services of the priesthood there—not for the multitudinous sacrifices and burnt offerings, but for God—the living God. He only rightly prizes the sanctuary who prizes it in proportion as a living God is found within its walls.

Let us this morning dwell for a short time on the desire of the heart and flesh, as expressed by the psalmist. We will note first, *the nature of this desire:* 'the living God'. Then we will ask you to observe, *the strength of this desire:* 'my heart and my flesh crieth out for God'; and then, if we have time, we will note, lastly, *the comfortable assurance that this desire may give us.* If you and I can say, 'My heart and my flesh crieth out to God', it shows that we belong to David's tribe. There must be something of the grace of God in us, or we should never know such longing.

I. Let us observe then, first, THE DESIRE OF HEART AND FLESH—
THE LIVING GOD. It is old Master Sibbes, one of the sweetest of
the Puritanical writers, who well observes that the desires of the
heart are the best proofs of saintship; and if a man wishes to know
whether he is really a saint or no, he can very soon find out by
putting his finger upon the pulse of his desires, for those are things
that never can be counterfeit. You may counterfeit words; you may
counterfeit actions; but you cannot counterfeit desires. You cannot
always tell a Christian by his actions; for sometimes true Christians act in a very ugly style, and sometimes those who are not
Christians act in a very beautiful way, and hypocrites often act the
best. The whole of a hypocrite's life may be a simple counterfeit.
Nor are our words always a true test. Of course, a hypocrite will
lie in his throat; and often the most beautiful experience, as far as
language goes, is the experience that falls from the lips of a man
whose heart knows nothing about the grace of God. And, even
with no hypocrisy in us, our language is not a very safe test. It is
possible to mix with God's children until you pick up a sort of
Christian dialect, and talk of others' experiences as though they
were your own. Just as a man sojourning in a foreign country will
learn a good deal of the language of its inhabitants by simply
hearing it talked, so it is possible to dwell among Christians until
their language is in great measure acquired. Talking a language
does not constitute a nationality. But there is one thing which
cannot be picked up or counterfeited, and that is a desire. Let me
know my desire, then do I know myself; for I can no more counterfeit a desire than I can counterfeit fire. I think it is the same old
Puritan who says, 'Dost thou want to know what thou art? Go ask
thy desires, and they will tell thee. Dost thou wish to know where
thou art? See whither thy desires tend.' A good action may be done
without any love to that action; and, on the other hand, an evil
may be avoided—not from any hatred to that evil. The good action

may be done from an impure motive; the evil may be avoided simply from a selfish motive; but the desire of the soul—that is the immediate issue of the heart, and let me find my desire, then do I find myself. A caged bird cannot fly: does it therefore cease to be a bird? No; that it does not fly is because it is in a cage. Open the door: see, now, how quickly it darts through the opening, and flies, skimming through the air, heavenward. It has the bird's nature. It had the desire for flight even when the cruel wires kept it in. And so is it with the child of God. Often does he get caged, and if you were to judge simply by appearances, you would say, 'Surely he has not the nature of the Christian within.' Only open the door. Only give him a chance of flight; you will see then that, after all, the desire of his soul has been towards God, for, in the language of my text, he says, 'My heart and my flesh crieth out for the living God.'

Having noted, then, that the desire of a man is the best proof of his saintship, let us go a step further, and observe that the desire of the true saint is after God himself. 'My heart and my flesh crieth out for—*for God.*' Oh, here is a marvel of grace! Surely it is unnecessary to go farther than this in order to prove that, when a man is converted, he receives altogether a new nature! He *must* be a new creature in Christ Jesus! Fancy!—the desire of a man's heart finding expression in the words—'for God'. Scripture tells me that poor human nature wishes anything rather than God, for 'there is none that seeketh after God'; and, so far from desiring God, the natural heart would like to do away with him; and as he cannot do away with the throne of God in heaven, he seeks to abolish the throne of God from his mind, and, therefore, tries to forget God. If the natural man can banish God from his thoughts and from his reckonings, he will; and, therefore, if I can honestly say before the Lord this morning, 'My desire is for God', I need no other proof —no other magnificent demonstration—that there is a something wrought in me which is not of the world. It is this which puts the line of demarcation between the real saint and the counterfeit. A man who is born of God can not do without God.

Now, I want you to note that this desire swallows up all others. Supposing, as in all probability is the case, that David is the penman of this psalm; see how beautifully this thought comes out. The desire for God drowns all others. I can imagine that when he penned this psalm he was out on one of the many wars that occupied him, or else, maybe, a fugitive before his own son Absalom. Any way, we know he was away from the courts of the sanctuary, and yet I do not find him saying, 'My heart and my flesh crieth out for my home.' Yet David was essentially a home man, for he always returned, when he could, to bless his household. He was certainly a man with plenty of patriotism in his heart, but I do not hear him saying, 'My heart and my flesh crieth out for Jerusalem.' No, nor even for the sanctuary itself. His soul longed for it; but it was not the edifice. It was not the costly service. It was not the priesthood. It was not the reared altar. It was not the sacrifice. It was God himself for whom his soul cried out. Methinks there is a lesson here to many who are devotees either to a building or to a style of worship. My dear friend, if you really have the grace of God in your heart, all that will concern you is to have God in the service. You may, of course, have your likes and dislikes; you prefer one style of building to another; but it will be to you a matter of supreme indifference whether you worship in a place with a steeple or without. Much as some of us may object to steeple-houses, we would sooner far worship in a steeple-house, and have God, than in this tabernacle if we had not a sense of his presence. But who, on the other hand, would not rather worship in the plainest building that could be put up, with bare whitewashed walls, and have the Lord, than worship in the grandest cathedral that the art of man or the wealth of a nation ever produced, and yet lack the presence of a living God? All these mere externals, beloved, are of very, very little worth. Choose your building if you like; but after you have reared it, think but little of it. It is the God in the building who must be the object of the soul's delight. And as for the order of service, I care not. Only give me a service which has plenty of God in it. If hymns are sung that praise him, I mind not whether they be long, short, or common metre, exquisite in composition, or homely rhymes. If a sermon only brings me up to God, I mind not whether it be preached with polished periods or in rough, rugged sentences. If the service only leads me nearer to a living God, you may begin with the sermon and leave off with a hymn, or begin with a hymn and leave off with the sermon. All these mere *etceteras* are nothing. It is 'My heart and my flesh crieth out for God', for nothing less than God can satisfy the craving of a believer's soul. There is a hunger in the heart of the saint which only God himself can satisfy. Thou mayest fill its mouth with everything thou canst think of, and it will yet hunger and cry out for 'God! God! God!' If you are really a believer—a saved man—the world cannot make you content, let it try its utmost. If all the wealth of the universe were yours, and all the honours that society can give were lying at your feet—if everything a natural heart can wish for were in your possession, you would be as wretched as hell with it all if you had not a living God by your side. If, on the other hand, you are a child of God, and walking in the light of his countenance, though trade may be bad—though children may be sick—though sorrows may come like Atlantic billows one after another, in ceaseless roll, you will yet be able to say, 'My soul rejoiceth in God.' He who hath the divine presence, and nothing else, yet knows he is rich to all the intents of bliss. He that has all things else, but lacks the realized presence of his God, feels unutterably poor. All the experiences of the Christian resolve themselves into this: 'My heart and my flesh crieth out for God.'

There may be some one who says, 'How do you account for this?' Well, I think there are three things quite sufficient in themselves to account for this desire God-ward; and the first and chief is that *every saint has within his breast that which is actually born of God, and therefore it cries out after its own Father*. It is no figure of speech —no symbol—no type—when we read in the Gospel of John that we are 'born of God'. It is a positive fact. There never was a more actual or real birth in any home than there is within the breast when the Spirit of God comes to a man in regenerating power. There is a new nature begotten of God by the incorruptible seed of the word. There is something within the believer's breast which nature never put there—which self did not put there—which the world did not put there. It comes directly from God, and has a divine parentage. Do you marvel, then, that this holy thing which is born of God is always tending towards its original? It must. You cannot show me anything in nature but what tends to its original.

Water will always try to rise to the level of its spring. Fire will ever flash upwards, because, in the first instance, it came from on high. The sun's rays long buried in those submerged forests, and imprisoned in coal, will leap upward to their source in tongues of fire the moment their dungeon door is opened. And child of God, you and I have that within the breast which is restless until it reaches its original. Born of God, I must fly to God. The new nature he has begotten can never rest short of him, and so heart and flesh crieth out for God. This accounts for the misery of a backslider. I have often been astonished when such have asked me so simple a question as 'How is it, sir, I am so miserable? I feel as if I were being torn in two.' Of course you do. The new nature never dies out when once it is within a man, however much it may be slighted and neglected. There it is in the heart, crying, 'God! God! God! God!' and there is the old nature shouting with loud voice, 'The world! the world! the world! the world!' and the unhappy man is dragged between the two, the new nature struggling God-ward, the old nature earthward, until he cries out in his pain and anguish.

Poor soul hast thou wandered, and lost thy joys? Thank God for thy misery, while thou deplorest thy wanderings, for it is one of the best proofs that, after all, the birth of the divine nature has taken place within you.

Then another reason is that *every believer has the Spirit of God dwelling within him, and if he has the Spirit of God dwelling within him, it is only natural that he should desire God.* I hope and believe that, in preaching to you this morning, I am speaking to those who believe that it was no mere figure of speech on our Lord's part when he said, 'And we will come and take up our abode within him'; or on the apostle's part when he said, 'Know ye not that your body is the temple of the Holy Ghost?' Within the breast of every believer there dwells the third person of the Trinity, the ever blessed Spirit. The moment you remember this, you can understand the desire of my text. What is the one great work of the Spirit which I tried to show you the other Sunday morning? Is it not to glorify Christ? Surely it is, and the great work of Christ was to glorify the Father. Therefore, if I have the Spirit within my breast, it will always be leading me up to God through Christ. Long as ever the Spirit of God dwells within the breast, all its motions, all its teachings, all its tendencies are to the eternal Father through Jesus. Therefore, 'My heart and my flesh crieth out for God.'

But once more, and I will leave this point. Do not you think this desire after God *becomes intensified by earth's experience?* I ask you to mark the words I employ—'becomes *intensified* by earth's experience'. It is not that the experience of earth makes you long for God, but I believe the experience of earth often makes you long *more* for God. After you have discovered the hollowness, the emptiness, the disappointing nature of the world—after you have had a little experience of the amount of sham there is abroad when, perhaps, over and over again, you have been most bitterly disappointed in the one you trusted most—when all things, too, begin to fail you and you feel that troubles huge are coming on apace, then it is that the soul cries out more earnestly than ever for God. Oh for something real in a world of unreality—for something true in a world so false! Oh for something abiding in a world which is so fleeting! And so the very experiences of earth inflame the soul's desires after God. As I was listening to a brother praying at a recent prayer meeting here, I remarked to a friend of his, 'I never heard him pray like that before.' 'No', was the answer, 'he never had so much trouble before.' I could tell, all the way through that prayer, that there were cries and groanings after God, which, though begotten by the Spirit, had been intensified by earth's bitter experiences. Perhaps if the psalmist had not been out on the mountain side, away from the courts of the Lord's house, there would not have been so deep an emphasis on this cry—'Oh for God!'

II. Now, only for two or three minutes, I want you to observe THE INTENSITY OF THIS DESIRE. 'My heart and my flesh crieth out.' Do you see, heart and flesh being both mentioned, we are taught that it is the desire of the whole man. Every faculty of the mind and every affection of the heart crieth out. Now, this word 'crieth out'—what does it mean? In the original it means the cry of a company of soldiers as they fall on to the foe. When the word of command is given for the battle to commence, a wild cry rises up from the ranks—the cry of the men as they dash forward. There is expectation, eagerness, desire, all concentrated in its note.

For a moment look at it in this light. This desire after God has intensity. All the soul, the heart, the flesh, join in the cry. A man never knows how he can cry to God until he cries *after* God. You may put that down as certain. No man knows how intense prayer can become until the subject of the prayer is God himself. Then he is startled by his own eagerness—almost afraid at his own earnestness. The idea of our text is also a cry of distress—such a cry as I should imagine would break from the lips of one who had been wandering late in the afternoon along a seacoast and become caught by the advancing tide. He is not acquainted with the shore, and does not know that the tide runs round inside the bank on which he is walking. As he wends his way, the shadows of the evening come down, and he can see in the distance the lights of the spot where his temporary home is. But the tide has come in between him and the shore. He climbs from rock to rock. The waters rise. He can go no further. Nothing but a boat can save him. How he wishes that the evening were not advanced! It is no use waving his handkerchief now. He cannot be seen. But lights are moving about on shore. Now listen to him. There is anguish in the cry which he sends across the waste of waters. *'Help!* HELP! HELP!' 'My heart and my flesh crieth out for God.' Nothing but God can meet the exigencies of the case.

It is an intensity that drowns all other desires—'crieth out for God'. I passed a little child the other day being led by the hand by a kind-faced policeman; and as the little thing walked by his side, I could hear it, amidst its sobs, continually crying, 'Father! father! father! father!' Yes, in this great city—full of people, the only face the child wanted to see was the face of its father. He knew he had lost a father's hand, for he had wandered from a father's side, and he wanted father back again. 'My heart and my flesh crieth out for God.' Just as a lost child cares not for a million faces it may meet along the road—it wants to look at its father's face—so the true born child of God can rest satisfied with nothing short of a sight of his God. 'My heart and my flesh crieth out for God.'

Once more, it is an intensity of desire that *creates pain.* The language of our text is the language of a soul which can bear its anguish no longer in silence. It is a cry extorted by inward pangs.

We will not dwell on our last points—(as our time is gone)—but only say there are some *very comforting assurances to be gained from this subject.* Have you been able to say, step by step, 'Yes, I know this—I have borne that—I have gone right through that—the pastor has just been describing my experience this morning'? Then let me say here, lift up the hands which hang down, and let the feeble knees be confirmed, and the sad heart be glad. You say, 'Be glad because I am so miserable'? Yes, be glad because you are wretched without God. That longing after God is a more infallible proof you are God's, than your longest prayers, your most zealous services, or the very best of your actions. These might be counterfeit: this longing after God cannot be. And if there is within your soul an aching void that nothing but a living God can fill, write it down, 'I am born of God'; for none but those who are born of God know aught of this sweet pain. Oh what must heaven be! If all the desires of a saint are concentrated in this one for God, what must the satisfaction of heaven be when it is all God—God on the throne, God before me, God leading me, God delighting my eyes, God in my songs,—the world, its cares, its sorrows, its worries, all gone—a heavenly atmosphere of God all round! How unutterably deep the satisfaction! My heart and my flesh will no longer cry out for God, but will eternally rejoice in him.

Dear Reader,—Let me earnestly ask you to join me in prayer for a gracious revival of God's work throughout our land. It is sorely needed now, for in many parts 'Zion languisheth.' The spirit of the world is gaining entrance, and therefore spiritual power declines. Let us plead together.—Yours affectionately,

ARCHIBALD G. BROWN.[1]

---

[1] This note appeared after the sermon as printed in *The Penny Pulpit, New Series.*

PAST FINDING OUT[1]

His ways are past finding out.
Romans 11:33.

THESE words form part of the adoring exclamation that leaps from the lips of the Apostle Paul after a prolonged study of divine procedure. He has been dwelling upon God's plan of governing the world, and God's method of bringing about his purposes, and, as he has gazed upon this mighty theme, its immensity has grown upon him. The 'many-folded wisdom' has in measure been unfolded before the apostle's eyes. He has done now with argument, and takes to worshipping. He is like the Alpine climber who has at last reached the summit of the peak. During the upward climb he has passed by many a crevasse deep and dark; he has peered down many a black gorge, seemingly the home of the thunder-cloud. Over and over again his path has skirted some awful precipice, down which he has tremblingly gazed until his brain has grown dizzy with the sight. He has passed through the clouds that belt the lower part of the mountain, and now he is right up on the summit, and from that point he looks down, and, lo, the clouds have melted, and two burning rays of light illumine the deeps that lie beneath. These two rays of light are God's wisdom and God's knowledge, and from the mountain-top he sees that all the dark gorges, deep precipices, and black spots, are now illumined; and, falling upon his knees, he worships

[1] February 7, 1897, East London Tabernacle.

THIS GOD OUR GOD

and exclaims, 'Oh, the depths of the riches of the wisdom and the knowledge of God! His ways are past finding out.'

Thus far I have taken the passage as if it were simply a note of adoration. There is adoration, but I am not quite sure that there is not something else as well. It seems to me to be *adoration accompanied with a shudder,* if these two things can be linked together; and therefore, I will alter my illustration and give you another aspect of the subject. It seems to me that Paul has been standing in thought on the shore, gazing out upon the boundless ocean of divine purpose and divine plan; and at last he ventures to thrust his skiff out just a little way from the shore. But no sooner has he done so than the mists of the ocean wrap him round about. He lets out his fathoming line, and finds no bottom; and then he hastens his return to shore, and exclaims with a shudder, whilst at the same time he worships, 'Oh, the depths of the riches of the wisdom and knowledge of God!'

What is it that Paul has been contemplating? We have it in the whole chapter. It is God's method of redemption as regards both Jew and Gentile. Read from the 28th verse: 'As concerning the gospel, they [that is, the Jews] are enemies for your sakes; but, as touching the election, they are beloved for the fathers' sakes. For the gifts and calling of God are without repentance. For, as ye in times past have not believed God, yet have now obtained mercy through their unbelief [ah, there is a mystery for you, the Gentiles finding mercy through the unbelief of the Jew], even so have these also now not believed, that through your mercy they also may obtain mercy, for God hath concluded them all [both Jew and Gentile] in unbelief, that he might have mercy upon all.' Do you catch the thought? Paul sees Israel chosen and blessed, but apostatising, and then he sees that, through the very apostasy of Israel, a door is thrown open before the Gentile hosts. And then he sees how that, through mercies shown to the Gentile, blessing is to come to the

Jew; and ultimately the Jew is to receive the Messiah, and he is to accept the One from whom the Gentiles apostatize. Then through the Jew the world is to be blessed. And, when Paul looks at these dark gorges and precipices that he has skirted, he can only say, 'Oh, the depth of the riches of the wisdom and the knowledge of God, who, by a heavenly chemistry, brings good even out of ill. Truly, God is not be judged. His ways are past finding out.'

Is it not a mercy that, *when we cannot understand, we can still worship,* and that, when we cannot comprehend, we can still adore? When my poor tired head grows worthless, and is unable to do its work in the way of understanding, it is a choice blessing that I am free to take to my knees. When it is maddening to be a student of divine procedure, it is delightful to be a worshipper. We all often come like Jacob to a place that is full of stones, and the stones all round are hard facts, and those hard facts are often most mysterious. There are various ways of dealing with them. If you like, you can get into a pet with them, and kick them, but you will only lame yourself. Facts are awkward things to kick. Or you may go blundering about them, despairingly, falling over them, wounding your feet, and bruising your shins. But there is a third and better way. Take these hard facts, and build them up into an altar, anoint them, and worship God at them. That is what Paul did. When he saw facts and mysteries which he could not explain, he worshipped God, and said, 'Oh, the depth of the riches of the wisdom of God. His ways are past finding out.'

The thought which has been working in my mind, so far as anything has been able to work there this week, is that the characteristic—may I say the chief characteristic—of God and of God's ways and of God's works is that they are past finding out, and that that is the verdict at which we must ultimately arrive. Oh, what fools we are, and how slow to accept this truth! If God's ways are past finding out, why do I waste my hours, and tease my brain, and run the risk of breaking my heart, by trying to do what God says cannot be done. Happy is the man who accepts the verdict, 'past finding out', and says, 'Lord, I believe it, and I am not going to try. If thou sayest, "past finding out", I am not going to try to pick the lock. I will rather worship and adore.'

I.—Is NOT THE TEXT TRUE OF GOD HIMSELF IN HIS BEING: 'past finding out'? I am not departing from my text. I am perfectly aware that the sentence is, 'His ways are past finding out'; but I am sure that he whose ways are past finding out will himself be the same. You cannot imagine a being who is inferior to his ways. If God's ways are inscrutable, his being must be, and so of God we say, 'past finding out'.

What a little word that word 'God' is. You have taught it to your child, and I suppose that most of us learned to spell 'G-O-D' when we were little ones at our mothers' knees. So easily spelt; so quickly uttered; yet, who is there who could venture to say what he means when he says 'God'? *It is the one name which, when mentioned, is not accompanied by any mental form. No figure rises to my mind's vision* when I say 'God'. But do you say, 'Who is God? What is God?' I know until you ask me. 'He is past finding out.' It has been so in the saintly experience of all ages. We find Job saying, in the 11th chapter, at the 7th verse, 'Canst thou by searching find out God? Canst thou find out the Almighty unto perfection? High as heaven, deeper than Sheol. What canst thou know? The measure thereof is longer than the earth, and broader than the sea.' Thus in the earliest book of Holy Scripture there is this solemn note rung out, 'past finding out'. Thou mayest search, but thou canst not discover. There are no data to start from. There is no standard by which you may compare; and therefore, God says, 'To whom, then, will ye liken me, or shall I be equal? saith the Holy One.' Do you marvel that God's holy ire was poured out upon idolatry? Oh, the madness of the sin of trying to set forth in wood, or stone, or metal, a Jehovah whose glory lies in the fact that he is past finding out. 'No man can see me and live' is the language of deity. Clouds and darkness are round about him; and then, in singular contrast, he 'maketh light his garment'. Light can hide as fully and completely as darkness. Is it not Milton who, with a splendid touch of genius, says that God is 'dark with insufferable light'? Arrayed in light, God in his being must ever remain past finding out.

O eternal God, we love to think of thee! Thou boundless ocean of being! Our little skiff of thought may float on thee. It does so now, this moment, with delight. But explore thee? Never! Does someone here say, 'I cannot believe in a God that I cannot understand'? Well, sir, I cannot congratulate you on your common sense. For my own part, I could not believe in a God that I could understand. I could not have any confidence in a God that I could comprehend. I should be greater than my God. A God that could be comprehended would be smaller than the man who comprehended him; and therefore, let faith be strengthened, and not staggered, by the utterance, 'He is past finding out.'

II.—BUT GOD IS PAST FINDING OUT, NOT ONLY IN HIS BEING, BUT IN HIS WORKS. Turn once more to the Book of Job, the 9th chapter, and the 10th verse, where, speaking of God, Job says, 'which doeth great things past finding out'. You see that here it is not the being of God that we have to deal with, but it is the doing of God. It is that the Almighty doeth great things past finding out. If you look at the context you will see that the statement is made with reference to nature. Read from the 8th verse: 'Which alone spreadeth out the heavens and treadeth upon the waves of the sea, which maketh Arcturus, Orion, and Pleiades, and the chambers of the south, which doeth great things past finding out.' I do not think that there is a child here who will not be able to follow me in this simple line of argument. When I meet with a being who is past finding out, I need not be surprised if he does that which is past finding out. His actions are likely to be in harmony with himself. Gaze for a moment upon this wondrous illustration which Job introduces, namely, that we have only to lift our eyes up and behold nature in order to see that there is something past finding out. Oh, what wonders there are all round about us. Who are we? Where are we? Well, we are living on a little world, for, after all, the earth which we think so much of is rather a small commodity amongst the other worlds. We are living, I say, on a little world that is slung up on nothing. Earth floats in a limitless ocean of space. But she is not alone, for if, when you go away from this service, you look up, you will see that there is a fleet of a myriad other vessels, and that they are all navigating the same wide sea. Do the inhabitants of these different worlds act as the crews of the vessels? Is there any human hand at the helm? The answer is, 'No, there is no human steersman. All the beings that are on these worlds are but passengers.' Who, then, is Captain? and the voice comes from heaven, 'By the greatness of his might, for that he is great in power, not one faileth.' And, as Job marked Arcturus and Orion and the Pleiades, he did what any man who is not blinded by sin will do. He worshipped, and he said, 'Lord, thy works, like thyself, are past finding out.'

But in this little world in which we live are we not ever finding that we are governed by laws which are only beginning to be discovered? Science does not invent anything. Science only discovers, and the discoveries of science are but so many testimonials to the verdict, 'past finding out', for each discovery only reveals that there is more to be discovered. Oh, the many-folded wisdom of God. Marvellous are all his works, from the mountain range to the insect's wing.

III.—I have no doubt that I shall carry you all with me in my third point, because it touches everyday life and everyday experience. It is that GOD IS PAST FINDING OUT IN HIS WAYS. Here, as you will see, we come to the actual meaning of our text: 'How unsearchable are his judgments, and his ways past finding out.' I wish that I could say a word that might be a help to some poor dazed brain that is here tonight. Am I speaking to any who have seen strange things in life? They are called 'providential dealings'. They have been, perhaps, seemingly very contradictory one to the other, and quite inexplicable. Have you begun to doubt? Have you come here with your faith, if not prostrate, yet beginning to stagger? I should be very glad to be the means of confirming some feeble knee. At all events, whatever other qualification I may not possess for dealing with this point, I have one, and that is the fitness that is gained by personal experience. But need we be surprised if God's ways are past finding out? Listen for a moment. You have acquiesced in the truth that his being is past finding out. You are certain that his works are. Then, surely, there is no reason to be surprised if his methods are the same. Faith finds her tonic in the very fact that God's ways are so far above our own. Listen. Does not Jehovah say, 'As high as the heavens are above the earth, so high are my ways above your ways, and my thoughts above your thoughts'? And yet sometimes we criticise God. I say 'we', though, perhaps, I have no right to include you. But I would not dare to say that I have never criticised God, and, in all probability, you have to make the same confession. But, oh, what folly! As I turned this thought over, I imagined that I entered into a study, and found there a man of mighty intellect. I looked round the apartment, and there were ponderous tomes, books about deep, mysterious things; and on the table there were delicate instruments, and I could see that the student often rose from the books to test something by a complicated experiment with the finest of instruments. Looking up, I saw that away in the corner of that study a little web had been spun, and there was a spider viewing all from his watch-tower; and that spider, from his exalted position, looked down upon the student at the table, and said, 'What a strange being he is; what useless actions he is over performing. There is nothing practical about him. He neither spins a web nor does he eat flies.' And the spider saw a fly alight upon the table, close to the student's hand, but the man took no notice of it, and positively he did not even try to catch it. And the spider said, 'How foolish he is! The idea of letting slip an opportunity like that!' Ah, spider, thou hast more ability to enter into the deep thoughts of that student, and to understand the purpose of his most intricate experiments, than I have to comprehend the thoughts and ways and purposes of God. Easier far for the spider to understand the action of the chemist, than for me to understand the why of God in doing this or that. The moment we go in for 'whys' and 'wherefores', we hurl ourselves into a prickly hedge. To analyse God's 'why' and 'wherefore', is like trying to get through a hedge of prickly pear, such as I saw in the sunny clime a few days ago. You will tear your garments to pieces, and lacerate yourself. I can imagine some persons here saying, 'But *why* should that child die? *Why* should that hope of the family be stricken down! *Why* should that dear lad, who seemed called of God to do such a gracious work, be laid low? *Why* should that loving wife be swept into the grave? It does seem so hard.' Ah, 'wait a wee,[1] and dinna weary'. Judge him not. It is not within your province to do so, for his ways are past finding out. God has his loving purpose, and he is carrying along everything towards it.

Last summer as I was travelling up from the West of England in a railway carriage, we pulled up at a station, and, the window being down, I noticed that in tripped a little fly, and I found that I was going to have a railway companion. I said to myself, 'I wonder

[1] A short time.

whether that fly knows where he has got in, and whether he knows where he will get out.' For about two hundred miles I let the fly talk to me. He did not attempt to go out. No, he was thoroughly at home in that carriage, and he made little excursions to and fro. There was a grease spot on the back of the carriage, and he went and made an inspection of that, and I think that he found in it something sweet to his taste as a fly. He flew backwards and forwards, and rested on the lamp. Sometimes he was on the ceiling, and sometimes on the cushion, and now and again upon the floor; but I am perfectly sure that, while he was making these excursions, he was altogether unaware of the fact that he was being carried on by the train to a pre-determined goal. *He might make his journeys within the carriage, but the carriage itself was whirling along the lines.* So, as God's children, we make our little excursions, and we do this and that, and we live in our own little world; but, thank God, our little world is only part of the big train of divine purpose, and, whilst I fly and whilst I rest, I am being borne on, unconsciously to myself, to God's terminus. God's ways are past finding out.

IV.—I want to take you now one step further, and it will be the last. As God is past finding out in his being and in his works and in his ways, does it not stand to reason that there will be THE SAME CHARACTERISTICS IN HIS SALVATION, so that, when God saves man, the salvation of God, like its Author, will have about it much that is past finding out? In the 3rd chapter of the Epistle to the Ephesians, we read, at the 8th verse, of 'the unsearchable riches of Christ'. The word there translated 'unsearchable' is precisely the same word that we have in our text, 'past finding out'; so that the passage means 'the riches of Christ that are past finding out'. When God provides a Saviour, he provides a Saviour the fulness of whose riches is past finding out. What are those riches that cannot be tracked,—those riches that never can be fully discovered? Why, riches of merit, riches of grace, riches of love, riches of saving fulness. 'It pleased the Father that in him, Christ Jesus, should all fulness dwell.' Why, I wonder that you do not leap up from your seats and sing,

Hallelujah, what a Saviour!

Here is a Saviour so fully equipped by the Father that his provision as such is simply past finding out. Be of good cheer, for he saved the 'chief of sinners'. Paul came, and he found that there was enough and to spare, and so he speaks of 'unsearchable riches'. We cannot trace them out. They defy all search. Millions of sinners since Paul's time have come to Christ, and they all say that there is enough and more than enough. I will guarantee that the man in this Tabernacle who has been a Christian longest, and who knows Christ most fully, is the man who will have discovered most that Christ is past finding out. Oh, he is a fair country that has no frontier. He is an ocean that has no shore. There is always an infinite fulness, a *pleroma*, about him. Come, sinner, you need not be afraid with such a Saviour as this, for in him there is a saving ability that is past finding out.

I think you will see that it must logically follow that, if Jesus, as my Saviour, is past finding out in his fulness, *all that he gives me will have the same characteristic.* If the Lord gives a *pardon*, what sort of a pardon will he bestow? Listen to the language of the Holy Ghost in the 103rd Psalm. 'As far as the east is from the west, so far hath he removed our transgressions from us.' How far does the pardon go? Oh, it is past finding out. How far is the east from the west? Actually there is no ultimate east, and there is no final west. Space is boundless in each direction. There are no limits. You may travel for ages yonder, and you will find nothing to stop you. And so it is with the pardon you may get tonight. Believer, that is the sort of pardon which you have received. It is a forgiveness past finding out.

And what is *the acceptance* that he gives us? When he forgives our sins, what position does he bring us into? 'Complete in him.' At your leisure turn to the 2nd chapter of the Epistle to the Colossians, and read the 9th verse in this connection. 'It pleased the Father that in him should all fulness dwell, and ye are complete in him.' Imagine it. Complete in all fulness. How much does that include? We cannot say. It is past finding out. I only know that the acceptance of every saint here tonight is an acceptance according to the righteousness of God. The believer is made the righteousness of God in Christ, and he may sing,

> So near, so very near to God,
>   I cannot nearer be,
> For in the Person of His Son,
>   I am as near as He.

His acceptance is past finding out.

And God gives believers *a peace*, does he not? And what sort of a peace is that? You will find the answer in the 4th chapter of the Philippians, and the 7th verse. 'In every thing by prayer and supplication, with thanksgiving, make known your requests unto God; and the peace of God which *passeth all understanding* shall keep your heart and mind.' We are not at all surprised at this. If God who is past finding out gives me peace, I may anticipate that that peace will also be past finding out. Look at John Huss. He is blazing away in Constance, but what a glory there is in his countenance. As an onlooker says, 'His face did shine as if heaven shone into it'; and he sang a psalm until his head bowed down in the flames. It is a peace that passeth understanding. Why, some of you who are here have had a peace that you could not understand. When death has invaded your home, or when sickness has laid you low, there has been within your own soul a quiet and a rest that have defied explanation. It has been 'past finding out'. 'Ah', says someone over there, 'I will tell you of one thing that I object to in you Christians.' Well, what is that? 'You are such a miserable set.' Well, I dispute it. I believe that the Christian is the happiest man on God's earth; and, more than that, he can say concerning his joy what no worldling can say, for in the language of Peter, it is *a joy unspeakable* and full of glory'. It is past finding out. The Christian possesses a happiness which he cannot exactly put into words. There is not a worldling here who could not very easily describe the greatest joy of his happiest moment, but there are hundreds of God's children here who can say that there is a delicious joy in Christ which cannot be described. There is an exquisite bliss. There is a nectar which the Lord puts to a believer's mouth, so sweet that it causes the lips of them that sleep to speak. There is a strange inner joy that makes all the bells inside to ring; a happiness that overloads the chariot of language. It is unspeakable. And why? Because it is charged with glory.

And *the heaven* that he gives is also past finding out. It is bound to be so. If even the foretastes of it are past finding out, namely, the peace and joy which the Christian possesses here, we may be quite sure that the full final glory will also be past finding out. 'I am persuaded', says the apostle in the 8th of Romans, 'that the sufferings of this present time are not worthy to be compared with the glory that is to be revealed.' Why, Paul, how much glory do you expect? 'Oh, it is past finding out. There is an exceeding weight of it.' Beloved, how many have worshipped in this Tabernacle, and have since discovered the bliss that is past finding out. They have forded the river and gone up the shining steps on the other side, and they have had their welcome from the Master, and they are now just slowly learning what it is to be in heaven. I suppose that for ever the joy must deepen, the glories unfold, the bliss intensify. The awful delight of being with God—oh, this we cannot tell. No poet has ever reached the height of describing heaven. All Scripture imagery seems to fail, for even in the Book of Revelation the Holy Ghost does not tell us what heaven is: he only tells us what it is not. He does not tell us what is there; but he tells us what is not there. There is no sickness; there is no crying; there is no weariness; there is no dying; there is no sighing; there is no parting; and there is no night there. But he does not tell us what there is, for I suppose that it could not be put into language. It is past finding out.

Now, if such a gospel as this be preached to you, and if there be offered unto you a Christ so full of saving power and love that the fulness thereof is past finding out, do you not think that there is something else past finding out if you reject it? Do you say, 'I do not quite follow you, preacher. What do you mean?' If you reject Christ, who, in his saving power, is past finding out, do you not think that there is something attaching to you which also is past finding out? I will tell you what it is. I mean *your responsibility;* for listen: 'How shall we escape if we neglect so great salvation?' That is a question which has never yet been answered, and it never will be, and God himself cannot answer it. It is past finding out. The responsibility of the sinner who rejects such a Christ and such a salvation is past all discovery.

Oh, come and cast yourself down at the feet of the adorable Lord, the high, the holy, the lofty One, the eternal I Am, who, in his being and in his works and in his ways, is past finding out. Go, see him in Christ. Behold the One who is past finding out hanging in sweat of blood upon the cross. He is there for you. Oh, here is love past finding out. Here is grace past finding out. Go cast yourself on him, believe in him, and you shall be saved, and you shall go away from this Tabernacle saying, 'Hallelujah, I have found the Saviour, and, oh! he is past finding out. Hallelujah, I have found a peace, and that is past finding out. Glory be to God, a joy has come into my soul which is unspeakable: it, too, is past finding out. Hallelujah, just a little way ahead I see, through the gloom and mist, an open door into the glory. I hear the music of the redeemed coming through it. I hear my Saviour's voice saying, "A little while, and thou shalt enter here, and thou shalt find that these glories through all ages are past finding out." God grant that it may be so with all of us, for Jesus's sake. Amen.

ARCHIBALD BROWN TITLES

FROM

THE BANNER OF TRUTH TRUST

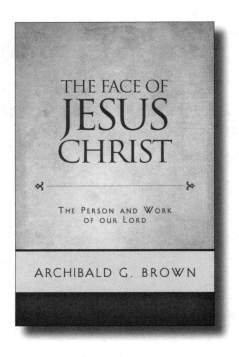

The Face of Jesus Christ
Sermons on the Person and Work of Our Lord

Archibald G. Brown

paperback, 296 pp. ISBN: 978-1-84871-147-1

Archibald Brown was a man utterly stricken with the beauty and glory of his Lord Jesus—and his sermons are infectious.

WORLD MAGAZINE

I have enjoyed several so much that I have read them twice. They provide an excellent model for textual preaching.

FREE CHURCH WITNESS

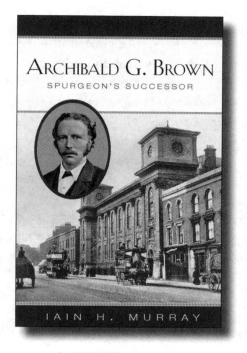

Archibald G. Brown
Spurgeon's Successor

Iain H. Murray

clothbound, 432 pp. ISBN: 978-1-84871-139-6

Beautifully produced, the book is a compelling read.
EVANGELICALS NOW

. . . the life and ministry set before us in these pages is simply thrilling.
EVANGELICAL PRESBYTERIAN

. . . a masterly biography . . .
EVANGELICAL TIMES